Religions and Discourse

Edited by James M. M. Francis

Volume 43

PETER LANG

Oxford • Bern • Berlin • Bruxelles • Frankfurt am Main • New York • Wien

Sue Yore

The Mystic Way
in Postmodernity

Transcending Theological Boundaries
in the Writings of Iris Murdoch,
Denise Levertov and Annie Dillard

PETER LANG

Oxford • Bern • Berlin • Bruxelles • Frankfurt am Main • New York • Wien

Bibliographic information published by Die Deutsche Bibliothek
Die Deutsche Bibliothek lists this publication in the Deutsche National-
bibliografie; detailed bibliographic data is available on the Internet at
<http://dnb.ddb.de>.

A catalogue record for this book is available from the British Library and from the
Library of Congress.

ISSN 1422-8998
ISBN 978-3-03911-536-5

© Peter Lang AG, International Academic Publishers, Bern 2009
Hochfeldstrasse 32, Postfach 746, CH-3000 Bern 9, Switzerland
info@peterlang.com, www.peterlang.com, www.peterlang.net

Printed in Germany

This book is dedicated to Mum and Dad (Betty and Ken) with love

Acknowledgements

I would like to extend my thanks to a number of people who have supported, advised and encouraged me throughout the process of completing this book. First, I must acknowledge that the original idea grew from a conversation with my first PhD supervisor Professor Ann Loades. In particular, Ann guided me toward the theological insights in the writings of Iris Murdoch, Denise Levertov and Annie Dillard whose work was unknown to me at that time. She also provided much needed moral support and conviction that this was a worthy project. Second, I would like to extend my sincere gratitude to my second supervisor, Professor Philip Sheldrake, who helped me to focus my thinking and steer me through the academic requirements of completing a doctoral thesis following Ann's retirement. I must also thank colleagues in Theology and Religious Education at York St John's University for their continued support and encouragement. I would like to make particular mention of Pauline Kollontai for her practical and moral support, as well as Professor Sebastian Kim, Dr Chris Maunder and Louise Redshaw who all read through the manuscript at various stages of completion and offered helpful suggestions. I should mention that this book was made possible due to a bursary from the Arts and Humanities Research Board that supported me through my doctoral studies. Finally, I would like to thank my family and friends for their love and encouragement throughout the process of bringing the book to completion.

Contents

Introduction

A chief characteristic of the postmodern world, in the opinion of British theologian Mark McIntosh, is that a 'pseudo-spirituality that deals in escape, in avoidance of the reality of the other'[1] is replacing organised religion. Because of a lack of community and outward looking generally that is inherent to such spirituality, such a spiritual practice is more likely to become idiosyncratic and the follower of such a path apathetic towards political and social concerns. However, the upside of this movement away from traditional organised religions is that women have found space to explore and express their spirituality; but at the other end of the spectrum, we are currently witnessing a resurgence in extreme or fundamentalist forms of religion globally in a backlash against this trend. By comparison to adherents of a personalised pseudo-spirituality, the adherents of these fundamentalist movements espouse political agendas that stifle freethinking, curtail women's (and marginalised peoples) self-definition and contributions to public life, and discourage theological enquiry that questions accepted 'truths'.

Philip Sheldrake, a British theologian who is concerned with these polarities, argues that '[t]he most important lesson that postmodernity can teach spirituality is the need to reject an unhealthy division between the sacred and the secular', which has left two main options for mainstream Christians – to 'assimilate Christianity to surrounding culture or, like some radical fundamentalists, reject human culture entirely'.[2] Of course, neither of these suggestions offers a satisfactory solution, as Christianity would cease to be a living and dynamic religious tradition in both scenarios. Among the underlying premises of this book is an agreement with both McIntosh and Sheldrake, but further, I want to suggest that contemporary literary texts, specifically those with a mystical orientation, have the potential to subvert such

---

1   Mark A. McIntosh, *Mystical Theology* (Oxford: Blackwell, 1998), 5.
2   Philip Sheldrake, *Spirituality and Theology: Christian Living and the Doctrine of God* (London: Darton, Longman & Todd, 1998), 12.

religious schisms through addressing the dilemmas peculiar to post-modernity.

The notion that mystically enlivened literature can provide alternative and renewable resources to the received tradition as represented by biblical texts is nothing new. David Jenkins observed back in 1964 that

> the dreadful thing about so much theology is that, in relation to the reality of the human situation, it is so superficial. Theological categories (really theological formulae) are 'aimed' without sufficient depth of understanding at life insensitively misunderstood. Theologians need therefore to stand *under* the judgments and insights of literature before they can speak with true theological force, of and to, the world this literature reflects and illuminates.[3]

Jenkins suggests here that literature provides the starting point for theological reflection.

In view of the perceived inadequacy of religious language to address contemporary concerns, there has indeed been a growing trend to look to literature as a resource for theological and religious insight. Without doubt, the primary language of religion has historically centred on the poetical, metaphorical and mythical; but unfortunately, the importance of this fact has often been misunderstood, overlooked or denied. The need for the Church to maintain clear doctrinal teaching has the unfortunate side effect of literary language becoming subsumed and transmogrified into theological language. Furthermore, the institutionalised elements of religion tend to marginalise or strictly control the voices of mystics who typically use language idiosyncratically in creative and progressive ways, as opposed to official theological language, which can become static. I shall argue that literature with a conscious mystical orientation not only 'reflects and illuminates' reality but also avoids the 'superficiality' that Jenkins concedes is part of most theological texts. As a stay against the abusive potential of authoritative religion based on immovable sacred texts, this study seeks to demonstrate that the literary writer, as a mys-

---

3   David Jenkins, 'Literature and the Theologian', in John Coulson (ed), *Theology and the University: An Ecumenical Investigation* (Baltimore: Helicon Press, 1964), 219.

tic, is able to bridge the gap between the personal and communal, the body and the spirit, beauty and tragedy. This study will assert that it is primarily through extending their imaginations that women in particular have posited theological insights that point beyond dogmatism and irrelevancy.

The writers chosen for this task are Iris Murdoch (1919–1999), Denise Levertov (1923–1997) and Annie Dillard (1945–). There are three primary reasons for this selection. The first and more general is that there is an obvious and definite mystical focus and sense of being on a spiritual quest in the work of these writers, an overt attempt to explore human meaning and ethical action in relation to the sacred. Literary critics, theologians and philosophers alike have, in various contexts, labelled Murdoch, Levertov and Dillard as 'mystics' as well as locating them within a more specific continuity of Christian and Platonist mysticism. The second, more specific and unifying factor in this choice of writers is that they all appear to empathise with Julian of Norwich on a number of spiritual, theological and existential levels. Given their emulation of Julian, it seems appropriate to suggest that they are consciously located within the same trajectory of female mystics. The third and more practical consideration is that our writers have popular appeal among Christians and non-Christians alike. Like Julian, who wrote for 'my fellow Christians'[4] and chose (we presume) to live her life between the Church and the ordinary folk in her anchorhold, our writers cannot be easily situated – religiously, socially, artistically or intellectually – within culture, Church or Academy. They engage with all aspects of the culture at various times in distinct and creative ways and thus evade easy categorisation.

In relation to this, mystical experience in postmodernity is a sense of 'seeing' and holding the sacred and lived reality in creative tension, as opposed to the more traditional notion of mysticism as a cloistered avocation. Consequently, postmodern mysticism has more to do with a deepening of being than the classical understanding of mystical experience, which will inevitably present problems concerning definitions of mysticism. To this end, I propose to map out the

---

4   Julian of Norwich, *Showings*. Trans. Edmund College, O.S.A. and James Walsh, S.J. (Mahwah, New Jersey: Paulist Press, 1978), 155.

essentials of the mystic way by drawing on the writings of Murdoch, Levertov and Dillard, who I will argue are postmodern mystics. Relying on my discernment of their own self-understanding and motivations, I suggest that these writers self-consciously resist postmodern meaninglessness by actively locating themselves within a trajectory of mystical consciousness that accompanies all religious expressions historically.

In this regard, while the use of literature to express or explore theological concepts is nothing new, this book develops several areas beyond current scholarship. First and foremost, it takes literary writers seriously as theologians in their own right through questioning the traditional marginalisation of women's mystical insights. In my view, there has been an overemphasis on the influence of male forerunners and not enough attention paid to women's unique contribution. With regard to Murdoch, Levertov and Dillard, this discussion identifies a common agenda in those who seek spiritual meaning through a synthesis of imagination and intellect in dialogue with mystical traditions. The spiritual or mystical dimension of their work, although acknowledged by a range of literary critics, is rarely recognised as a source for theology despite the fact that all three engage with that discipline and its texts throughout the corpus of their work. Those who do pay attention to the religious significance of these writers' work tend to see it in subjective terms. In contradistinction, I suggest that if theologians incorporated insights from literary writers, such as those examined here, into their own discourse, it would help to keep the discipline dynamic and speaking to the age.

Secondly, and as noted previously, this book argues that Murdoch, Levertov and Dillard are mystics in their own right, outside a particular theological tradition (although all three are conversant in various religious traditions, particularly Christianity). While the mystical outlook of their work is acknowledged by a number of authors, there has not been any systematic attempt to surmise what this means for theology. For this task, I will draw on the thinking of selected theologians, of whom Grace Jantzen, Dorothee Soelle and Sallie McFague are the main conversation partners. All these women have in the past held a distinct feminist position but appear to have broadened their conceptual horizons to be more inclusive.

14

To date, there has been only tentative scholarship linking the writers to be discussed in this book with either the mystical tradition or the suggestion that they are engaging in theology. One of the more significant works to deal with such spiritual matters is *Iris Murdoch: Work for the Spirit* (1981) by Elizabeth Dipple, who in her preface refers to the subject of this work as being that of a 'radiant mystic'.[5] Although written as literary criticism, the book focuses on Murdoch's religious and moral impulses that emerged from her concerns with what she perceived to be an increasingly godless, secular society. Dipple provides a close analysis of the religious themes in novels up to and including *Nuns and Soldiers*. The other noteworthy work is *Iris Murdoch: Figures of Good* (1990) by Suguna Ramanathan, who delves systematically into Murdoch's exploration of goodness and the de-mythologisation of Christianity. In particular, she demonstrates how Plato's the Good undergoes 'a distinct Christian transmutation'[6] in Murdoch's hands. She provides an impressive analysis of novels up to and including *Message to the Planet*. More recently, there is Robert Hardy's *Psychological and Religious Narratives in Iris Murdoch's Fiction* (2000), wherein the author examines the relationship between religious and psychological narratives in Murdoch's fiction with reference to the theories of Freud and Jung. Other scholarly experts on her work from the literary fields – such as Peter Conradi (2001), Kum Kum Bajaj (2001), Hilda Spear (1995), and Bran Nicol (1999) (2004) – incorporate a discussion of her religious ideas into a wider schema for her work. However, none engages solely with her mysticism.

In a similar manner, the majority of criticism about Levertov's work is based on the discipline of literary studies. The only work that explores her religious ideas explicitly is a small publication entitled *Poetry as Prayer* (2001) by her friend Murray Bodo, but there is a sizeable body of literary criticism that deals with her religious poetry in collections of essays edited by Albert Gelpi (1993) and Linda Wagner-Martin (1991). Otherwise of note is the fact that a whole edi-

5   Elizabeth Dipple, *Iris Murdoch: Work for the Spirit* (London: Methuen, 1982), x.
6   Suguna Ramanathan, *Iris Murdoch: Figures of Good* (Basingstoke: Macmillan, 1990), 4.

tion of the journal *Renascence* (1997/1998) was devoted to articles exploring religious ideas in her poetry.

To date, the most extensive discussion of Dillard's mystical capabilities is found in Sandra Humble Johnson's *The Space Between* (1992). Although written very much with a view to linking Dillard's epiphanic moments to earlier Romantics such as William Wordsworth and T. S. Eliot, the book provides the keenest sense of her mysticism. Humble Johnson explores her desire to capture her allusive and momentary illuminations in language with close reference to the transformation of the reader. Eugene H. Peterson points to the 'spaces between' implied in the title as referring to the epiphanic moment that words generate through creating a space between temporal and eternal time. He further suggests that, via Dillard, Humble Johnson offers a detailed demonstration of this process and that 'pastors and professors especially need books like this'.[7] In fact, Humble Johnson makes frequent allusion to the mystical routes of the *via positiva* and *via negativa* in Dillard's work, tying it into the Western mystical tradition.

Literary critics have a tendency to regard the topic of mysticism as an esoteric, perhaps idiosyncratic literary category that may be applied to a few writers like those under discussion. On the contrary, I argue that mysticism is a term which bridges the gap between literature and theology and offers a more reasonable way of dealing with theology and spirituality. Within the Christian tradition, both Mark McIntosh (1998) and Philip Sheldrake (1998) argue passionately that the split between spirituality and theology has been a damaging one. There are also a significant number of key thinkers in the Christian tradition, Rowan Williams and Karl Rahner being but two examples, who are renowned for their arguments calling for the urgent renewal of mystical consciousnesses as a prerequisite for the survival of Christianity.[8] On a broader level, it is apparent that contemporary spiritu-

7   Eugene Peterson, 'Annie Dillard: Praying With Her Eyes Open', in *Theological Students Fellowship Bulletin*, 1985: 7–11, 11.
8   See for example, Karl Rahner, *Theological Investigations*, volume 5 (London: Darton, Longman & Todd, 1966) and Rowan Williams, *Teresa of Avila* (London: Geoffrey Chapman, 1991), Chapter 5 'Mysticism and Incarnation'. See also Mary C. Grey, *Prophecy and Mysticism: the Heart of the Postmodern Church* (Edinburgh: T. & T. Clark, 1997).

ality has become a highly fragmented phenomenon that has led to a revival of interest in 'the mystical'. David Tacey (2004) is among those who have done detailed studies of spiritual trends and has noted the mystical resurgence.[9] This of course has its own problems in a consumer culture, as spirituality then becomes a commodity as opposed to a way of being. I propose that the mystical insights of Murdoch, Levertov and Dillard can help address some of these dilemmas and pressing concerns associated with contemporary spirituality and theological irrelevance in postmodernity.

In order to address these questions and to move towards a more holistic outcome for these divisions, the book is divided into three thematic parts to help facilitate the process from imaginative or mystical contemplation to theological expression. Part One (Chapters One to Three) will explore the conceptual and practical foundations for following the *via mystica* in postmodernity, while Part Two (Chapters Four and Five) takes a closer look at the mystical processes involved along the way, and Part Three (Chapters Six and Seven) integrates mystical insights from Murdoch, Levertov and Dillard into theological reflection.

Chapter One provides a provisional outline of what a mystic in postmodernity might be like and argues for a conceptual and spiritual connection to the contemporary writer. In doing so, this discussion invokes Grace Jantzen's construction of a postmodern anchoress in particular. This chapter will be concerned primarily with methodology but will also include an overview of the lives of the three writers under discussion with an introduction to their sense of vocation as writers. In this chapter, there will also be an introduction to our main theological conversation partners: Grace Jantzen, Dorothee Soelle and Sallie McFague.

Chapter Two is concerned with the methods and practice of contemplation in postmodernity. As such, the discussion revives the medieval notion of the *via contemplativa* that includes the *via activa* and

---

9   David Tacey, *The Spirituality Revolution: The Emergence of Contemporary Spirituality* (Hove, New York: Brunner-Routledge, 2004). See also Paul Heelas et al. *The Spiritual Revolution* (Oxford: Blackwell, 2003) and Grace Davie et al. *Predicting Religion* (Aldershot: Ashgate, 2003).

explores what it means to write and read mystically. The second part focuses specifically on Murdoch, Levertov and Dillard's engagement with Julian of Norwich to argue that they revision her role in post-modernity through empathetic reading. Lastly, I will evaluate the metaphor of vision as an elementary theological tool that enables and instigates mystical insight for these writers.

Chapter Three develops the links between the self-understanding of the creative writer and the mystic. In particular, the discussion investigates the role of the imagination in the search for beauty, truth and unity. The existential role of the creative artist parallels the mystics on many fronts, notably the ability to withdraw to another level of consciousness and a readiness to exist on and transcend accepted conceptual and existential boundaries. Julian's phrase 'being endlessly born' will be taken to represent the creative possibilities latent in human effort, or what Jantzen (1998) terms 'natality'. The creative and mystical search for meaning, unlike systematic theology, accepts incompleteness. Both these perspectives evoke a mystical calling for humans to become what McFague (1993) more specifically describes as co-creators with God.

Chapter Four explores the *via positiva* as the first stage of this mystical path. On this 'stage' along the path, the mystic/writer seeks to rekindle a sense of awe, wonderment and passion that has largely been obscured in postmodernity. Whether the subject matter is found in the natural world or in ordinary experience, such literary works always give way to praise and amazement. This pilgrimage then is not experienced in any elite sense, but is, in the words of Murdoch, experienced in all 'our minute relations with our surrounding world' – even stones.[10] Indeed Murdoch's notion of love and eros will receive specific attention, as will Levertov's sense of *joie de vivre* and the prevalence of the concept of extravagance found in Dillard's work. Unfortunately, the *via positiva* has its darker side, however. Notably our writers acknowledge a horror of the contingent and the stark reality of suffering, the fact of our mortality and humanity's injustices to each other. It will be argued that the avoidance of these realities in

10   Iris Murdoch, *Metaphysics as a Guide to Morals* (London: Penguin, 1992), 474.

18

the past has led to a false perception of human ontology by placing hope outside this world.

Chapter Five starts with an outline of the postmodern emptiness that characterises our age. It then goes on to identify how taking small moments out of everyday living can enable epiphanic experiences. The negative way conventionally refers to the fact that human speech ultimately fails to talk about God. For Soelle (2001), the *via negativa* must take on a more political edge of resistance, which means to acknowledge the potential for evil that is latent within all of us. Murdoch, Levertov and Dillard acknowledge and work through the traditional 'dark night of the soul' with detailed emphasis on human feelings of doubt, despair and hopelessness. The result is a readiness to lose the ego, an acceptance of mystery, the knowledge that humans are powerless in the face of contingency, and that language ultimately trails off as the intellect fails and mystical perception starts. In a mystical sense, this results in the mystic desire for God, and theologically speaking, is expressed by Soelle as a 'hermeneutic of hunger', which she believes captures the essence of human longing for 'a different spirituality'[11] in postmodernity.

Chapter Six proposes how the preceding insights can be integrated into a non-dualistic theology. The notion of wholeness, both personal and collective, dominates this chapter. Julian provides an example of a mystic/theologian who integrates bodily, cognitive and spiritual insights. The works of Julian and Murdoch, Levertov and Dillard (these latter writing over five hundred years after the former) can be characterised by the fact that these writers create bridges between self and the Other. As such, they espouse a *via media* that continually blurs conceptual boundaries between love and knowledge. Theological reflection developed in the light of these insights will by necessity combine theory and praxis through personal insight and communal vision. A model of relationship evokes the change of consciousness that these ideas imply.

Chapter Seven examines the implications of incorporating mystical insights from literary texts into theological reflection. The overall

---

11   Dorothee Soelle, *The Silent Cry: Mysticism and Resistance* (Minneapolis: Fortress Press, 2001), 48.

intention is to transcend existing doctrinal and conceptual boundaries in order to move towards possible futures. First, the discussion will include an evaluation of the correlation between Murdoch, Levertov and Dillard's major impulses and that of Soelle, Jantzen and McFague, with particular attention to transformation. Next, there will be an analysis of the nuanced ways the Bible operates as a living text for imaginative thinkers and an overview of what this all means for theology. I cite McFague's 'parabolic theology' as a method that links contemporary writers, mysticism and theology whilst at the same time opening up trajectories into the future. I will suggest that to understand humans as mystic writers and readers is to imagine them as continually in a process of becoming, which in turn promotes an optimistic and hopeful attitude towards the future.

The broad aims of this book are threefold. In the first instance, rather than dismiss the term 'mystic' as problematic as does Alister McGrath because of its 'unhelpful associations' and 'anti-intellectual approach',[12] I seek to establish that mysticism is a vital category that links the creative imagination and theological discourse. Moreover, this discussion will challenge the limited association of mysticism with ineffable and inexplicable religious experience by suggesting that Murdoch, Levertov and Dillard embody mystical consciousness as a life process and mode of being. Second, I wish to demonstrate that literary writings of, in this case, women who demonstrate a mystical sensibility can facilitate the advancement of a potentially more democratic, holistic and tenable theology. As such, this proposition does not seek to impose a theological agenda on to literature or use it as a means to explore confessional faith, but rather, by the end, I intend to demonstrate that a mystical orientation functions effectively as connecting principle between theological scholarship and creative texts that are themselves on the mystic way.

---

12   Alister E. McGrath, *Christian Spirituality: An Approach* (Oxford: Blackwell, 1998), 6.

Part One

Chapter One
The *Via Mystica*: Mysticism in Postmodernity

Near the end of the fourteenth century, twenty years after reflecting on one of her original visions received during a period of intense illness, the medieval anchoress Julian of Norwich wrote:

> [God] showed me something small, no bigger than a hazelnut, lying in the palm of my hand, as it seemed to me, and it was as round as a ball. I looked at it with the eye of my understanding and thought: What can this be? And it was answered generally thus: It is everything that is made. I was amazed that it could last, for I thought that because of its littleness it would suddenly have fallen into nothing. And I was answered in my understanding: It lasts and always will, because God loves it; and thus everything has being through the love of God.[1]

Here Julian makes a statement that is essentially mystical in that it derives from her direct experience of God's presence, but the assertion is also theological given that it grapples with the doctrine of Creation. The small thing in her palm is a metaphorical image of the world held safe in the loving hand of God, and it is at the same time representative of the unitive nature of the relationship between the Creator and the created world as she sees it. On a subjective or micro level, the metaphor is the connection between Julian's experience and her understanding. The image also becomes a link between the micro world of personal spirituality and the macro world of communal theology due to the fact that her writings were intended as, and have indeed become, popular reading. It is because of this capacity to connect spiritual concepts to the world via seemingly simple, but in actuality multi-layered, metaphors, and her ability to do so with a woman's sensibility, that Julian's writings have become hugely popular within contemporary spirituality and feminist theology.[2]

1   Julian, *Showings*, 183.
2   See for example Kerry Hide, *Gifted Origins to Graced Fulfilment* (Collegeville, Minnesota: The Liturgical Press, 2001); Grace M. Jantzen, *Julian of Norwich*

The word 'anchoress' derives from the Greek word *anachōreō*, which means 'to withdraw'. Such religious solitaries appear to be mostly a British phenomenon, and although there were certainly male anchorites, it was more likely to be a position taken up by women. The author of the early thirteenth century text *Ancrene Wisse*, or 'Guide for Anchoresses', played on the word 'anchor', emphasising the traditional sense of being anchored to something, which in their case was the church building. Medieval anchoresses were 'anchored' to a completely enclosed living space within which they became interned during a solemn ceremony. Once inside, they would only emerge in their coffin. So the anchorhold became literally both womb and tomb.

We do not know for sure why Julian became an anchoress. Apart from her individual writings, the only surviving records that mention her are wills from the period written on behalf of benefactors who left her money after their demise and a brief mention by Margery Kempe.[3] To suggest that Julian's religious vocation provided her with the means to circumvent male control inside and outside of the Church, as a feminist interpretation would, is a somewhat moot point and can only remain at the level of speculation. What we can be sure of, however, is that the Church would have strictly censored women's voices – to step beyond the boundaries of orthodoxy would have been to court death. The equivalent to an anchoress in postmodernity has more freedom, and circumstances dictate that she must anchor herself to the contingent world. Frederick Bauershmidt argues that Julian, like us, lived at the edge of modernity as a 'fellow boundary dweller' and can therefore offer an invaluable resource for coping with the shift between modernity and postmodernity.[4] Also, in as much as she was, as far as we know, the first woman to write a book in the vernacular in England, it seems appropriate to explore the writings of women who

---

(London: SPCK, 2000); Sheila Upjohn, *In Search of Julian of Norwich* (London: Darton, Longman and Todd, 1989) and *Why Julian Now?* (London: Darton, Longman and Todd, 1997); Joan Nuth, *Wisdom's Daughter* (New York: Crossroad, 1991).

3   Jantzen, *Julian of Norwich*, 3.
4   Frederick Bauerschmidt, 'Order, Freedom and "Kindness": Julian of Norwich on the Edge of Modernity', in *Theology Today* 60 (2003), 63.

consciously follow in her footsteps along the *via mystica* in post-modernity.

The first aim of this chapter is therefore to make clear the sense in which I understand the mystic way in postmodernity. Secondly, I will introduce the work of Iris Murdoch, Denise Levertov and Annie Dillard and demonstrate the grounds on which I believe I can describe them as postmodern mystics. Lastly, there will be an overview of the key aspects of our three theological conversation partners – Sallie McFague, Grace Jantzen and Dorothee Soelle – who, as fellow 'boundary dwellers' or 'postmodern anchoresses', are going to further my argument concerning the transformation of theology based on mystical expression found in selected literary writers.

Mysticism in Postmodernity

To suggest that a popular published literary writer offers insights into 'the mystic way in postmodernity' in a theological context raises a number of definitional problems. Both the words 'postmodernity' and 'mystic' defy easy explanation or classification. Variations of the terms 'mystic' function in everyday language in a colloquial sense, but the term is also the subject of intense academic debate and scholarship. Furthermore, using the term is problematic in relation to Murdoch, Levertov and Dillard in the context of Christian mysticism. They do not wholly comply with accepted doctrines of the Christian Church (not at all in Murdoch's case), and indeed, their religious beliefs can be described as somewhat unorthodox. Experiences of the direct presence of God are not intrinsic to their mysticism as I am defining it either, although Dillard constantly tries to instigate beatific experiences. As a result, these writers do not conform to classical definitions of mysticism in the Christian tradition that focus on direct experience of the presence of an all-powerful, loving God. Obviously, three important questions arise out of this initial preamble that need to be answered: First, in what sense am I using the terms 'mystic' and 'mysticism'? Second, what do I perceive 'postmodernity' to be? And lastly, on what grounds do I claim that Murdoch, Levertov and Dillard as creative writers are 'postmodern mystics'?

What is Mysticism?

Identifying the distinctive elements of mysticism has proved problematic across the disciplines of theology, sociology, psychology, anthropology and the history of religions. Apart from the fact that mysticism is concerned with the invisible and unknowable aspect of reality, there is also the difficulty of multiple and varied practices and beliefs in the history of world religions. Moreover, there is an increasing tendency to use the term 'spirituality' interchangeably with mysticism, which further complicates any attempt at a definition in our time by diluting previous definitions. In the end, I have chosen to reject the word 'spirituality' because increasingly the term indicates what Paul Heelas and Linda Woodhead have termed 'the subjective turn' in spirituality.[5] In fact, I have opted to use 'mysticism' due to its tradition of renewal and subversion at the heart of major religious traditions, which has been just as much outward looking as inward. In order to deal with the elusive nature of the concept, the intention here is to contribute to this transportation of the mystical from what Michael Kessler and Christian Sheppard call the 'outer eddy of the theological mainstream' in an attempt to repair separations between public and private spirituality.[6]

Generally, the classical definition of mysticism is *cognitio Dei experimentis*, or knowledge of God gained through experience.[7] The first definition that the *Oxford English Dictionary* offers is that mysticism represents a belief in the possibility of 'union with the divine', which has a tendency to conjure up images of the human soul fleeing

---

5   Paul Heelas and Linda Woodhead, *The Spiritual Revolution: Why Religion is Giving Way to Spirituality* (Oxford: Blackwell, 2005), 2–6. For a defence of the public side of Christian spirituality, see Philip Sheldrake 'Christian Spirituality as a Way of Living Publicly: A Dialectic of the Mystical and Prophetic', in *Spiritus*, 3 (2003), 19–37.

6   Michael Kessler, and Christian Sheppard, *Mystics: Presence and Aporia* (Chicago and London: University of Chicago Press, 2003), ix.

7   Soelle, *The Silent Cry*, 45.

corporal existence in favour of the 'higher' spiritual realm. A second definition suggests a more grounded understanding by defining mysticism as the 'reliance on spiritual intuition or exalted feeling as a means of acquiring knowledge of mysteries inaccessible to intellectual apprehension'.[8] This definition could include both theistic forms of mysticism (as in Christianity, Judaism and Islam) as well as non-theistic or monist approaches wherein ultimate reality is non-personal (as in Buddhism). In existential terms, mysticism refers to specific 'opinions, mental tendencies, or habits of thought or feeling' that constitute religious belief and practice.[9] In other words, it is about an attitude or way of living a spiritual life which accepts that 'God transcend[s] human comprehension'.[10] As we proceed, it will become apparent that this does not mean we should abandon rational thought however.

More commonly, understandings of mysticism range widely from an 'obscure or confused belief or thought'[11] to more esoteric beliefs and practices. Indeed, Jewish and Islamic mysticism is rapidly being popularised in the West in the form of Kabbalah and Sufism, and Buddhist meditation is increasingly a practice that many people in postmodernity find appealing due to its focus on changing consciousness without the requirement to adopt theistic beliefs that are increasingly problematic in a world of rational science. Likewise, contemporary spiritual seekers are actively reinventing (or appropriating, depending on your point of view) indigenous religious traditions such as shamanism and witchcraft. Practices such as yoga and tai chi, which are often attempts to cope with lives that are progressively more stressful, are also religious practices at root. However, it is my contention that Murdoch, Levertov and Dillard continue, although somewhat eccentrically, to write within a mainly Christian context. They are well versed in the key mystical texts within the Christian tradition, as well as the Bible, and thus these writers are, in some sense, on a continuum spir-

8   *The Oxford English Dictionary*, 2nd Edition, Vol. X (Oxford: Clarendon Press, 1989), 176.
9   Ibid.
10   Ibid., 175.
11   *Collins English Dictionary* (Glasgow: Harper Collins, 1994), 1033.

itually and intellectually with previous mystics such as Julian. However, Murdoch, Levertov and Dillard write in a pluralistic world, and consequently draw insights from other mystical traditions found in world religions.

There is a long history of individual mystics whose personal search for God transformed their lives and those around them.[12] Ursula King, who provides a broad overview of the Christian mystic throughout the ages, describes a mystic as

> a person who is deeply aware of the powerful presence of the divine Spirit: someone who seeks, above all, knowledge and love of God and who experiences to an extraordinary degree the profoundly personal encounter with the energy of divine life. Mystics often perceive the presence of God throughout the world of nature and in all that is alive, leading to a transfiguration of the ordinary around them. However, the touch of God is most strongly felt deep within their hearts.[13]

In short, mysticism is principally intuitive and outside of rational control, which makes all the more poignant the fact that our current primary understanding of mysticism derives from the work of the philosopher and psychologist William James. At the turn of the twentieth century, James defined mysticism as a subjective experience of ineffability that involves an altered state of consciousness and direct contact or experience of the sacred.[14] However, it is largely due to James' focus on extraordinary mystical experience that subsequent interpretations of the lives of medieval mystics have been somewhat skewed.

---

12 Apart from Julian of Norwich, examples could include Bernard of Clairvaux (1090–1153), Francis of Assisi (1181–1226), Hildegard of Bingen (1098–1179), Catherine of Sienna (1347–1380), Mechtild of Magdeburg (c.1210–1297), Marguerite Porete (d.1310), Meister Eckhart (1260–1327), Ignatius Loyola (1491–1556), Teresa of Avila (1515–1582), John of the Cross (1542–1591), Jacob Boehme (1575–1624), Simone Weil (1909–1943), Pierre Teilhard de Chardin (1881–1955), and Thomas Merton (1915–1968). See Ursula King, *Christian Mystics: Their Lives and Legacies throughout the Ages* (London and New York: Routledge, 2001), for an introduction to key figures.

13 King, *Christian Mystic*, 3.

14 William James, *The Variety of Religious Experience*, 1902. See particularly lectures XVI and XVII for his definition and explanation of mysticism.

De Certeau (1992), Turner (1995), McGinn (1991) and Jantzen (1995) (1998) are among contemporary thinkers who have critiqued James' perspective as he conveyed it in *The Variety of Religious Experience* (1902) by re-examining mystical writings themselves for a fuller understanding of the term.[15] Michel De Certeau, a French Jesuit priest, viewed mysticism through an eclectic interdisciplinary lens. Key to his thought was his view that mysticism was a social practice for these early writers rather than a life of exclusive interiority. In this view, the individual who might be called a mystic engages fully with the public world. De Certeau also focused on the notion of 'desire' as the force that drives the spiritual seeker ever onward and upward.[16] Although this is somewhat tangential to our understanding of how I will use the term mysticism in this study, it is nevertheless relevant in terms of what motivates our mystic-poets. De Certeau also made some interesting connections between the fluid, incomplete or fragmented self in postmodernity, poetic insight and mystical practice that I will incorporate into this discussion.[17]

Denys Turner, until recently the Norris-Hulse Professor of Theology at Cambridge, argues that the modern turn towards experience has led to a misinterpretation of the self-understanding of mystics such as Julian, suggesting that, according to contemporary definitions of the term 'mysticism', they would be distinctly *'anti-mysticism'*. This is, he suggests, because their choice of metaphorical language was a deliberate one, in order to 'deny that they were terms descriptive of experiences'.[18] He also points out that, for Julian, and indeed all mystics in the Christian tradition, the original experience, if any, is not the goal in itself except as something that stimulates deeper contemplation over a lifetime.

---

15   I have chosen these writers as the pre-eminent scholars in the field from a theological perspective.

16   Michel De Certeau, The *Mystic Fable*, trans. Michael B. Smith (Chicago and London: The University of Chicago Press, 1992), 299 and 'Mystic Speech', in Michael De Cerrteau, Heterologies: *Discourse on the Other*, trans. Brian Massimi (Minneapolis: University of Minnesota Press, 1995).

17   De Certeau, *The Mystic Fable*, 295–99.

18   Denys Turner, *The Darkness of God* (Cambridge: Cambridge University Press, 1995), 4.

Along similar lines, Bernard McGinn, who has produced a trilogy of books studying the history of mysticism, is convinced that the separation of mystical experience and mystical theology rests on a misunderstanding, a severance he has not found throughout the history of Christian mysticism but only in our historical moment.[19] He is helpful in his suggestion that, rather than trying to define mysticism, it is more useful to think of it under three complementary headings: 'mysticism as a part or element of religion; mysticism as a process or way of life; and mysticism as an attempt to express a direct consciousness of the presence of God'.[20] In reality, the current definitional emphasis has remained on the third aspect, but this study seeks to examine the possibilities of stressing the second because a focus on the immediacy of experience does not tell us anything about the preparation or communication of mystical consciousness.[21] In this vein, the focus here will be on the process of writing in the life of a postmodern mystic in order to understand how texts act as ways of communicating what McGinn prefers to define as 'mystical consciousness'. Mysticism in this understanding pertains to a disciplined psychic state that both invites such experiences and is able to respond to them imaginatively, as opposed to first order mystical experience, which is more passive by nature.

The passive element of mystical experience is one among several dangers that portraying these women writers as mystics presents. Grace Jantzen (1995) (1998) has challenged what she defines as the 'male' understanding of what we mean by the term mystic by showing that the term has undergone major changes in different historical periods. In particular, she has highlighted the connections between power and gender. Despite indications to the contrary, she suggests that McGinn defines mysticism 'essentially in terms of intense, private, subjective experiences' as the basis of the study of mysticism.

---

19   Bernard McGinn, *The Foundations of Mysticism* (1992), *The Growth of Mysticism* (1996), *The Flowering of Mysticism* (1998) (London: SCM Press, The *Presence of God* series).
20   Bernard McGinn, *The Foundations of Mysticism* (London: SCM Press 1992), xv–xvi.
21   Ibid., xviii.

As Jantzen notes, he would not consider any ordinary 'process or way of life or element of religion [lacking in extraordinary experiences] as mystical'.[22] This effectively keeps women's experiences of the sacred on the margins of theological discourse in the same way it has throughout history.

That is, the Church has historically controlled 'who counts as a mystic'.[23] During the high and late Middle Ages, for example, women were increasingly able to claim authority through visions, but not surprisingly, women also underwent intense scrutiny by Church authorities who distinguished between real and false mysticism. Frequently, a woman's claim to mystical experience was condemned as blasphemous whereas a man's experience was deemed to be more authentic. Once the secular state took control, it was safer for women to practise mysticism, although this was in a strictly private or domesticated context. In fact, Jantzen argues that the socio-religious construction of both women and mysticism has historically been private and personal and underpinned the Victorian ideal of 'Angel of the House'.[24]

Modern expressions of mysticism still present the same dangers for women because they may reinforce stereotypes of passivity. Too much focus on a woman's capacity to turn inward and withdraw from society is problematic because it tends to marginalise and disempower women. More generally, this focus could deflect attention from the magnitude of the social, religious, economic and ideological barriers that have obstructed women's self-realization in the public world. In the academy, the focus on the scientific study of mystical experience reinforces rational, and by extension male, control to the question of who counts as a mystic.[25] So whether it is the male hierarchy of the

---

22 Grace M. Jantzen, *Power, Gender and Christian Mysticism* (Cambridge: Cambridge University Press, 1995), 6.

23 Ibid. This is a question that runs throughout Jantzen's discussion. See for example pages 15, 23, 335, 341.

24 Grace M. Jantzen, 'Feminists, philosophers, and mystics', *Hypatia*, 9:4 (1994), 186–206.

25 Ibid. This is not to suggest that women are not rational, of course, but rather refers to the classical social distinctions between the psychologies of men and women: the former as rational and the latter as intuitive. In short, these clichés are nevertheless emblematic of societal realities.

institutionalised Church or the scientific focus on the individual post-Enlightenment, women's status as 'mystics' has basically been pre-scribed outside their own self-understanding.

Despite surface differences, the key theoretical approaches mentioned above all tend to downplay experientialist readings and posit mysticism as a phenomenon that reshapes the sense of self in relationship to others. An unbalanced preoccupation with interiority is strongly discouraged as unhealthy. Literary writers understand this because they know that 'the limits and interest of introspection are soon reached'.[26] I find it intriguing that, as far as I can ascertain, literary critics do not have the same hesitations when talking about mystics, mysticism or the mystical, however. No doubt, this is because any sense of the Transcendent is not bound up with truth claims to the same extent that theology and the social sciences are; or perhaps, as the poet Elizabeth Jennings reminds us, because the poet as mystic writes *unconsciously*, and too much analysis impairs the spontaneity and artistic achievement.[27]

So, what can we say specifically about the term mysticism in order to outline its meaning in postmodernity? I find a useful starting point in Dorothee Soelle's *The Strength of the Weak* (1984), wherein she argues that mysticism is

> an awareness of God gained not through books, not through the authority of religious teachings, not through the so-called priestly office but through the life experiences of human beings, experiences that are articulated and reflected upon in religious language but that first come to people in what they encounter in life […] an experience that breaks through the existing limitations of human comprehension, feeling, and reflection.[28]

Soelle is keen to emphasise that these 'experiences' do not necessarily have to be 'something extraordinary' by suggesting that it is more appropriate to think of mystical experience as a commonly felt notion of 'wholeness' or a 'sense of being at home in the world'. Neither is it

26   Elizabeth Jennings, *Every Changing Shape: Mystical Experience and the Making of Poems* (Manchester: Carcanet, 1996), 19.
27   Ibid., 14. My italics.
28   Dorothee Soelle, *The Strength of the Weak: Towards a Christian Feminist Identity*, trans. R. & R. Kimber (Philadelphia: The Westminster Press, 1984), 86–87.

of any importance whether the articulation of these encounters happens within a theistic or non-theistic context. But what is vitally important for Soelle is that we need to find the language to communicate these experiences and reflections.[29]

Don Cupitt offers an elucidation of this language indicating that the search for mystical language is more complex than Soelle initially suggests. He proposes two opposing but mutually interacting ways of defining mystical knowledge based on broadly Platonic and Neo-Platonic starting points:

> the divine nature is utterly incomprehensible to us, and can be known by us only by unknowing and in a state of utter darkness; or that God is the most readily knowable and universally known object of all, the knowledge of him being the foundation or underpinning of all other knowledge whatsoever. The first line of argument leads to a conclusion that nobody can really know God, and the second to the conclusion that there can be nobody who does *not* know God. The two conclusions must coincide, the knowledge of God being something so deep and dark and transcendental that in one way nobody has it, and yet in another way everybody has it.[30]

Cupitt outlines two 'ways' of apprehending God – one that accepts God as completely unknowable and the other within which humans have the ability to perceive and describe God at all times. I shall argue that these are essentially different sides of the same coin rather than being opposing paths.

In relation to Plato's cave myth, which is arguably the foundational narrative of Western philosophy, this means either looking at the shadows and reflections in the cave or looking straight at the sun. Like the prisoners chained to the wall of a cave who can only see shadows on the wall cast by a fire, so all our attempts to name God or reality fail to truly grasp the essence of the Divine, which remains beyond words and images. It is only when we move allegorically towards the sun, beyond such images and towards the blinding light that true vision occurs. Cupitt's suggestion that these two paths must inevitably 'coincide' diminishes the reality of mysticism. The way of the mystic is always a paradoxical one involving strange encounters.

29   Ibid., 88–89.
30   Don Cupitt, *Mysticism after Modernity* (Oxford: Blackwell, 1998), 4.

The *via negativa*, which is characterised as the way of not knowing and darkness, and the *via positiva*, that knowledge of God that is wholly evident, are better thought of as being in perpetual tension. The mystical theology of Pseudo-Dionysius describes how it is possible to discover God in the outpouring of himself in creation. Yet, at the same time, the mystic must ultimately pass beyond all images and names of God.[31] Therefore, language employed by the mystic to speak of the sacred is both apophatic and cataphatic. Apophatic language reflects the theological assumption that God is ultimately beyond all symbols and concepts,[32] and the use of cataphatic language is the opposite in that it describes God through affirmations of what he/she is. In the Christian tradition, as well as other mystical strands in world religions, mystical experience represents a breakthrough in these differences, and more specifically, between the knowing subject and the object.

In many ways, the attempt to define mysticism (or anything for that matter) in the context of postmodernity can never reach a point of precision. Indeed, a key aspect of postmodern philosophy, according to Zygmunt Bauman, is the acknowledgement that definitions tend to conceal as much as they reveal, because they have a tendency

> to maim and obfuscate while pretending to clarify and straighten up. It also accepts the fact that all too often experience spills out of the verbal cages in which one would wish to hold it, that there are things of which one should keep silent since one cannot speak of them, and that the ineffable is as much an integral part of the human mode of being-in-the-world as is the linguistic net in which one tries (in vain, as it happens, though no less vigorously for that reason) to catch it.[33]

---

31 Dionysius the Areopagite, *Mystical Theology and The Celestial Hierarchies*, trans. The Editors of the Shrine of Wisdom (Godalming, Surrey: The Shrine of Wisdom, 1949) 7–16.

32 E. A. Livingstone, 'Apophatic theology', *The Concise Oxford Dictionary of the Christian Church*. (Oxford: Oxford University Press, 2000) http://www.Oxford reference.com/views/ENTRY.html?subview=Main&entry=t95.e330 02/02/06

33 Zygmunt Bauman, 'Postmodern Religion?', in Paul Heelas (ed), *Religion, Modernity and Postmodernity* (Oxford: Blackwell, 1998), 55. Bauman is no doubt referring to Wittgenstein's famous phrase, 'What we cannot speak about we must pass over in silence', from Ludwig Wittgenstein, *Tractatus Logico-Philosophicus*,

This sense of meaning slipping through the net of language is, of course, a chief characteristic of postmodernity. Despite this inherent constraint, for the purposes of this study, the mystic is someone who is 'seized by time [... and] erupts and transforms' and feels compelled to write or produce what De Certeau defines as 'mystic fable', even though they recognise that the journey never realises its aim.[34] In this regard, there is a clear link between what Bauman describes as the fluidity of meaning in postmodernity and De Certeau's description of mystics as those who 'point out pathways to get lost'.[35]

The use of the term 'mysticism' here maintains the classical tension between the *via negativa* and the *via positiva*, but rather than being an extraordinary or ineffable experience available to a few lucky individuals, mysticism is also here a radical engagement with the Other, whether it be God, the natural world or other living beings. In other words, mysticism is a way of being in the world or an orientation of consciousness towards that which remains utterly inexplicable. However, the postmodern mystic is also something of a prophet in that he or she calls people back to God or ethical conduct and envisages possible futures. In short, just as their predecessors were pointers for lived religion, inspiring others to prayer if nothing else, the mystic in postmodernity envisions alternatives to the fragmentation of postmodern life, which is by definition, a similarly radical engagement. The *via mystica* is a challenge to think creatively in this unique time we call postmodernity.

What is Postmodernity?

Again, like mysticism, postmodernity tends to be notoriously difficult to define or explain in any wholly satisfactory way. As Cupitt notes,

---

trans. D. F. Pears and B. F. McGuinness (London: Routledge & Kegan Paul, 1963), 151. Wittgenstein was influential in Murdoch's thought – so much so that her first published novel *Under The Net* was a direct allusion to his view that all our thoughts and ideas inevitably fall through the 'net' of language.

34   De Certeau, *The Mystic Fable*, 11–13.

35   Ibid., 17. De Certeau points out that this may just mean 'losing' certain types of knowledge.

the term 'postmodern' is best understood, not as indicating that we have shifted to a new mode of understanding, but on the contrary, that we are in a transitional period wherein 'we have a name for what is gone [the Modern Age] but not for what is coming'.[36] More specifically, for the purposes of this study, I define postmodernity as a period in history characterised by disintegration of religious, political and social institutions and the mores to which they previously laid claim, the questioning of the overarching ability of reason, and the recognition that all knowledge is partial and contextual. I particularly endorse Sheldrake's celebration of postmodernity as a hopeful and rewarding time for theology because it

> frees the notion of 'God' from the constraints of rational philosophy and the need to justify belief in rational terms. [… It also] implies a rejection of any kind of literalism. It also rejects authoritarianism and prefers dialogue with strangers and what is 'other' rather than to colonize alien experiences or to convert those who understand the world differently.[37]

In other words, postmodernity is a time when human beings are peculiarly open to the subversion of narrow, literalist interpretations of religion, a time characterised by the need to defend the otherness, differences and particularities not only of people but all living beings.

The traditional theological stance in monotheistic religions such as Christianity, Judaism and Islam is that meaning resides principally in long-established supernatural categories and values, wherein 'the transcendent is seen as standing *above* or *behind* human and natural reality'.[38] At the other end of the spectrum, there are postmodern viewpoints espoused by philosophers such as Jacques Derrida, Roland Barthes and Michael Foucault who argue that humans construct all knowledge. What has become known as the 'linguistic turn' includes the assertion that there is no meaning prior to or outside of language.[39]

36 Cupitt, *Mysticism After Modernity*, 1.
37 Sheldrake, *Spirituality and Theology*, 10.
38 Jerry H. Gill, *Mediated Transcendence: A Postmodern Reflection* (Macon, Georgia: Mercer University Press, 1989), 2.
39 See Richard Rorty (ed), *The Linguistic Turn: Essays on Philosophical Method* (Chicago: University of Chicago Press, 1992) for a good introduction to the emphasis on language in philosophical theory. Jacques Derrida's most influential

Cupitt (1998) openly embraces postmodern ideas about the death of God and rejects modernist claims for objective truth in favour of relativism. However, this book will argue for the continuation of an idea of some form of the transcendent, albeit a somewhat unorthodox one. That is, mystical experience is presumed to be precisely the direct apprehension of the transcendent in everyday reality. Otherwise, such 'experience' must of necessity merely fit into some hyper-relativised version of experience.

McFague helpfully describes postmodernity as a shift in assumptions wherein there is

> a greater appreciation of nature, linked with chastened admiration for technology; the recognition of the importance of language (and hence interpretation and construction) in human existence; the acceptance of the challenge that other religious options present to the Judeo-Christian tradition; a sense of displacement of the white, Western male and the rise of those dispossessed because of gender, race or class; an apocalyptic sensibility, fuelled in part by the awareness that we exist between two holocausts, the Jewish and the nuclear, and perhaps most significant, a growing appreciation of the thoroughgoing, radical interdependence of life at all levels and in every imaginable way.[40]

What McFague depicts here is an overview of the attitudes that arise within postmodernity. She also implies that theology and personal spirituality cannot be divorced from these pressing concerns.

Paul Lakeland suggests that postmodernity is an interplay between the given and the novel, or what has been and what might be.[41] Like Cupitt, Lakeland locates postmodernity as a time of transit between past and present, but he goes further by suggesting it is a creative time wherein humans have the opportunity to participate in the future. Lakeland goes on to identify three types of humanity in postmodernity. The first type is the obvious consumer of postmodern culture and consists of the large numbers of people who do not ask about

---

book, wherein he outlines his now famous deconstruction theory, is *Writing and Difference* (London: Routledge, 2001) or for a critique of postmodernism, refer to Terry Eagleton's *The Illusions of Postmodernism* (Oxford: Blackwell, 1996).

40   Sallie McFague, *Models of God* (Philadelphia: Fortress Press, 1987), x.

41   Paul Lakeland, *Postmodernity: Christian Identity in a Fragmented Age* (Minneapolis: Fortress Press, 1997), 1.

the meaning of life, tend to idolise money or sex, and effectively live solely for the present. The second group he refers to are those he defines as being both postmodern and premodern at the same time. Those under this heading accept the trappings of postmodernity but have a nostalgic longing for older beliefs and values and are inclined to have a sentimental view of the past. Within this group are Protestant Christian fundamentalists such Pat Robertson, the charismatic US evangelist, or neo-conservatives like the ex-Tory Prime Minister Margaret Thatcher. The third category is representative of individuals who recognise that they live in a postmodern world but are 'critically present' in that world.[42] Murdoch, Levertov and Dillard fit into the third group as writers who work within the tensions between modern and postmodern ideologies.

The Postmodern Mystic

Postmodernity, rather than being a wholly negative state of affairs as regards belief and religious experience as might be perceived, offers the potential for mysticism to flourish. However, Melvyn Matthews argues that contemporary Christians engage inappropriately with medieval mystics owing to modern presuppositions regarding the self and its possessions,[43] which means that postmodernity represents a correction in this regard. In fact, for mystics such as Julian, there was no sense of the self as we moderns understand it. The postmodern turn toward decentring the self as represented by the 'death of the subject' is, according to Matthews, 'a way of bringing the over-inflated view of the self into the light of reality, a way of deconstruction so that a proper humility about the place of the self is restored'.[44] In short, although this move in our time has overtones of nihilism, a discussion that exceeds this current study, there is a link between philosophical

---

42   Ibid., 9–11.
43   Melvyn Matthews, *Both Alike to Thee: The Retrieval of the Mystic Way* (London: SPCK, 2000), 90.
44   Ibid., 91.

deconstruction of self in postmodernity and medieval awareness of the seductive nature of the self.

Mystics have historically understood the impossibility of talking about God, knowing that God 'surpasses speech and defies conceptual control'.[45] Similarly, postmodern thought acknowledges the difficulties of definition and reality of the continual reconstruction of meaning. Postmodern mysticism therefore openly embraces paradox and ambiguity and accepts that the sacred remains perennially beyond our grasp. At the same time, there is a clear attention to every detail of lived reality. In fact, postmodern mysticism represents a complete reversal of classical theology, philosophy and literalist religions that seek the truth in the higher realms of abstraction or divine revelation.

Soelle proposes in *The Silent Cry* that mysticism is a sensibility caught up with everyday life, thereby implying that the sacred exists as part of the ordinary world. In short, she wishes to democratise mysticism.[46] An acknowledgement of the immanent nature of the sacred naturally forces the mystic in postmodernity to engage with the larger social, ecological and political issues, a move that becomes even more important within the context of globalisation, wherein the knock-on effects of Western wealth on developing countries is only too apparent. The tendency to associate mysticism with inferiority not only ignores the reality of others but also provides a fragmentary account of the self. Indeed, much of the focus in the current trend that is self-help manuals pivots on the belief that there is an inner, real self that is waiting to emerge. In contradistinction, Sheldrake insists, following his reading of Rowan Williams, that 'the real self is found or made from the very beginning in human communication and interaction'.[47] In other words, our identities are formed in relation to others – a point that will prove to be important later in this discussion. This assertion subverts the stereotypical image of the spiritual recluse who goes ever

---

45   Kessler & Sheppard, *Mystics*, viii.
46   Soelle, *The Silent Cry*, 9–22.
47   Philip Sheldrake, 'Christian Spirituality as a Way of Living Publicly', 19. Sheldrake draws on Rowan Williams, thought from 'Interiority and Epiphany: A Reading in New Testament Ethics', in *On Christian Theology* (Oxford: Blackwell, 2000), chapter 16.

deeper into a private, inner quest for meaning by suggesting that an active involvement with the wider community is not only a moral and mystical task but essential for self-development. Jantzen has demonstrated that mystics of the Christian Church have, in fact, always been at the forefront of social concern. Hermits and anchorites of the Middle Ages had an enormous ministry of personal counselling or spent themselves caring for the sick and social outcasts; others were not afraid to speak up for the powerless and marginalised.[48] Thus, this discussion seeks to contribute towards the rediscovery of this other side to mysticism, its active, social and political component, in postmodernity.

Murdoch was not by any means ignorant of social and political issues; she rather enjoyed political debate and was not shy about offering political opinions in interviews. In her fiction, however, she preferred to focus her energies on changing individual consciousness and the development of individual virtue through her 'moral fables' or parables. In reality, Levertov is the closest politically to both McFague and Soelle as a large proportion of her work is politically motivated. In response to suggestions that such poetry might be of a lesser aesthetic value, she responds:

> A poetry of anguish, a poetry of anger, of rage, a poetry that, from literal or deeply imagined experience, depicts and denounces perennial injustice and cruelty in their current forms, and in our peculiar time warns of the unprecedented perils that confront us, can be truly high poetry...[49]

---

48 Grace M. Jantzen 'Ethics and mysticism: Friends or foes?', in *Nederlands Theologisch Tijdschrift* 39 (1985), 315–16. She particularly refers to Francis of Assisi and his mission to lepers; those among the Beguines who worked to alleviate suffering during the plague; Vincent de Paul who, among other things, worked to lessen the suffering of the slaves who manned French galleys. She also considers the more political activities of well-known mystics such as Meister Eckhart. He attacked the exploitation and social injustices of north Germany in the 14th century in his preaching. She reads John of the Cross as someone who protested against 'the smug triumphalism of the Spain of the *conversos* and the conquistadors, finding the insecurities of the "dark night" preferable to the certainties of the Grand Inquisitor'.

49 Levertov, 'Poetry, Prophecy and Survival', in *New & Selected Essays*, 143–44.

The central themes of Levertov's political poetry include protests against nuclear proliferation, war atrocities and the ecological crisis. Her poetry, like McFague's theology, affirms all life – not just the human but plants and animals too. Dillard's work, by her own definition, is noticeably lacking in ethical concern, but as will become apparent as we proceed, rather than being a serious omission, a lack of didactic assertion is, surprisingly, one of its strengths.

Contemporary writers who rely on their imagination and experience of the world provide a non-authoritative and self-reflexive means of exploring what it means to be human in relation to the sacred. What is interesting for this study is that Murdoch, Dillard and Levertov resist both the postmodern trend towards 'anything goes', a scenario wherein everything is relative, and the tendency at the other end of the spectrum to formalism, or a 'by the book' mentality. It will become apparent in this discussion that, in many ways, Murdoch, Levertov and Dillard subvert stereotypical images of female mystics, while at the same time it is possible to locate them within a female pattern of mystical consciousness that subverts the dominant ideology. In this context, the task of the postmodern mystic is to resist postmodern relativity and the subsequent loss of transcendental or religious mystery.

The Writer as a Mystic

David Tacey, Associate Professor in Psychoanalytic Studies at La Trobe University, Melbourne, admits that 'religion needs the poetic imagination and the contemporary arts, because they are major ways in which "eternal" truth or the holy become revived and made relevant to the times'.[50] Historically, this has been the task of both the prophet and the mystic. The more emotive, imaginative and intuitive language in literary and poetic writing counterbalances the more scientific or technological jargon of the social sciences. Creative writing is also a way of surviving psychologically and spiritually as well as being a compulsive response to a life spent in pilgrimage. For writers of integ-

---

50   David Tacey, *The Spirituality Revolution: The Emergence of Contemporary Spirituality* (New York: Brunner-Routledge, 2004), 161.

rity, the aesthetic literary quest is equally a spiritual quest to discern transcendent meaning and purpose in human life.

This is not to state emphatically that all literary writers are mystics. There are, I suggest, three key discernable characteristics of a mystic-writer. First, their life is exemplified by dedication and immersion in religious traditions, the lives and works of mystics and sacred texts. Second they work in a tension between pragmatism and mystery or concrete and social realities and an imaginative attempt to grasp the unseen, transcendent realm. Third, writers with a mystical orientation, past and present, become renowned for the forceful ways they inspire people to become more spiritually and ethically aware. Although I would want to be wary of making value judgments about other fictional writers, I would suggest that these factors demarcate the writing of the mystic-writer from the writer whose work may merely entertain, titillate or facilitate an escape from the world of the everyday into one of fantasy.

There is a clear parallel between the attempts by many literary writers and mystics to understand how the universe functions and their longing for spiritual perfection. Moreover, a wondrous appreciation of beauty in art or the natural world parallels and overlaps religious faith or spiritual fulfilment. Thus, it seems natural that mysticism and beauty find expression through the arts. Although language ultimately fails to express the sacred adequately, this does not mean that the effort should discontinue. The imagination is the faculty that links the creative artist and mystic, and it is through language that the creative writer conveys mystical perception for the rest of us, no matter how insufficient literary forms might be to carry out the task.

An extended imagination, according to Noel D. O'Donoghue, may produce visions such as those recorded in Julian's *Showings*, but the imagination might also be manifested as poetic, artistic, symbolic, philosophical and theological visualisations and insights.[51] Creative writing or mystical language has the potential to go further than the confined language of philosophy and theology because it has a freedom denied to rational thought. In many ways, it also remains part of

---

51   Noel D. O'Donoghue, 'Mystical Imagination', in James P. Mackey, *Religious Imagination* (Edinburgh: Edinburgh University Press, 1986), 187–88.

subjective experience and therefore beyond the control of others. Yet this freedom does not come without commitment, moral responsibility and self-giving.[52] Without the latter, creative texts could become potentially dangerous to the degree that they espouse oppressive and restricted doctrines and ideologies (that is, as propaganda for a given perception of the real). This is a serious problem that warrants more discussion but falls outside the scope of this argument.

It is particularly the use of metaphoric language that links the mystic, the poet and the theologian. Metaphors essentially act as a bridge between what is known and what cannot be known by operating in a dialectic between 'is' and 'is not'. By necessity, in order to achieve any level of understanding, metaphorical language plays on a dialogue between an image and a concept. Julian's small thing 'no rounder than a ball' appears as such but is in reality something else that escapes human perception; metaphor both reveals and conceals at the same time. It is only by conjuring up an image based on her perceptions that an understanding of the unseen mystery Julian calls God becomes apparent.

Poetry and fiction both rely on image and metaphor, and sacred texts are resplendent with them. The key difference is that monotheistic religions have a tendency to literalise metaphors such as 'Father' for God, whereas in creative writing, metaphors remain a means of understanding something beyond our reach through reference to something we recognise from experience. In monotheistic religions, the *literary* has a tendency to become confused with the *literal*. Literary and mythical texts in polytheistic or monist worldviews are arguably more predisposed to being fluid and flexible as regards meaning, and these texts are recognised as a human, and therefore fallible, effort to grasp what lies beyond human perception. Mystics have a long tradition of utilising metaphorical language, and this study is an attempt to assess metaphorical language for its theological import in what might be termed 'postmodern mysticism'.

Towards the end of the twentieth century, some seven hundred years after Julian wrote, Jantzen asks an interesting question in her introduction to the new edition of *Julian of Norwich* (2000): 'What

52   Ibid., 191–92.

does it mean to be an anchoress in postmodernity?' She acknowledges that a postmodern anchoress would not be the same as late medieval anchoress such as Julian, but she asserts, a postmodern anchoress might share the position of 'standing at an angle to the certainties and preoccupations of the world [with] an openness to the divine in a world that has given itself to the mundane'.[53] In practical terms, this requires the time and space to withdraw from the social world for contemplation and engaged thought. In theoretical terms, it suggests a critique of the Enlightenment ideals that were premised upon 'certainties'.

The purpose of such a postmodern anchoress, Jantzen suggests, is 'to discern the death dealing structures and practices of modernity and to be open to ways of new life and flourishing'.[54] The mystic in postmodernity has to work against a radically different social, cultural, religious and political background to Julian's. For Jantzen, the postmodern mystic has to resist 'the practices of modernity', which she believes have contributed to a destructive and nullifying ideology. There are a number of ways that Murdoch, Levertov and Dillard mimic Julian the medieval anchoress in postmodernity, and this will be explored more fully in Chapter Two. Broadly speaking, however, this parallel is discernable in a comparable pattern of mystical engagement that involves contemplation and reflection. Furthermore, as Cupitt notes, a mystical sensibility, significantly and almost without exception, appears to lead to the act of writing.[55] The crucial distinction between creative writers and traditional mystics is that theological or spiritual insight, more often than not, emerges within the text as it progresses for the latter. Rather than being separated as a conceptual thought or extraordinary experience that predates it, illumination happens during the process for both the writer and the reader. Mystical insight in creative and expressive writing will be implicit and ambiguous as opposed to explicit and prescriptive. Therefore, it follows that a writer's choice of language, particularly the use of metaphor, may not be immediately recognisable as theological, because the term creative

---

53   Jantzen, *Julian of Norwich*, vii.
54   Ibid., xxii.
55   Cupitt, *Mysticism After Modernity*, 60–66.

writer and not theologian or religious contemplative more accurately defines their role in the world. Murdoch, Levertov and Dillard allow the distinction to blur because of their extensive knowledge and experience of Christianity, other mystical traditions and classical writers in the literary tradition.

To conclude, postmodernity is a time wherein dualistic thinking (either/or) is being replaced by a more dialectical relationship (both/ and). Increasingly, we are witnessing a move from the dominance of Western philosophical hegemony to a celebration of ancient wisdoms. In other words, there is a tension between past, present and future or in academic terms between premodern, modern and postmodern. Mysticism does not pertain to isolated ineffable experiences of the presence of God, but rather, denotes a way of actively longing for and experiencing the sacred reality rooted in everyday experience. A mystic in postmodernity is someone who thinks dialectically, has 'an openness to the Divine' and actively works for the transformation of individuals and society. As such, they are in a position of critiquing the excesses of modernity and seeking to overcome the destructive ideologies of its aftermath in postmodernity, and therefore, mystics in postmodernity become strangers in their own land.

Three Literary Mystics

Although Murdoch, Levertov and Dillard all think and write within a 'mystical' framework, distinctive features of their work defy any easy categorisation and are uniquely characteristic to each. Murdoch was centrally concerned with how to be religious (as she perceived it) in a non-religious age. Being religious, to her mind, was inextricably enmeshed in being moral. It is for this reason that I have called her a 'moral mystic'. Above all, she challenged the meta-ethical post-structural concern with language in postmodern enquiry by striving to recover a perception of human consciousness with morality as a central element. Further, she considered consciousness to be unavoidably oriented towards the idea of the Good, a notion she developed chiefly through the depiction of characters in her novels who wrestle with their own conscience and moral integrity in their relationships with others.

From her own writing on the subject, it is clear that Levertov perceived herself to be on a spiritual quest or pilgrimage from the very start.[56] Undoubtedly, her journey was one of paradox and unresolved conflict, although not one devoid of faith or hope. Like the mystic, she grappled with both joy and pain. Her poetry reveals that she often despaired, but at other times, she was also ecstatic; and all the while, the real world remained a tangible presence throughout her work. I have described Levertov as a 'wandering' mystic because of her Jewish ancestry, from which I have drawn on the archetype of the wandering Jew and the fact that she shows a personal fondness for the metaphor of walking and wandering to denote spiritual development in her poetry.

In a similar manner to Levertov, Dillard largely seeks and relays wisdom through personal encounters with a chaotic world. Her first major publication, *Pilgrim at Tinker Creek*, which reflects her eclectic interests, overtly parallels the medieval mystic way of the *via positiva* and *via negativa*. I have coined the term 'mystic at the edge' to denote her fascination with 'the fringe', or the place between temporal and non-temporal worlds as a place of illumination, and the difficulty of pinning her style to one discipline or genre.

Iris Murdoch: Moral Mystic

Peter Conradi describes the process of writing Murdoch's biography as 'the charting [of a] journey from brilliant bohemian youth towards the wise serenity, celebrated in Tom Phillip's iconic portrait of her in the National Portrait Gallery'.[57] Undoubtedly, it is chiefly through her novels that she became a public celebrity. John Bayley, her husband

---

56   Levertov, 'Some Affinities of Content', in *New & Selected Essays*, 3.
57   Peter J. Conradi, *Going Buddhist: Panic and Emptiness, the Buddha and Me* (London: Short Books, 2004), 156.

of many years, recalls in his biography that she had one main and concise agenda throughout her writing career, which was 'to write something for everyone'.[58] She wrote a total of twenty-seven novels spanning four decades, from 1954 to 1995, publishing her first book, *Sartre: Romantic Rationalist*, in 1953 and her first novel, *Under the Net*, the year after. In addition to her novels, Murdoch also published four works of philosophy, four plays, some poetry, and a sizable number of essays on philosophy and literature that Peter Conradi has collected into one volume entitled *Existentialists and Mystics*.

In recent years, unfortunately, Richard Eyre's film *Iris* has set up a dichotomy between 'young Iris bonking and old Iris bonkers'.[59] An emphasis on the details of Murdoch's sexual encounters as a young woman and her decline into the darkness of Alzheimer's disease has overshadowed a brilliant career as a writer and loving acquaintance of those who knew her best.[60] Although I will draw on biographies where relevant, the focus of this thesis is Murdoch's own writing.

Murdoch was born in Dublin on July 15th 1919. When she was nine, her Anglo-Irish parents moved to London, where her father joined the civil service. She began writing stories at this time 'to provide herself with imaginary siblings'.[61] Like many before her, and no doubt for many to come, her initial attempts at writing were 'strateg[ies] for assuaging anxiety or loneliness'.[62] By the age of seventeen (1936),

---

58   Audio tape, *Iris: A Memoir of Iris Murdoch* (UK: Clipper Audio:2002).
59   Don Cupitt, 'Iris and the Death of God'. Cupitt records a conversation with an unnamed person. http://www.guardian.co.uk/comment/story/0,3604,672531,00. html
60   The film and John Bayley's books about their life together (on which the film is based), *An Elegy for Iris* and *Iris: A Memoir of Iris Murdoch*, have both received mixed reviews due to the fact that intimate details about her life are the central concern. A. N. Wilson is particularly scathing of both books in *Iris Murdoch as I Knew Her* (London: Hutchinson, 2003). There has been much speculation about Bayley's motivations for writing his biographies especially as he was somewhat in the shadow of his wife's success throughout their life together.
61   Peter J. Conradi, *Iris Murdoch: A Life* (London: Harper Collins, 2001), 46.
62   Ibid.

however, she was certain that she wanted to be a writer.[63] She attended Badminton School in Bristol and read Greats at Somerville College, Oxford where she gained a First in 1942. After taking her finals, she followed her father into the Civil Service, becoming an assistant principal to the Treasury, where she stayed until 1944. Following this appointment, she joined the United Nations Relief and Rehabilitation Administration, working with refugees from Belgium and Austria. Afterwards, she received the offer of a scholarship to study in the United States of America but could not take it up as she had briefly belonged to the Communist Party when she was a student, and much to her chagrin, could not gain permission to enter the country. So instead, she successfully took up a Sarah Smithson studentship in philosophy at Newnham College, Cambridge in 1947. The following year, she became a fellow of St Anne's College, Oxford as a tutor in philosophy – a post she held for fifteen years.

In retrospect, bearing in mind her phenomenal success as a writer, it is hard to imagine the young Murdoch who struggled with internal and external difficulties that hindered the realisation of her dream. She wrote several novels before *Under the Net* was published in 1954,[64] submitting her second novel to Faber & Faber in 1944, which was rejected by T. S. Eliot himself. She later commented that he was right to do so as her early novels were 'too personal', and she soon learnt to 'burn the confessional and subjective out of her writing'.[65] There was one person seemed to give her both the freedom and stability that were to prove essential to enable her to pursue her career.

In 1956, she married the writer and literary critic John Bayley, whom she lived with in Steeple Aston for thirty years, moving to Oxford for the latter part of their long and happy marriage. They never had children. In 1976, she was awarded the CBE, and in 1987, a DBE in the New Year's Honours List. Among her many awards and hon-

---

63 Ibid., 56. Conradi tells us that she was on the mail-boat in the summer of 1936 to Dublin when a family friend asked her what she wanted to do in life, to which she replied, 'Write'.

64 Ibid., 170. Conradi has not been able to establish the exact number. The number appears to be between four and six, some of which were destroyed by Murdoch in 1986.

65 Ibid.

ours, she received the Booker Prize for the novel *The Sea, The Sea* in 1978. During the last years of her life, she was tragically afflicted with Alzheimer's and died in 1999 at age seventy-nine.

For most critics, nearly all the narrators and protagonists in her novels are obviously the voice of Murdoch. If Conradi's biography is accurate, in spite of her previous assertion about burning away her subjectivity, it is clear that Murdoch's personal life experiences do provide the basis of much of the characterisations, plots and human dilemmas depicted in her novels. In effect, she intended her readers to learn from her own distractions from reality, her many sorties into the world of enchantment.

Her passionate ambition to write is apparent in 1944 when she shares her literary ambitions with Frank Thompson in their long correspondences during the war years:

> I have no time to live my own life – at a time when my own life feels of intense value & interest to me. Jesus God how I want to write. I want to write a long, long & exceedingly obscure novel objectifying the queer conflicts I find within myself & observe in the characters of others. Like Proust I want to escape from the eternal push and rattle of time into the coolness & poise of a work of art.[66]

Writing for Murdoch was initially a form of escapism and therapy, a way of making sense of the world she inhabited. This period of her life sees her adrift, at a stage when she had to act decisively. By now, thanks to her education at Oxford, she was also an intellectual who, under her mentor Donald MacKinnon, had gained a highly developed perspective on a philosophy of life. Earlier in 1943, when writing to Thompson, she quoted Aldous Huxley's doctrine that, for a writer, 'it is not what one has experienced but what one *does* with what one has experienced that matters'.[67]

It was not until the end of the war that she rekindled her interest in philosophy by reading Sartre's *L'Etre et le Néant*. In Murdoch's personal philosophy, there are influences of Platonic, Buddhist and Christian thought that she applied to her lifelong search for the 'Good'. Two philosophers, Simone Weil and Plato, are both tangible

66   Ibid., 171.
67   Ibid., 155.

presences throughout Murdoch's oeuvre.[68] Plato's notion of the Good informs her own formulation but undergoes 'a distinct Christian trans-mutation'.[69] And Weil's notion of 'attention' in her ethic of love is a continual undercurrent in both Murdoch's novels and her philosophy. Her interest in Buddhism and Hinduism are also apparent in her work.

Her first novel, *Under the Net*, contained most of her important ideas that she was to elaborate on in subsequent works. Specifically, it introduced her idea of the 'existential and mystical hero' (or 'saint and artist') in the guise of Jake Donaghue and Hugo Bellfounder. Jake as the first person narrator tries to cover the chaos of reality with philo-sophical dialogue, while Hugo struggles to be good. By the end of the novel, Hugo gives up the search for wisdom and decides to be a watchmaker, to honour the world's details. As such, Conradi suggests that he stands for 'a loving empirical curiosity about particulars, for reverential attention'.[70] Indeed, at one point, Hugo proposes to Jake that he 'renounce…the search for God – in favour of the local – seeing life as a task, as blundering on'. 'Blundering on', or 'struggle' as she uses elsewhere,[71] are both fitting metaphors to characterise the on-going mystical quest for the Good in Murdoch's own life and in her novels.

In was in her essay 'Existentialists and Mystics' that Murdoch developed this by exemplifying two sorts of novels: the existentialist with its lonely brave godless hero (who represents the man of reason) and the mystical novel that seeks to reconcile the divisions of self experienced by humans in the twentieth century. She represents post-modernity as a time in which many are increasingly 'frightened and alone' because 'God, Reason and Society' are being 'quietly wheeled

---

68   I refer the reader to Gabriel Griffin, *The Influence of the Writings of Simone Weil on the Fiction of Iris Murdoch* (New York: Edwin Mellen Press, 1993) for a detailed analysis of Simone Weil's influence on Murdoch.

69   Siguna Ramanathan, *Iris Murdoch: Figures of Good* (Basingstoke: Macmillan, 1990), 4.

70   Peter J. Conradi, *Iris Murdoch: The Saint and the Artist* (London: Harper Collins, 2001), 6.

71   Murdoch, *Metaphysics as a Guide to Morals*, 317.

off' the scene.[72] To resist the nihilistic tendency that this scenario encourages, she extols the virtues of the 'the mystical hero' in narrative as someone who 'retains[s] a conception of God' and attempts to express 'a religious consciousness without the trappings of religion'. Mystics, then, are those who no longer have the support and comfort of traditional notions of a personal God and support of religious institutions, as they 'inhabit a spiritual world unconsoled by familiar religious imagery'. Although the postmodern mystic is ridden with angst, he/she is not devoid of hope because they are still 'haunted by the sense of reality and unity of some sort of spiritual world'.[73]

Although her skill as a novelist developed over the course of her output, there is remarkably little difference between her mystical perception of the good life in her first novel and what was to be, sadly, her last, *Jackson's Dilemma*. It is, of course, now common knowledge that, unfortunately, by the time she wrote what was to be her final novel, she was in the early stages of Alzheimer's disease.[74] Written at a time when Murdoch was still grappling, not altogether successfully, with Heidegger's philosophy, it poignantly reveals that her own religious and philosophical dilemmas were still largely unresolved.[75] The central character, Benet, who is writing a book on Heidegger, is therefore a reflection of Murdoch herself, who tried to relay what this great philosopher meant by 'truth'.

Again, the dominant theme of both her novels and her personal philosophy is the quest for the Good, which she perceives to be a

---

72 Iris Murdoch, 'Existentialists and Mystics', in Peter J. Conradi (ed), *Iris Murdoch: Existentialists and Mystics* (London: Penguin, 1997), 224.

73 Ibid., 225–26.

74 The diagnosis was confirmed in a post mortem after her death in 1999. In order to understand the ailment further, researchers at University College London have done extensive analysis of three of her novels: *Under the Net, The Sea, The Sea* (which is deemed to represent the pinnacle of her career) and the last, *Jackson's Dilemma*. Their findings reveal that there were a smaller number of word-types and that the vocabulary was more commonplace in the latter. http://newsvote.bbc.co.uk/mapps/pagetools/print/news.bbc.co.uk/2/hi/health/4 05860

75 Murdoch worked for six years on a book about Heidegger's philosophy. It was in proof form by 1993, but she decided that it was no good and should be abandoned. Conradi, *Iris Murdoch*, 586.

magnetic force that is intuitively known by everyone but transcends normal everyday experience. As an ideal of perfection, the Good exists as a focal point of attention and is known through love and the imagination. Murdoch preserves a sense of mystery, some sense of the divine that remains unknowable, ungraspable, which I argue is akin to mystical knowing. The imaginary world Murdoch created is inhabited by an assortment of bizarre characters, through which she explores the possibility of discovering an ethical transcendence by providing the reader with a 'quasi-religious alternative in the vision of the good'.[76] Ultimately, she assumed that most people would find connections between the characters and plots in her novels and their own lives in order to extract both meaning and sustenance. This is endorsed by the British theologian David Jasper, who succinctly characterises Murdoch's fiction as representative of an individual's search 'for his or her true self [which] emerges as an attempt to rediscover a metaphysic structured upon recognizable images of traditional belief'.[77] It is clear, according to Murdoch's reasoning that Christianity has prevented moral and spiritual growth by promoting images and doctrines that have been taken 'for real' and served to create 'a mythological barrier' that divides the tradition from ordinary people and prevents the 'free movement of spirit' by inserting a 'full-stop barrier'.[78] As a consequence, one of Murdoch's primary concerns was that the substance of theology needs to be extracted from its ideological and analytical abstractions and restored to the real 'stuff' of human life.

76   Ann Loades, 'Iris Murdoch: the vision of the good in the *via negativa*', in *Culture, Education and Society* 40:2 (1986), 147.
77   David Jasper, *The Study of Literature and Religion: An Introduction*, 2nd Edition. (London: Macmillan, 1992), 141.
78   Murdoch, 'The Fire and the Sun: Why Plato Banished the Artists', in Conradi, *Existentialists and Mystics*, 447.

Denise Levertov: Wandering Mystic

Denise Lynch describes Levertov's work as capturing 'the rhythms of a spiritual life centring on mystery'.[79] Levertov's occupation with the pilgrim's quest for meaning was, to some extent, inherited from her father's interest in the mystical traditions of his Jewish origins.[80] Levertov believed that her vocation as a poet was a vocation to build 'an archway, a bridge, an altar' to the transcendent through her poetic vision.[81] In support of this, Charles Altieri proposes that Levertov endeavours throughout her *oeuvre* to 'slip beyond, to a sense of the infinite depth and mystery at the horizon of what is sharply seen'. [82] The final volume of Levertov's last poems, *This Great Unknowing*, which were published posthumously following her death in 1997, continues her dedication to seeking traces of the transcendent in nature. As a mystic who held a deep respect for every living thing, the poem 'Beyond the Field' in particular summarises the insights of her life's quest – the only truth human beings can say with any certainty. 'The mind's far edges twitch / sensing kinships, beyond reach. / Too much unseen, unknown, unknowable'.[83] Throughout her poetic career, it was clear that she did not see her role (or that of any human) to define the nature of world, but rather, to be in awe of the splendour of being.

Levertov was born in Ilford, Essex, England in 1923. Her father was a Russian Jew named Paul Philip Levertoff who converted to Christianity and became an Anglican clergyman. Her mother, Beatrice Spooner-Jones, was a Welsh singer. Her parents educated Levertov

79   Denise E Lynch, 'Denise Levertov and the Poetry of Incarnation', in *Renascence* 50: 1–2 (1997/1998), 49–64.
80   Charles Altieri, 'Denise Levertov and the Limits of the Aesthetics of Presence', in Albert Gelpi (ed), *Denise Levertov: Selected Criticism* (Ann Arbor, MI: The University of Michigan Press, 1993), 128.
81   Denise Levertov, 'Vocation', in *Oblique Prayers* (Newcastle upon Tyne: Bloodaxe Books, 1986), 31.
82   Altieri, 'Denise Levertov and the Limits of the Aesthetics of Presence', Albert Gelpi (ed), *Denise Levertov: Selected Criticism* (Ann Arbor, MI: The University of Michigan Press, 1993), 128.
83   Denise Levertov, 'Beyond the Field', in *This Great Unknowing* (Tarset, Northumberland: Bloodaxe Books 2001), 16.

solely at home, so she never went to school as such, although she did attend ballet lessons for many years. She published her first poem, 'Listening to Distant Guns', which she wrote 'during or just before Dunkirk',[84] in *Poetry Quarterly* in 1940. She tells us that she could hear the guns across the channel from her home in Buckinghamshire.

During the war years, she worked as a civilian nurse in St Luke's Hospital, London from 1943 to 1944. After this, she worked in an antique and bookshop in London during 1946 – the same year she published her first book of poetry entitled *The Double Image*, poems mostly written when she was between eighteen and nineteen years of age.[85] On hearing the news that her work had been accepted for publication, she remembers going into a 'church somewhere in Soho to kneel in awe because my destiny, which I had always known as a certain but vague form on the far horizon, was beginning to *happen*'.[86]

The next year, in 1947, she served as a civilian nurse in a British hospital in Paris, France where she met and married the writer Mitchell Goodman. The couple moved to New York in 1948 and had a son, Nicolai, in 1949. Fortunately for her, some of her poems were included in an anthology edited by Kenneth Rexroth (whom she credits with discovering her) entitled *New British Poets* (1947), and she published poems in the magazine *Origin* and the *Black Mountain Review*.[87] It was during this year that she began a lifelong friendship with another poet, Robert Creeley. From 1950 to 1951, the family lived in Europe, where Levertov devoted a substantial amount of her

---

84 Denise Levertov, *Poems 1940–1960* (New York: New Directions, 1979), vii.
85 Ibid.
86 Ibid., viii.
87 Levertov became associated with the Black Mountain poets, named after an experimental college in North Carolina that was presided over by Charles Olsen as rector. Levertov along with Robert Duncan and Robert Creeley were among those new poets whose poetry first appeared in Don Allen's anthology entitled *The New American Poetry* (1960). Although Levertov never attended Black Mountain College, she accepted their aesthetic ideals, and her association with these poets gave her an outlet for work that was contrary to acceptable literary forms of the time. As peers, Duncan and Creeley inspired and confirmed the work she was doing at the time.

time to study and writing. The next year, they returned to New York where she eventually became a US citizen in 1955.

Like Murdoch, Levertov read widely and started to write as a young child. She felt that the lessons she received at home from her mother greatly benefited her craft, because she 'never had to read anything [she] didn't want to read, or write anything [she] didn't feel like writing'.[88] Additionally, her background contained some interesting cultural and religious combinations. Notably, her father's Hasidic background provided a profound influence on her religious outlook. Furthermore, she had varying degrees of European and American influences throughout her life due to moving between continents on several occasions. In summarising the opus of Levertov's work, Bobby Caudle Rogers states, '[h]ers is a poetry of moments, a poetry of small, luminous surprise'.[89]

Levertov herself refused to be categorised as anything 'except as mish-mash'.[90] Lacey suggests that the earlier part of Levertov's career typifies the notion of a 'hopeful, confident pilgrim, led by a guide or muse'. Later, after reflecting deeply on the world's sorrows, she takes on the air of a 'baffled and despairing wanderer'.[91] Yet, by the time she writes 'The Cold Spring',[92] she has become 'the tested, resilient blend of pilgrim/wanderer, formed by a provisional religious faith, always in the darkness, always prone to despair, but persisting in the guides she has found'. She did in fact, become progressively more religious in her outlook. In her poetry of the 1960s, Levertov shows an intuition of the 'mystery of the living thing; of the thing's vital energy'.[93] At this point, she does not name the mystery; nor does she

---

88   Nicholas O'Connell, 'Levertov's Final Interview: A Poet's Validation', http://www.english.unic.edu/maps/poets/g_l/levertov/oconnell.htm

89   Bobby C. Rogers, 'Denise Levertov's Poetics of Process', in D. J. N. Middleton, *God, Literature and Process Thought* (Aldershot: Ashgate, 2002), 207.

90   Gary Pacernick, 'Interview with Denise Levertov', in Anne Colclough Little, & Susie Paul, *Denise Levertov: New Perspectives* (West Cornwall, CT: Locust Hill Press, 2000), 91.

91   Paul A. Lacey, 'Wanderer and Pilgrim; Poet and Person', in Little & Paul, *Denise Levertov*, 245.

92   Denise Levertov, *Poems, 1968–1972* (New York: New Directions, 1987), 6.

93   Gelpi, *Denise Levertov*, 4.

refer to any theological reality or tradition.[94] Later, after her conversion to Roman Catholicism, this mystery is associated with the Holy Spirit. Collections of poems such as *Candles of Babylon*, *Oblique Prayers*, *Breathing the Water* and *A Door in the Hive* illustrate that she has given the mystery a name: the Christian Incarnation, a 'term that bridges the rupture between individual epiphany and public calamity'.[95] It also provides a clear statement about the role of the mystic/poet in postmodernity. Like Murdoch, Levertov was 'antagonistic' to confessional poetry that she thought tended to 'exploit the private life'.[96] She held the opinion that such poetry usually entails 'just telling a personal story and feeling better for having told it', and that the impulse of such poets to 'unburden themselves' means that inevitably 'the aesthetic considerations are disregarded'.[97]

De Certeau describes mysticism in terms of wandering, which parallels how I have decided to describe Denise Levertov.[98] Spiritual wanderings are the subject of a number of her poems. For example, the first line of the poem 'Overland to the Islands' (1958) states, 'Let's go much as that dog goes',[99] which in retrospect might be interpreted as a metaphor for Levertov's pilgrimage through life.

> Under his feet
> rocks and mud, his imagination, sniffing,
> engaged in its perceptions – dancing
> edgeways, there's nothing
> the dog disdains on his way,
> nevertheless he
> keeps moving, changing
> pace and approach but
> not direction – 'every step an arrival'.

94   Ibid., 4.
95   Ibid., 5.
96   Michael Andre (1971/72) 'Denise Levertov: An Interview', in Jewel Brooker Spears, *Conversations with Denise Levertov* (Jackson, MS: University Press of Mississippi, 1998), 65.
97   Sybil Estess, 'Denise Levertov', in Spears, *Conversations with Denise Levertov*, 98.
98   De Certeau, *The Mystic Fable*, 299.
99   Levertov, *Poems 1940–1960*, 55.

The sense of following a path with a clear goal is evident despite changes in direction and pace. The phrase 'every step an arrival' is directly quoted from Rilke and is best explained by Rodgers, who surmises that it 'suggests the gaining of wisdom, an instant of hope, an epiphanic moment'.[100] This does not denote the finding of conclusive answers, but rather, brief and treasured moments of illumination that punctuate the journey. Each moment is a 'new arrival' or a new gleaning of insight. But ultimately, as Bobby Rogers reminds us, 'there is not ultimate arrival that negates or diminishes any next step'.[101] Conversely, perhaps paradoxically, this can also imply a 'perpetual departure'.[102] Either way there is a sense of movement, continual motion and non-closure.

Both in life and in poetry, an overriding aim that becomes obvious from reading Levertov's work is her desire to unite the inner and outer worlds. The inner world relates to intuition and conscience while the external involves observation, sensual experiences, and perceptions of other people, the natural world and inanimate objects. In other words, she tries to follow a path attuned morally and spiritually to her sense of who she is whilst being tangentially a poet who is fully engaged in the world. This clearly locates her within the mystical continuum. As Turner specifies, the mystical path is by definition also a dialectical path so that there is 'no longer any distinction at all between the "exterior" and the "interior"'.[103] Annie Dillard likewise blurred the distinctions between these two worlds.

---

100 Audrey T. Rodgers, *Denise Levertov* (Rutherford; Madison; Teaneck: Farleigh Dickson University Press, 1993), 213.
101 Ibid., 209.
102 De Certeau, *The Mystic Fable*, 99.
103 Denys Turner, *The Darkness of God* (Cambridge: Cambridge University Press, 1995), 253.

Bruce Ronda describes Dillard as 'a mystic for our time',[104] and in fact, Dillard consciously locates herself within the Christian mystical tradition. Radaker identifies a tripartite basis of Dillard's mysticism in *Pilgrim at Tinker Creek* as represented by the three images of the Eskimo, Newton and Buddha, which he identifies as the 'primitive, scientific and mystical epistemologies'.[105] Of the three writers here discussed, perhaps Dillard's epistemological and existential stance most aptly represents the postmodern mystic. That is, her work is the result not only of abstract reason but also an older and a timeless direct experience of the world that transcends reason.

Dillard was born into an affluent family on 30 April 1945 in Pittsburgh, Pennsylvania. Her father, Frank Doak, ran the family firm but later left in order to pursue more pleasurable activities such as taking a boat down the Mississippi after 'his reading went to his head'.[106] Her mother was called Pam Lambert Doak, whom Dillard speculates 'must have cut a paradoxical figure in her modernist living room, with her platinum blond hair, her brisk motions, her slender, urbane frame, her ironic wit [and] her speech [that] was endlessly interesting'.[107] The portrait Dillard paints of her parents is as larger than life characters who engaged in existence to the fullest. Her parents shared their eclectic interests with their three daughters, which included telling and collecting jokes and diverse reading interests.

As a child, she was sent to private schools and preferred playing baseball and collecting rocks to the dancing lessons to which she was sent. From the age of seven, once she could memorise her telephone number, she was allowed to explore her hometown and would walk endlessly around the streets and parks of the surrounding neighbourhood. She attended a Presbyterian church with her family and was

---

104   Bruce A. Ronda, 'Annie Dillard and the Fire of God', in *Christian Century* 100:16 (1983), 483.
105   Kevin Radaker, 'Caribou, Electrons, and the Angel: Stalking the Sacred in Annie Dillard's *Pilgrim at Tinker Creek*', in *Christianity and Literature* 46:2 (1997), 124.
106   Annie Dillard, *An American Childhood* (New York: Harper, 1988), 6.
107   Ibid., 36.

instructed in the social skills expected of a young woman within the rigid social structure of her class and town. From a very early age, she became a keen observer of the natural world around her. She also became a voracious reader, making full use of the local library that she recalls with nostalgia in *An American Childhood*. Among her most favourite books was *The Field Book of Ponds and Streams*, which became a springboard for her long sojourns into the natural world.[108]

Generally, she rebelled against the Pittsburgh society in which the Doaks moved, and she reflects that she 'morally disapproved most things in America, and blamed my innocent parents for them [...]. When I was angry, I felt myself coiled and longing to kill someone or bomb something big'.[109] She tells us that she quit the church and 'wrote the minister a fierce letter'.[110] The minister, by lending her four volumes of the apologetic writings of C. S. Lewis, managed to lure her back into the church. She recalls being particularly impressed by *The Problem of Pain*, that she liked the way the question of suffering was defused through what she felt was 'a choice of fancy language that basically said, "Forget it"'.[111] It was at a Presbyterian Bible camp during adolescence that she first realised that she 'had a head for religious ideas'.[112]

Based on the advice of her headmistress, Dillard ended up at Hollins College in Virginia, where she apparently 'sent all her problem children'.[113] It was to be the turning point for Dillard as she was able to explore her writing potential in a supportive and creative environment. It was at Hollins that 'Doak [Annie Dillard] changed from being an angry daughter into a sister who competed with and supported her peers'.[114] Her interaction with other women at Hollins allowed

---

108 Ibid., 81–85. She refers to Ann Haven Morgan, *The Field Book of Ponds and Streams* (G. P. Putnam's Sons, 1934).
109 Ibid., 222.
110 Ibid., 226.
111 Ibid., 227–28.
112 Ibid., 133.
113 Nancy C. Parrish, *Lee Smith, Annie Dillard and the Hollins Group* (Baton Rouge, LA: Louisiana State University Press, 1998), 130.
114 Ibid., 131.

her to find a sense of peace as well as giving her an intellectual and creative space to develop her individual writing skills.

This was further advanced by her controversial marriage to her English professor, Richard Dillard, on 5 June 1965. His mentoring certainly contributed to her subsequent skill as a writer. Her marriage to one of her teachers was something of a rebellious act, yet she cites her husband as her 'best critic'. However, the marriage did not survive the winning of the Pulitzer Prize for *Pilgrim at Tinker Creek*. Apparently, the reasons for this stemmed from the fact that that their literary tastes were diverging in a way that was symbolic of the pulling apart of the marriage due to her continuing resistance to traditional roles expected of women at this time.[115]

Dillard gained both her undergraduate and Master's degree at Hollins. The subjects of her research were to form the two organising structures of *Pilgrim at Tinker Creek*. For her senior thesis, she studied the work of the poet Emily Dickinson, and for her Masters, she turned to Thoreau and *Walden Pond* (1854). Parrish concludes that it was from this early college work that Dillard learned how to conflate the genres of autobiography, novel, scientific treatise and religious meditation. She saw Tinker Creek as a metaphysical entity existing at the edge of infinity; and she studied a disciplined narrative voice that was part persona and part authorial. A writer who lived her life at the edge of conventional expectations discovered in these works the ideas and forms that would allow her to successfully blur and push the boundaries of her own writing.[116]

Following a serious bout of pneumonia, Dillard left for the wilderness to study nature for clues about God. *Pilgrim at Tinker Creek* is the book she wrote based upon that life-changing experience retrospectively drawing on her copious notes taken during the time she spent there observing nature through the seasons. Parrish alerts us to two important facts concerning the narrator of *Pilgrim at Tinker Creek*. Firstly, Dillard has created a narrator who is partly a fictional character and partly based on real autobiographical experience.[117] To some

---

115   Parrish, *Lee Smith, Annie Dillard and the Hollins Group*, 133.
116   Ibid., 147.
117   Ibid., 146–47.

extent, she invents an imaginary voice enabling her to write a spiritual autobiography that is subjective but also one that is able to transcend her own experience. Secondly, Dillard delights in stretching boundaries in her praxis. The fact that her work continues to defy conventional literary definitions is testimony to her innovative and radical approach to writing about things that matter in the contemporary world.

Following the break up of her marriage to her first husband, Dillard became writer-in-residence at Western Washington University. It was here that she wrote *Holy the Firm* and her only novel, *The Living*. During this period, she also met and married her second husband, Gary Clevidence, and had her only child, Cody Rose. From 1979 to date, she has been writer-in-residence at Wesleyan University, where she met and married her third husband, Robert Richardson. Her audience knows next to nothing about her marriages and divorces, or her experience of being a mother, yet conversely, they know a great deal about her life of the spirit.

She has, to her annoyance, been described as an essayist, and her work is often classed as spiritual autobiography. In fact, the only book that she claims can accurately be described as a collection of essays is *Teaching a Stone to Talk*. Her public often forget that she is also a poet. Her first publication, *Tickets for a Prayer Wheel*, was a collection of poems that took her five years to complete. To her dismay, this first publication was totally overshadowed by the public acclaim that *Pilgrim at Tinker Creek* attracted, which she wrote in just eight months.

Any attempt to classify her work as one particular genre fails to convey the full dynamics of her work. Creative non-fiction is perhaps more suitable as a category and captures Dillard's aesthetic approach to the 'perusal of illumination',[118] which incorporates the paradoxical nature of the relationship between creation and creator. Like Murdoch and Levertov, her spiritual progress entwines and interacts with her journey towards artistic integrity.

Pilgrimage is a central theme and the narrative structure of three of her early works: *Pilgrim at Tinker Creek*, *Holy the Firm* and *Teach-*

---

118   Sandra Humble Johnson, *The Space Between: Literary Epiphany in the Work of Annie Dillard* (Kent, Ohio, and London: The Kent State University Press, 1992), ix.

ing a Stone to Talk. In *Teaching a Stone to Talk*, Dillard graphically recounts the delusions, false trails and self-doubt that accompany the writer through the journey to bring each piece of work to maturity. Conversely, she also recounts the joys, exhilaration and love of the writer's life. There are no illusions of grandeur for her though – the ultimate meaninglessness and pointlessness of such creative endeavours are ever-present. In short, Dillard demonstrates a keen ability to operate within the dialectical tension of the *via positiva* and the *via negativa*. However, like Murdoch and Levertov, writing is also something of a vocation – a work of love – but as a postmodern mystic, she has devoted her life to seeking out the sacred hidden in creation, and to this extent, writing is a religious calling. In the spirit of nineteenth century Romanticism, Dillard attempts to gather her impressions and reflections on nature so that the end product is essentially a record of her own interior life.[119]

In her own words, Dillard refers to her religious attitude as 'shoddy Christianity'.[120] She says that her primary audience is not the committed Christian, but 'the skeptic, the agnostic [...] whom she aims to get to "acknowledge the supernatural"'.[121] However, she believes that even Christians are partly unaware of this realm and says, 'On the whole, I do not find Christians – outside of the catacombs, sufficiently sensible of conditions. Does anyone have the foggiest idea what sort of power we so blithely invoke?'[122] Fundamentally, Dillard sees the world as desacralised and in need of spiritual renewal, and in order to enact this renewal, she adopts an almost surreal form of writing that often resorts to magical realism. The unsuspecting reader is forced into noticing unexpected 'incursions' of the sacred through continual blurring of the boundaries of the real and unreal.

---

119   Bruce A. Ronda, 'Annie Dillard and the Fire of God', in *Christian Century* 100: 16 (1983), 1062.

120   Annie Dillard, 'Singing with the Fundamentalists', in *Yale Review* 74 (1985) 315.

121   Philip Yancey, 'Dispatches from the Ontological Frontiers: Annie Dillard's Magical Realist Essay', http://www.cam-and-heather.com/cam_new/academia/dillard.html

122   Annie Dillard, *Teaching a Stone to Talk* (New York: Harper, 1992), 53.

Twenty-five years after the publication of *Pilgrim at Tinker Creek*, Dillard returns to the non-fiction first person narrative in *For the Time Being*. Whilst in the former she focused on the microcosmic world of Tinker Creek, in the latter she takes in a macrocosmic or panoramic vision by virtue of incorporating a broad sweep of human history, science, geology, biology and theology. She moves haphazardly between moments of terror, illumination and joy, in a perpetual state of bewilderment. In between these random and chaotic glimpses of life on earth, she throws in snippets of wisdom from mystics she admires such as Pierre Teilhard de Chardin and Baal Shem Tov and her own experiences of visiting Israel and China. It is left up to the reader to make any connections. Instead of offering sustained analysis, she fills in the gaps between what seem entirely unconnected facts with a catalogue of numbers, such as how many people died in various natural disasters or at the hands of some tyrant. Mostly, the book charts her life's journey to date. There are 'real' reflections on visits to China and Jerusalem as well as encounters with various individuals. Overall, there is a disjointed or haphazard feel to the writing. Yet, despite the fact that Dillard is further from providing answers to life's big questions than ever, there is a sense of resigned optimism that avoids postmodern nihilism.

Her work fits in with the postmodern agenda in obvious ways, for example, her resistance to standard narrative forms and appearing on the surface to offer multiple and disconnected views of the world. A casual reading fails to yield a full comprehension of the inner connections that hold the postmodern feeling of angst at bay by holding oppositional ideas in tension. A closer investigation reveals that, like Murdoch and Levertov, she seeks a unified whole. In order to make 'real artistic meaning out of meaningless', the discerning artist has to rely on 'the old way, by creating a self-relevant artistic whole'.[123] The unifying device underlying Dillard's 'glittering collage of material' is the epiphanic moment.[124] And the epiphanic moment is the link between creative writing, mysticism and theology.

---

123   Annie Dillard, *Living by Fiction* (New York: Harper, 1988), 28.
124   Humble Johnson, *The Space Between*, 57.

Theological Conversation Partners

Whilst being somewhat unorthodox or eccentric at times, Murdoch, Levertov and Dillard continue to operate within the ambit of the Judaeo-Christian tradition despite the fact that they also bring insights from other religious traditions such as Buddhism, Hasidic Judaism and indigenous religions to bear on their 'theology'. Mystics such as Julian typically used common speech to produce theology that is accessible to ordinary people rather than operating solely at the level of private spiritual or scholarly discourse. It is on these grounds that I make theological claims for these writers. Murdoch, Levertov and Dillard, as published authors, have the potential to reach a wider audience than the narrow confines of theological discourse, and increasingly, theologians are recognising that they need the insights of artists if theology is to continue to be a living enterprise.

In order to access the work of these three writers theologically, the insights of three contemporary theologians in particular will provide the tools of theological reflection: Grace Jantzen, Dorothee Soelle and Sallie McFague. Although historically they all fall broadly into the category of 'feminist theology', their overall perspective is more holistic than it is narrowly definable and therefore mirrors the personal philosophies of Murdoch, Levertov and Dillard.

Grace Jantzen: Julian of Norwich and Natality

As noted previously, Jantzen has been at the forefront of critiquing William James' definition of mysticism as an intense psychological state and highlighted the dangers this poses for women. Additionally, she has done some impressive interpretation of the life and work of Julian of Norwich, who figures in the work of all three of these writers, and she has explored mysticism in postmodernity within a feminist framework.

On a philosophical level, in *Becoming Divine* she draws attention to the danger of metaphors such as 'salvation' when they become literalised.[125] In particular, she grapples with traditional Christianity's penchant for necrophilia, its focus on death, suggesting that 'natality' as a metaphor offers more promise for 'human flourishing'. Such 'a person "in full flourish" is a movement or person that is vibrant and creative, blossoming and developing and coming to fruition'.[126] Underpinning this suggestion is the idea that the language theologians and philosophers of religion choose reflects social and political order as much as it conveys any religious reality.[127] She argues that the concept of salvation in Christian theology denotes human beings as passive and perennially trapped in terrible circumstances from which they need to be saved. Jerry Gill agrees, suggesting that 'words have consequences' and that 'the language we acquire and adopt, with various "root metaphors" and conceptual orientations inherent within it, directs and colours the way we construe and interact with the world around us'.[128] Through the creative and flexible use of metaphor in which creative writing rejoices, Murdoch, Dillard and Levertov are able to make a positive contribution towards Jantzen's notion of 'flourishing' by disclosing new ways to imagine our relation to the sacred. In theological terms, these literary writers do not focus on life after death but life in the here and now.

In the Christian tradition, especially since the changes brought about by the Protestant Reformation, there has been an emphasis on inward spirituality, which 'invited people to ponder their personal eternal destiny'.[129] To counteract the individualism and consequential disregard for the Other that characterises modernity, Jantzen has proposed a 'theology of flourishing' as a more useful metaphor than that of salvation. What is crucial for this new model is that the inner and outer lives, including the political, are inseparable because

---

125 Grace M. Jantzen, *Becoming Divine, Towards a Feminist Philosophy of Religion* (Manchester: Manchester University Press, 1998), 159–62.
126 Ibid., 160.
127 Ibid., 161.
128 Jerry H. Gill, *Mediated Transcendence* (Macon, Georgia: Mercer University Press, 1989), 123–24.
129 Grace M. Jantzen 'Feminism and Flourishing: Gender and Metaphor', in *Feminist Theology* 18 (1995), 91.

a plant which flourishes does so from its own inner life, 'rooted and grounded' in its source. If that inner life is gone, the plant withers and dries up, no matter how good its external circumstances [...] there is no flourishing of the plant while its 'body' withers in intolerable weather conditions. A theology built on the model of flourishing is one whose spirituality is holistic, rather than the privatized, subjectivized spirituality so characteristic of contemporary Christianity.[130]

In the introduction to the new edition of *Julian of Norwich*, Jantzen surmises that we need postmodern anchoresses (which I understand to be the same as mystics) to help mend the 'violent and fragmented world'. They would represent a 'radical otherness to contemporary culture and its values'. A postmodern anchoress is someone who 'stands at an angle to the certainties and preoccupations of the world around her' to offer 'an interrogation of modernity' and an 'openness to the divine in a world that has given itself over to the mundane'. In particular, this means to turn towards the world rather than away from it. As such, she argues against privatised spirituality that turns to an 'unengaged and safe cocoon'.[131] Above all, she argues that a postmodern anchoress or mystic needs to offer visions to enable human flourishing. The enclosed space of the medieval mystic becomes, in postmodernity, a willingness to think independently from accepted cultural, academic and religious norms – whether they be modern or postmodern.

In practical terms, this means a withdrawal from the world for contemplation and engaged thought, which parallels the life of the creative writer whose craft requires temporary solitariness. That is, however public the consumption of a written product might be, however interactive the text once read, writing is a private act performed in solitude. However, the writings of such postmodern mystics also subvert the privatisation of spirituality, which Jantzen suggests diverts our attention away from social and political injustices by preserving the status quo,[132] by conveying their private experience as a potential revelation for readers. The mystic in postmodernity cannot afford to

130   Ibid., 101.
131   Jantzen, 'Feminists, philosophers, and mystics' 186–206.
132   Ibid.

66

live an utterly private life, but rather, must reach out to others. Conversely, in as much as theology represents the public realm, it cannot ignore individual experience and endeavour.

Given that women's voices historically have been marginalised in Christian theology, or firmly restrained to the non-rational or mystical strand, the modern turn inward also poses a new threat to women's ability to be effectual. Jantzen (1995) argues that such categorisations have served to maintain hierarchical power structures as well as leading to a misguided view of mysticism as a wholly privatised, experiential and individual affair. Dorothee Soelle, the next of our theologians to be discussed here, energetically resists the same introspection.

Dorothee Soelle: Mary, Martha and the Mystic Way Today

In *The Silent Cry*, Soelle develops Karl Rahner's notion that the only way that religion is likely to survive in postmodernity is in a mystical sense.[133] Although she hesitates to define mysticism in this work, obviously her conception of the term includes radical engagement in the social and political issues of postmodernity. As such, mysticism is the antidote to counteract the rampant individualism of the West that allows the individual ego to inflate and the 'Other' to diminish. According to Sarah Pinnock, Soelle was not a 'radical' postmodern theologian but her methodology nevertheless demonstrates postmodern traits. Certainly, her desire to name global injustices would appear to resist the relativism that has become characteristic of postmodernity. Pinnock further describes her as 'moderate postmodern theologian' who rejects

> modern epistemological assumptions about the autonomous self and the priority of pure reason, as well as the possibility of epistemic foundations or proofs for theological claims. Instead, moderate postmodern theologians locate truth of theology in its self-reflexive relationship to Scripture and tradition, and its libratory potential. [Soelle recognised] that theology is constituted by language embedded in culturally conditioned means, [and that] the role of theology is to

133 See Karl Rahner, *Theological Investigations* Vol. VII (1972). Soelle died in 2003.

articulate the worldviews and practices of faith communities in a specific social context.[134]

What is more, Soelle alerted us to the ways in which language functions to promote dominance, which 'serves the exercise of power, control, and possession [...] where there is a separation of the one who commands and the one who obeys'.[135] By way of contrast, the mystic seeks a 'language of oneness' that is totally free from 'purpose and control'.[136] For this reason, Soelle readily adopts the narrative approach to theology, which is facilitated in *The Silent Cry* through drawing on the testimonies of mystics down the ages. Soelle's attempt to construct the mystic way for today is the underlying inspiration for the structure of this book. However, because she draws predominantly on texts written by mystics in the past, she does not fully contextualise her theology within postmodernity, which this study seeks to redress by drawing on the literary insights of three contemporary writers.

It will become apparent as we move through this discussion that Murdoch, Levertov and Dillard as postmodern mystics seek this 'language of oneness'. In particular, Sallie McFague's notion of the metaphorical nature of theological concepts and models as well as her constant concern that theology must be relevant to the times will contribute much to our discussion of postmodern mystics.

Sallie McFague: Metaphorical and Planetary Theology

I chose McFague as a theological conversation partner mainly because of her focus on religious language and metaphorical theology. She also has a clear sense that theology is always, like mysticism, a continuing and fluctuating process. Almost as a bonus, McFague, as far as I am aware, is the only theologian who explicitly incorporates all three of our writers into her theological expression. She also recognises that metaphorical language used by mystics 'is radical in relation to the

134 Sarah K. Pinnock (ed), *The Theology of Dorothy Soelle* (New York: Trinity Press International, 2003), 130–31.
135 Soelle, *The Silent Cry*, 63.
136 Ibid., 62–63.

tradition of patriarchal language' and that there is an inextricable relationship between human and divine images.[137] Metaphor is therefore the mechanism that links the creative writer, the mystic and the theologian.

As a result, McFague's concept of theology differs significantly from the inherited traditions. McFague suggests that the premise of postmodernism undermines two major characteristics of theology, that of universalism and subjectivity.[138] This is a result to be welcomed, however, because the universal concept of God is understood to deny pluralism while the modernist focus on the subject denies cultural and social factors. Obviously, history is awash with the dire consequences of the presumptuous and imperialistic undertones of these previous premises.

McFague also makes the point that any theological statements we make are not factual in an empirical sense and that

> Theological language is necessarily metaphorical, and this means relying on the relations, objects, and events in our familiar world as metaphors for what we do not know how to articulate. Poets use metaphors to express experiences and love and loss, death and grief, friendship and betrayal, joy and sorrow – our most important but hard-to-define experiences. Likewise, all theistic religions use metaphor to speak of God.[139]

The ability of metaphor to operate within a dialectic of universal and subjective knowledge makes it vitally essential to the creative writer, the mystic and theologian alike. Moreover, parables, which are for all intents and purposes extended metaphors, help us to understand and speak meaningfully about theological matters. Finally, McFague reminds us that religious language needs a concrete religious context, or otherwise it becomes both idolatrous and irrelevant. In her words:

> It becomes *idolatrous* because without a sense of awe, wonder, and mystery, we forget the inevitable distance between our words and divine reality. It becomes

---

137 Sallie McFague, *Metaphorical Theology: Models of God in Religious Language* (Philadelphia: Fortress Press, 1982), 175.
138 Sallie McFague, *Life Abundant* (Minneapolis: Fortress Press, 2001), 26.
139 Ibid., 30.

irrelevant because without a sense of the immanence of the divine in our lives, we find language about God empty and meaningless.[140]

For a postmodern mystic context is everything therefore. As we proceed it will become apparent that Murdoch, Levertov and Dillard maintain both points: the sense of mystery and belief that the divine empties itself out into the materiality of our lives.

Towards Mysticism in Postmodernity

So what aspect does the mystical way take in postmodernity? From a theoretical perspective, it must be interdisciplinary. Indeed our writers draw on a wide range of literary, philosophical, cultural, scientific and theological resources and function as a result within a different range of epistemological strategies. Secondly, it must be political in that mystics are those who present 'creative and courageous efforts at pushing back the boundaries of thought and action so that liberation can be achieved'.[141] They represent an alternative tradition, one that does not pander to the hierarchical powers of the Church. David Tracy puts it more succinctly when he states that 'the real face of postmodernity [...] is the face of the other [...] God's shattering otherness, the neighbour's irreducible otherness'. He also predicts that 'the recovery of mystical readings of the prophetic core of Judaism and Christianity is one of the surest signs of a postmodern sensitivity'.[142] In his view, theology will never again become systematised. He also envisages a 'wisdom grounded metaphysics' joining with an aesthetics to create some form of prophetic ethics such as that found in the thought of Murdoch.[143] Here, then, is the suggestion that the mystic-as-prophet-as writer has an important role to play in this strange time

140   McFague, *Metaphorical Theology*, 2.
141   Jantzen 'Feminists, philosophers, and mystics', 186–206.
142   David Tracy, 'Theology and the Many Faces of Postmodernity', in *Theology Today* 51:1 (1994) 114.
143   Ibid.

we call postmodernity. This chapter has suggested that Murdoch, Levertov and Dillard can be described as postmodern mystics who present theological insights through their creative writing. In the next chapter, we will explore more fully what it means to be a contemplative in postmodernity.

Chapter Two
The *Via Contemplativa*: Seeing the Sacred

In the last chapter, I proposed that the concept of mysticism in post-modernity is increasingly less about the focus on subjective mystical experience and more about an orientation of being or 'mystical consciousness'. This chapter develops this assertion by exploring what it means to follow the contemplative path, or *via contemplativa*, in post-modernity. As viewed relative to the work of Murdoch, Levertov and Dillard, following this path entails some distinct and key conceptual differences to the classical path of contemplation, but the essence of what constitutes the life and works of a mystic remains much the same – particularly their unorthodoxy.

The post-Enlightenment Western conception is that salvation is dependent on what an individual believes,[1] and in turn, belief is reliant on the rational self to discover and accept the truth about God. Luther rejected the idea that Christians could gain knowledge of God through supra-rational or mystical means, and consequently, the contemplative mode in the Protestant tradition was subordinated to the life of action and love of one's neighbour as characterised in the 'Protestant work ethic'.[2] Indeed, there was little support for mysticism by Protestant theologians in the twentieth century. Karl Barth, for example, stated categorically that there could never be an experience of union with Christ induced by any form of contemplation or change in human

---

1   Grace M. Jantzen, 'What's the Difference? Knowledge and Gender in (Post) Modern Philosophy of Religion', in *Religious Studies* 32 (1996), 21.
2   This refers to the Protestant belief that labour redeems humankind. Although the reformer John Calvin developed it, the phrase was established in a famous critique written by the sociologist Max Weber, *The Protestant Ethic and the Spirit of Capitalism* (London: Routledge, 2001), wherein he uncovers the influence of the Protestant work ethic on the development of capitalism. The Quakers are a Protestant denomination who retained a mystical way of knowing God in silence.

consciousness.[3] In the Protestant imagination, God is wholly other or transcendent. Even Paul Tillich, who had a lifelong interest in mysticism, concluded that 'the Protestant principle' of God's otherness would not fully accommodate it.[4] He was also deeply concerned that mysticism would provide a distraction from the fallen nature of humankind, but nevertheless mystical strands of Judaism and Christianity have persisted on the margins of the orthodox traditions. Individual mystics are, more often than not, prophetic and deeply moralistic individuals who prompt others to imitate and continue their insights and activities. Mystics also present challenges to the *status quo* through creative engagement with revelation and doctrine.

The variety of mystical expression and its development is far too varied and diverse to capture in such a short space,[5] but there is no doubt that Hellenistic thought, Plato chiefly, has influenced Western forms of mysticism as the early Christian mystics recognised that they shared the same focus on 'the soul's search for immediacy with God'.[6] As such, God or the Good are seen as existing outside of the soul. The alternative tendency is the reverse, to seek God or the transcendent *within* the human soul. This is the mystical way in Quakerism, Hinduism and Buddhism. This conception was also expressed in Gnosticism, which was eventually rejected by the Church as heretical. In Western mysticism, those of both inclinations, the search outward and the search inward, have described the search for the divine in terms of

3   See Karl Barth, 'The Doctrine of Reconciliation', in *Church Dogmatics*; Vol. IV, Part 3.2 (Edinburgh: T. & T. Clark, 1988), 538–49.
4   'The Protestant Principle' refers to the belief that God can only be known through Scripture or the spirit speaking through an ordained minister; any other medium can lead to idolatry or heresy. Bernard McGinn, with some reservations, cites Ernst Troeltsch (1865–1923) and Albert Schweitzer (1875–1965) as the most influential exceptions to the Protestant rejection of mysticism in theological discourse. *The Foundations of Mysticism* (London: SCM Press, 1991), 269–72.
5   I refer the reader to Bernard McGinn's trilogy for the Christian tradition. For a more inclusive overview of mysticism in different world faiths, see Geoffrey Parrinder's *Mysticism in the World's Religions* (Oxford: Oneworld, 1995).
6   Andrew Louth, *The Origins of the Christian Mystical Tradition* (Oxford: Clarendon Press, 1981), xiii. Chapter 1 provides a succinct overview of Plato's mysticism.

progressive stages. Notably, Louth outlines the contemplative path in the Christian mystical tradition as being characterised by three distinct stages of the soul's ascent to God: purification, illumination and union. In the purification stage, the soul empties in preparation for the second stage of receiving God's illumination. The soul then progresses through states of ecstasy and stillness (or 'the dark night of the soul') wherein the contemplative experiences feelings of loss and abandonment to an experience of union with God.[7]

Jantzen (1995) has been prominent in highlighting how this progression towards union with God was, for many of the male mystics, experienced solely in intellectual terms. The experience was also deeply hierarchical. That is, the pinnacle of spiritual attainment was imagined in a flight from the body to the purest part of the soul. Rather than a linear or logical sense of progression or ascent, however, I intend to focus on the *via contemplativa* as an attitude, motivation or way of being in the world that cannot fit so readily into a linear model. Jantzen's phrase 'becoming divine' is to my mind synonymous with the *via contemplativa*, which makes more sense when we recall that the word Plato used for contemplation was *theōria*, referring to the activation of the soul's natural divinity.[8] Furthermore, it is often overlooked that the purpose of escaping the cave and moving towards the light of the sun in Plato's cave myth was for the sole purpose of returning to guide others who were held captive.

Throughout the history of mysticism, there has been a tension between *theōria*, or watching and waiting, and *praxis*, or 'doing'.[9] In Greek philosophy this was the tension between philosophy and politics, and in Christian mysticism it has been represented by the tension between the *via contemplativa* and the *via activa* as characterised by Mary and Martha in the Gospels, which will be discussed in more depth in Chapter Seven. When I use the term *via contemplativa*, I intend it to incorporate both the above aspects because Murdoch's,

---

7   This is generally attributed to Origen. See Andrew Louth, *The Origins of the Christian Mystical Tradition* (Oxford: Clarendon Press, 1981), 54–61.

8   McGinn, *The Foundations of Mysticism*, 34.

9   Ibid., 106. Subsequently *theōria* has become 'theory', which refers to abstract knowledge or reason as distinct from practice.

Levertov's and Dillard's approaches to their personal quest for sacred knowledge exists alongside social and political action.[10] This chapter is concerned with their contemplative approach – how they look at and understand people and the world around them – which, I will demonstrate, is both active and passive.

In order to map out the *via contemplativa* in postmodernity, I will explore three key areas in the writings of Murdoch, Levertov and Dillard. First, I will review the feasibility of contemplation in post-modernity with particular reflection on how it is facilitated through a life of writing. Second, I will discuss reading the mystics in post-modernity, in particular, these three authors' intellectual, creative and existential engagement with Julian's works. The third issue addresses the methodological awareness evident in our writers as manifested in the notion of 'seeing', defined as relying equally on an outer sense of sight and an inner 'eye' of understanding. It will be argued that this double 'vision' is an essential ability for the mystic in postmodernity.

Contemplation in Postmodernity

Before the emergence of the problematical term 'mysticism', the common and much simpler term was 'contemplation'. Andrew Louth clearly concludes that, for early mystics such as Plato and Origen, contemplation was 'a stage on the way, not the end'.[11] Elsewhere he quotes medieval mystical theologian Richard of St Victor, who describes contemplation as 'a free and clear vision of the mind fixed upon the manifestation of wisdom in suspended wonder'.[12] The phrase 'free and clear vision' suggests that contemplation is a state wherein

---

10   I am aware that Dillard is not recognised as a political activist. The lack of attention to politics in her writings probably reflects her conclusion that nature has no concern for the rights of any living thing.

11   Louth, *The Origins of the Christian Mystical Tradition*, 85.

12   Andrew Louth, 'Theology and Spirituality', revised edition (SLG Press, 1978), 7, cited in McIntosh, *Mystical Theology*, 11.

the mind is free of the usual distractions and preoccupations. The requirement to become still in prayer or meditation does not change in postmodernity, despite the fact that it is not a familiar skill to many. Furthermore, this definition is clearly not about inner excitement, such as feelings of ecstasy. Rather it is indicative of a breakthrough of wisdom into the consciousness. A life of contemplation requires dedication, practice and motivation, which in turn, rewards the mystic with wisdom as it is achieved in just such increments.

Less dramatically, 'to contemplate' in common speech means 'to look at something thoughtfully and steadily', or equally, 'to think about something seriously and steadily'.[13] Mystical knowledge, by comparison, does not purportedly come about by human effort, but rather, by remaining passive and moving beyond concepts and images. For mystics such as John of the Cross, this is termed 'the dark night of the soul', which has typically been conceptualised by male mystics such as Eckhart as an outcome of long and dedicated mental processes. Louth provides us with a useful link to Greek ideas on mysticism using the Greek *nous*, which sheds a different light on the concept. Whereas we think of the mind as reasoning and thinking, the Greek verb *nous*, *noesis*, suggests 'an almost intuitive grasp of reality [...] or mystical union'.[14] It seems that in classical Greek there was an understanding of imagination and rational thinking working in tandem.

Etymologically, the word 'contemplation' comes from the Latin word *contemplātĭo*, which in turn comes from the root word '*templum*' – meaning an open place for observation. The more familiar understanding in English today is 'temple' – a sacred place dedicated to a deity. As such, Levertov reminds us that contemplation then means, 'not simply to observe, to regard, but to do these things in the presence of a god'.[15] The 'open place for observation' refers, I suggest, to both a literal place, such as a natural landscape or sacred building, as well as the imaginative space within human consciousness. The role of the imagination is fundamental to the discussion in Chapter Three. But for now, it is important to note that, for Murdoch,

13   *Microsoft Encarta Encyclopaedia* (2002).
14   Louth, *The Origins of the Christian Mystical Tradition*, xvi.
15   Denise Levertov, *The Poet in the World* (New York: New Directions, 1973), 8.

Levertov and Dillard, a life of contemplation involves seeing the sacred in whatever happens to be nearby as opposed to a transcendent reality outside of sensual perception. Neither is a contemplative life solely about finding the self. Mystics such as Julian felt the impulse to help others find spiritual contentment.

Rediscovering Contemplation

There are three crucial similarities between the traditional under-standing of the contemplative life and the mystic in postmodernity.[16] The chief aspect of the *via contemplativa* is a focus on the idea of a metaphysical perfection, which is the same objective for the literary writers under discussion, although they concentrate on its ontological manifestations. For Murdoch, in postmodernity, this is the Good, while Levertov and Dillard retain the Judeo-Christian concept of God. The notion of surrendering the self or diminishing the ego remains an intrinsic aspect of the life of a mystic, which is contrary to the individualist approach of modernism. This is equally essential for the creative writer of course. Last, but not least, the *via contemplativa* has always represented a movement towards love of the other. That is, this is not an attempt at possession of the other but loving awareness of the other, or the I–Thou relationship – an important aspect further developed in Chapter Six. Love is the connecting principle between the seen and unseen worlds, but love also enables humans to apprehend the reality of other beings. These various aspects of love will prove to be of importance in subsequent chapters, but at this point it is important to note that love is more about action than contemplation.

There are also some key differences between postmodern and classical mysticism that, broadly speaking, centre on critical issues of interiority and exteriority and the process of contemplation itself. The classical way of the mystic entails a clear focus on the result of union with God or Christ, or, in Plato's conception of the process, entry into

16   I have drawn on Dietrich von Hildebrand's general principles of the contemplative life for the traditional aspects. See *Transformation in Christ: on the Christian Attitude* (Fort Collins, CO: Ignatius Press, 2001).

the dazzling light of the Sun.[17] Mystical vision is described in terms of going inward, or 'the flight of the alone to the alone'.[18] In postmodernity, however, the journey includes a movement from the inner to the outer in as much as it is as members of communities that the postmodern mystic creates visions. A mystical experience implies that someone loses connection with the world around him or her, but in true mystical awareness thus defined, a movement towards others follows as the individual ego lessens its grip on the psyche. Lastly, there is an interesting difference in the idea of contemplation, which is a metaphor for seeing. The postmodern mystic needs a clear focus on what is literally in front of their eyes before they can see 'mystically'. Both aspects of postmodern mysticism are important in this discussion for methodological and theoretical reasons.

Plato held that a spiritual pilgrimage should be simultaneously intellectual, moral and religious, and arguably, his cave myth is the founding quest narrative of Western philosophy. Murdoch explains his metaphorical rendering:

> Prisoners in the cave are at first chained to face the back wall where all they can see are shadows, cast by a fire which is behind them, of themselves and of objects which are carried between them and the fire. Later they manage to turn round and see the fire and the objects which cast the shadows. Later they escape from the cave, see the outside world in the light of the sun, and finally the sun itself. The sun represents the Form of the Good in whose light truth is seen; it reveals the world, hitherto the invisible, and is also a source of life.[19]

For Murdoch, to journey fully into the light is a rare and dazzling experience, and indeed, it could even be an illusion, and therefore, to look at the sun would be to 'see nothing'.[20] Levertov refers to Plato's cave myth through the title of her second collection of prose essays

---

17   Plato uses the light of the sun, which both blinds and makes all things visible, as an allegory of the pure 'light' of the intellect which attains knowledge of the unknowable Good.

18   This is the well-known phrase from the fourteenth-century mystical text *The Cloud of Unknowing*, the author of which is unknown.

19   Plato, *Republic*, 514 paraphrased in Iris Murdoch, 'The Fire and the Sun', in Conradi, *Existentialists and Mystics*, 389.

20   Iris Murdoch, *The Sovereignty of Good* (New York & London: Routledge, 1970), 70.

Light Up the Cave (1981), and Dillard refers to fiction writers as 'thoughtful interpreters of the world [who] "doodle on the walls of the cave"'.[21] Philosophers, theologians, and mystic-poets are all, in one way or another, striving to see the 'light of the sun'.

Murdoch is something of a rarity in as much as she was both a successful novelist and philosopher. These disciplines require very different ways of thinking and writing. Indeed Murdoch herself was always keen to maintain a clear distinction between the two. She stated in an interview with Magee that the aim of philosophy is to clarify while the aim of literature is very often to mystify: 'The literary writer deliberately leaves a space for his reader to play in. The philosopher must not leave a space.'[22] In other words, literature leaves room for the imagination whilst philosophy engages the intellect only. It is on this basis that she frequently drew on the Bible.

One of Murdoch's favourite biblical phrases is Philippians 4:8: 'Whatsoever things are true, whatsoever, things are honest, whatsoever things are just, whatsoever things are lovely, whatsoever things are of good report [...] think on these things.'[23] This captures Murdoch's desire to contemplate the things of this world that retain an innocence uncorrupted by the 'greedy ego'. She remained optimistic at the possibility of living a life based on goodness, truth and beauty despite the evident decline in morals and religious belief in Western civilization. She believed that it was important not to lose sight of this possibility and to keep trying to achieve the Good, and she believed that it is the role of the novelist to help people work this out for themselves.

Levertov reminds us that poets write poems for the same reason that people read them. Individuals turn to poetry, she suggests, for 'illumination, for revelations that help them to survive, to survive in spirit not only in body'. Poems function for both the reader and writer as 'stepping stones in one's slow pilgrimage'.[24] For her, the work of a poet

21   Dillard, *Living by Fiction*, 13.
22   Iris Murdoch, 'Literature and Philosophy: A Conversation with Bryan Magee', in Conradi, *Existentialists and Mystics*, 5.
23   Murdoch, *The Sovereignty of Good*, 56.
24   Levertov, 'Poetry, Prophecy and Survival' in *New & Selected Essays*, 150.

in its entirety marks the spiritual journey through life as well as offering insights for others on the same quest. In an essay written in 1967 entitled 'A Sense of Pilgrimage' in *The Poet in the World*, Levertov explains her conviction that both life and work is a pilgrimage or spiritual journey. For her, the pilgrimage is 'essentially that of passage from one spiritual state into another'.[25] Later, in 1991, in her essay 'Some Affinities of Content', with the benefit of hindsight, she makes the point more lucidly when she states,

> [M]ore and more, what I have sought as *a reading writer*, is a poetry that, while it does not attempt to ignore or deny the ocean of crisis in which we swim, is itself 'on pilgrimage', as it were, in search of significance underneath and beyond the succession of temporal events: a poetry which attests to [a] 'deep spiritual longing'.[26]

This 'deep spiritual longing' characterises postmodernity. For Levertov, poetry is a form of prayer that seeks a resolution.[27] In 'For the Asking',[28] she offers a reflection on Augustine, whose 'soul / didn't become a mansion large enough / to welcome, along with God, the women he'd loved'. She suggests that God 'would never have felt / fully at home as his guest'. Nonetheless, she imagines that the power of prayer would have worked on his soul over the years, so that 'each word he set down, expanded, unnoticed; the roof / rose, and a skylight opened'. It is only the work of a contemplative over a lifetime that bears fruits of the spirit. This has to incorporate both intuition and inspiration as well as 'intellectual beliefs and opinions' because

> these intellectual commitments are not a system of dogmatic reasoning [and] to believe, as an artist, in inspiration or the intuitive, to know that without Imagination [...] no amount of acquired craft or scholarship or of brilliant reasoning will suffice, is to live with a door of one's life open to the transcendent, the numinous.[29]

---

25   Levertov, *The Poet in the World*, 71.
26   Levertov, 'Some Affinities of Content', in *New & Selected Essays*, 4.
27   See Murray Bodo, *Poetry as Prayer: Denise Levertov* (Boston: Pauline Books and Media, 2001). See Chapter 3 specifically.
28   Levertov, *This Great Unknowing*, 10.
29   Levertov, 'A Poet's View', in *New & Selected Essays*, 241.

Living 'with a door of one's life open to the transcendent' captures the life of a contemplative and recalls Julian in her anchoress' cell betwixt the sacred space of the church in Norwich and her window on the world. However, and as Murray Bodo's description of Levertov as 'an active contemplative' implies, in postmodernity the mystic tends to be actively involved in the world of politics.[30]

Dillard takes the life of spiritual contemplation far more literally. Most specifically, the three days she frames her contemplation around in *Holy the Firm* deliberately represent the three stages of the mystic way: purgation, illumination and union. Indeed, Dillard's fascination with the themes of pilgrimage or mystical quests is a continuous thread throughout her writing – she frequently juxtaposes her own spiritual path and travels with other journeys of note. Dillard's understanding of her vocation emerges most clearly in *Holy the Firm*, in which she explicitly describes herself as a blend of nun, thinker and artist. She explains: 'A nun lives in the fires of the spirit, a thinker lives in the bright wick of the mind, an artist lives jammed in the pool of materials.'[31] A life of contemplation requires three things: a spiritual passion and longing for the sacred, an active mind, and the ability to notice anything and everything.

Reading as a Mystical Task

As well as being successful writers, Murdoch, Levertov and Dillard were always avid readers. Reading and writing are inseparable from the mystic way in postmodernity.[32] McGinn argues that, due to the academic focus of recent decades on 'highly ambiguous experience', there has been a lack of analysis of the texts themselves, which consequently has created an unfortunate split between experience and its

---

30   Bodo, *Poetry as Prayer*, 5.
31   Annie Dillard, *Holy the Firm* (New York: Harper, 1988), 22.
32   Carl Keller suggests that mysticism should be defined primarily through writing. See *Mysticism and Language* (Oxford: Oxford University Press, 1992).

interpretation. He calls for a 'mystical hermeneutic'.[33] It is in this spirit that I read Murdoch, Levertov and Dillard.

Hans Robert Jauss summarises the reader-response element in literature thus:

> The experience of reading can liberate one from adaptations, prejudices, and predicaments of a lived praxis in that it compels one to a new perception of things. The horizon of expectations in literature [...] not only preserves actual experiences but also anticipates unrealised possibility, broadens the limited space of social behaviour for new desires, claims, and goals, and thereby opens up the paths of future experiences.[34]

So reading enables a re-visitation of the self and helps to promote changes in attitudes that in turn affect future ideologies and moral behaviour.

In order to deduce any meaning from 'mystical' texts, there is a requirement on the part of the reader to approach the text in a non-violent, receptive way in order that 'the integrity, the otherness, the wholeness of the text be respected and not violated by radical re-fashioning'.[35] Donovan describes this as an 'erotic responsiveness' whereby the 'interpreter must take the attitude of a 'receptive beholder'.[36] Whether facing a landscape, another being or a work of art, the 'beholder' should open themselves up to it to allow 'truth' to communicate itself. The act of interpretation, however, requires an intellectual engagement whereby we are forced, by entering into the world a writer creates, to recognise the difference of others and the fact of our own otherness.

33 McGinn, *The Foundations of Mysticism*, xiv. I will develop this in Chapter Seven in relation to Murdoch, Levertov and Dillard's approach to the Bible.
34 David Scott Arnold, 'Hermeneutic of Otherness: A Feeling of Deflection from a Viable Centre', in 'Reading A Severed Head', *Liminal Readings: Forms of Otherness in Melville, Joyce and Murdoch* (Basingstoke: Macmillan, 1998), 92 cites Hans Robert Jauss, *Toward an Aesthetics of Reception*, trans. Timothy Bahti (Minneapolis, Minnesota: University of Minnesota Press, 1982), 41.
35 Josephine Donovan, 'Ecofeminist literary criticism: reading the orange', in *Hypatia*, 11:2 (1996), 161–184.
36 Ibid.

Despite her strong political views about war, nuclear weapons and oppression of peoples in the developing world, Levertov did not believe that poetry as propaganda was a proper function of the genre. Rather, she thought that it 'sets in motion parts of people's being'.[37] By appealing to the reader's emotions and conscience, she hoped to affect change and resolve. Levertov was of the opinion that much of academic writing (literary criticism in particular) was too 'narrow' as if it 'had been developed from a thesis'. She prefers writers who 'love the work and plunge into it for their own pleasure', – writers who 'open doors for the reader'.[38] This seems crucial to the task of transformation, the issue broached in Chapter Seven – that a writer can instigate a change of consciousness in her readers.

Apart from one novel, Dillard's writing loosely falls into the category of spiritual autobiography – although we are never quite sure what is fact and what is fiction. In *Speaking in Parables*, Sallie McFague suggests that, 'like a good story, a good autobiography deals with the great unfamiliar, the mystery of the self, in and through the familiar, a multitude of events and circumstances'.[39] In particular, an autobiography that includes a mystical search deals with the self in relation to the sacred. People read autobiographies to find out about themselves. Rather than being an accurate account of facts and events in a person's life, a good autobiography is, according to McFague, a 'likeness or metaphor of the self'.[40] Dillard's 'autobiography' is, if we recall, partly fiction. Writing that can be termed 'mystical' steers away from the confessional approach and towards helping the reader to make sense of their own life by achieving the level of parable. For example, Dunn suggests that Dillard deliberately stalks her readers by 'approaching them in so many subtle ways that it is difficult to tell precisely when they have been "caught"'.[41]

---

37 Michael Andre, 'Denise Levertov: An Interview', in Brooker, *Conversations with Denise Levertov*, 64.

38 Ed Block, 'Interview with Denise Levertov', in *Renascence* 50 (1997) http://www.questia.com/PM.qst?a=o&d=5001524879

39 Sallie McFague, *Speaking in Parables* (London: SCM Press, 2002), 127.

40 Ibid., 131.

41 Robert Paul Dunn, 'The Artist as Nun: Theme, Tone and Vision in the Writings of Annie Dillard', in *Studia Mystica*, 1:4 (1978) 26.

Writing from the point of view of both a reader and a writer, Dillard asks:

> Why are we reading? If not in hope of beauty laid bare, life heightened and its deepest mystery probed? Can the writer isolate and vivify all in experience that most deeply engages our intellects and our hearts? Can the writer renew our hopes for literary forms? Why are we reading, if not in the hope that the writer will magnify and dramatize our days, will illuminate and inspire us with wisdom, courage, and the hope of meaningfulness, and press upon our minds the deepest of mysteries, so we may feel again their majesty and power? What do we ever know that is higher than that power which, from time to time, seizes our lives, and which reveals us startlingly to ourselves as creatures set down here bewildered? Why does death catch us by surprise, and why love? We still and always want waking. If we are reading for these things, why should anyone read books with advertising slogans and brand names in them? Why would anyone write such books? We should mass half-dressed in long lines like tribesmen and shake gourds at each other, to wake up; instead we watch television and miss the show.[42]

This passage captures Dillard's distinctive overview of the *via contemplativa* in postmodernity concisely. She wants to wake people up to mystical possibility.

Michael Sells, who writes about reading from a perspective of mystical language, identifies the moment when a reader gains insight as the 'meaning event' which

> indicates that moment when the meaning has become identical or fused with the act of predication. In metaphysical terms, essence is identical with existence, but such identity is not only asserted, it is performed. [...] The meaning event is the semantic analogue to the experience of mystical union. It does not describe or refer to mystical union but effects a semantic union that re-creates or imitates a mystical union.[43]

For Sells, this 'meaning event' is what defines a text as 'mystical'. Such a text provides a momentary glimpse of the sacred and opens up a trajectory that moves the reader beyond reason and to-

---

42   Annie Dillard, 'Write Till You Drop', http://www.nytimes.com.books/99/28/
      specials/dillard-drop.html
43   Michael A. Sells, *Mystical Languages of Unsaying* (Chicago and London: The
      University of Chicago Press, 1994), 9.

wards the unspeakable mystery. I would add that it could also provide that 'prick of consciousness' that jolts an individual out of apathy and perhaps towards action.

Mary or Martha?

Historically, the *via contemplativa* in the Christian tradition has been the vocation of those who spent their lives absorbed in spiritual matters through prayer and meditation with the ultimate goal to unite the soul with God. For most, this literally meant a life of seclusion shut away from the real world. But this was not the whole story for the medieval anchoress. Julian, for example, functioned for some of the time as a spiritual counselor who would speak to those seeking advice through a window that opened onto the outside world.[44] The *Ancrene Riwle* goes to some lengths to make it clear that this aspect of an anchoress or anchorite's life was of a lesser importance, ruling that:

> Ye anchorites have taken to yourselves as Mary's part, which our Lord himself commended. [...] Housewifery is Martha's part, and Mary's part is quietness and rest from all the world's din, that nothing may hinder her from hearing the voice of God.[45]

At the start of this chapter, it was established that a key characteristic of the *via contemplativa* in postmodernity, according to Soelle, is that the roles of Mary, the *via contemplativa*, and Martha, the *via activa*, are no longer separated and are understood to be of equal value. Postmodern mystics cannot divorce themselves from political or social concerns.[46] It is a primary assertion of this discussion that the act of writing is an action, or movement of love, that proceeds from contemplation.

---

44   One of the more notable people who sought her advice was Margery Kempe. Jantzen, *Julian of Norwich*, 29; 48–49, n9.

45   Ibid., 31. Jantzen cites James Morton (ed and trans.), *The Ancrene Riwle* VIII (London: Chatto & Windus; Boston: John W. Luce, 1907), 314–15.

46   See Janet K. Ruffing, R.S.M. (ed), *Mysticism & Social Transformation* (New York: Syracuse University Press, 2001) for a collection of articles reflecting on the connections between mysticism and social change.

For most people, contemplation usually involves some sort of prayer. Contemporary understanding of contemplative prayer is that this act is firmly in the private sphere and concerned with the relationship between the individual and God. Historically, it has been associated with long periods of silence and isolation. But in postmodernity, there is no longer the option of 'rest from all the world's din'; we do not have the luxury of remaining ignorant of the injustices and sufferings across the globe.

Kum Kum Bajaj draws attention to the paradox between a life of devotion and doing good through action that is found in several of Murdoch's novels. Specifically, Bajaj notices a connection to Indian thought, where the problem of finding the highest self and working in the world is discussed in terms of *Bhakti Marg* (The Way of Devotion) and *Karma Marg* (The Way of Action).[47] Murdoch's way is characterised as the way of love, which is both devotion and action. Perhaps one of the most memorable of Murdoch's mystical characters is Tallis Browne in *The Nice and the Good*, who demonstrates precisely this aspect. Characters that follow the path of love are those who can attend to the realities of others as well as acting when appropriate, which involves a degree of detachment and humility. Tallis genuinely tries to help everyone despite the suffering he experiences at the hands those around him for his efforts. He 'lives totally without illusion in the confusing complexities of the world'.[48] The Abbess in *The Bell* has the same attitude:

> Often we do not achieve for others the good we intend; but we achieve something, something that goes on from our effort. Good is an overflow. Where we generously and sincerely intend it, we are engaged in the work of creation which may be mysterious even to ourselves – and because it is mysterious we may be afraid of it. [...] Remember that all our failures are ultimately failures in love. Imperfect love must not be condemned and rejected, but made perfect. The way is forward, never back.[49]

---

47   Kum Kum Bajaj, *A Critical Study of Iris Murdoch's Fiction* (New Delhi: Atlantic Publishers and Distributors, 2001), 94.

48   Ibid., 98.

49   Iris Murdoch, *The Bell* (London: Vintage, 1973), 235.

In Levertov's view, something more than human effort is required: 'no amount of acquired craft or scholarship or of brilliant reasoning will suffice, is to live with a door of one's life open to the transcendent, the numinous. [*sic*]'[50] This suggests a position of receptive passivity that is only operative part of the time – as a committed political activist she equally trod the *via activa*. This inevitably creates a conflict.

Although Levertov sometimes invokes tasks as sacred that are traditionally seen as the purview of women, such as baking, sewing and knitting, she speaks of the difficulties women face trying to strike a balance between different roles.[51] One of Levertov's early poems that directly addresses this problem of women's divided nature is *The Earthwoman and the Waterwoman*[52] Here she refers to the maternal role women are expected to conform to and the internal conflicts this creates for those with other aspirations. In particular, it invokes the archetypal concept of the 'good' and 'bad' mother, or in Ostriker's words – the dualisms of a 'tame and wild self'.[53] Woman, especially we surmise the woman who is a poet, is sometimes the good mother who 'tends her cakes of good grain' and has well fed children. At other times, she is the bad mother who goes dancing in 'dragonfly dresses and blue shoes',[54] and whose children are 'spindle-thin'.[55]

In contrast to Levertov who either 'wanders' or 'dances', Dillard describes herself more assertively as 'stalking' the sacred in *Pilgrim at*

50 Levertov, 'A Poet's View', in *New & Selected Essays*, 241. 'The Sapphire in the Stream' as a metaphor for the goal of the mystic quest reappears as the title for a collection of her poetry centred on religious themes. See bibliography for details.

51 Sandra M. Gilbert 'Revolutionary Love', in Gelpi, *Denise Levertov*, 204. The metaphor of knitting appears in the early poem 'With Eyes in the Back of Our Heads', *Collected Earlier Poems, 1940–1960*, 86–87.

52 Levertov, *Poems 1940–1960*, 31–32.

53 Alicia Suskin Ostriker, *Stealing the Language: The Emergence of Women's Poetry in America* (London: The Women's Press, 1986), 79.

54 The fact that Levertov composed this poem in 1957 perhaps reflects the post-war culture that endorsed women's domestic roles.

55 Dancing is a spiritual practice in Levertov's thought, and probably links to the 'Hasidic dance of praise' that her father reportedly rose from his death bed to do shortly before his death. 'The Sense of Pilgrimage', in *The Poet in the World*, 70.

Tinker Creek, where she devotes Chapter Eleven to the topic. The verb conjures up images of a predator actively pursuing and watching its victim, and it is intentionally subversive and provocative when used in relation to a mystical quest. She explains that there are two paths, one active and one passive. She writes:

> The first is not what you think of as true stalking, but it is the *Via negativa*, and as fruitful as actual pursuit. When I stalk this way I take my stand on a bridge and wait, emptied. I put myself in the way of the creature's passage, like spring Eskimos at a seal's breathing hole. [...] I am Newton under the apple tree, Buddha under the bo. Stalking the other way, I forge my own passage seeking the creature. [...] I wander the banks; what I find, I follow, doggedly, like Eskimos haunting the caribou herds. I am Wilson squinting after the electrons in a cloud chamber; I am Jacob at Peniel wrestling with the angel.[56]

Not only does this passage capture the essence of the *via contemplativa* as being both active and passive, it also brings together the rituals of indigenous peoples, the vision of the scientist, and mystical experiences at the foundations of other major world faiths. Dillard associates herself with all three.

Rather than describing meditation solely as an emptying of the mind into the pure presence of God, she prefers to describe it as stalking. Through her practised self-control and ability to blend into her surroundings, she is able to actively seek out a relationship with the sacred through a careful and detailed exploration of specific aspects of nature. Alternatively, she also recognises that another way to attain knowledge of God is to rest or still the mind by 'gag[ging] the commentator'.[57] This closely parallels Buddhist meditative practices that seek to rid the mind of endless discussion, which allows the one who meditates to simply wait as an empty and passive being.

---

56   Annie Dillard, *Pilgrim at Tinker Creek* (New York: Harper, 1998), 186–87. Charles Thomas Rees Wilson (1869–1959) was a Scottish physicist and Nobel Prize winner who invented the Wilson Cloud Chamber, which showed the trails of particles and was particularly beneficial to the study of radioactivity. http://www.britannia.com. Jacob wrestling with the angel comes from the biblical account in Genesis 32. Buddha attains enlightenment under the Bodhi Tree in the Buddhist tradition. (Mahavastu, Volume III. 261, 268f).

57   Ronda, 'Annie Dillard and the Fire of God', 484.

The process of 'stalking the sacred' as ingeniously described by Annie Dillard in *Pilgrim at Tinker Creek* takes a lot of practice to perfect. McClintock argues that her method constitutes a meditative and ritualistic act, 'through ordinary activities such as walking, while – necessarily – one is open to aesthetic and spiritual experience'.[58] Her walking is preparation for the mystical experience or vision for which she longs. In addition, her other preparations for 'seeing' include diverse reading. She disciplines both her mind and her body in an attempt to gain a state of innocence, which will be relevant for Chapter Four. Next, however, we will explore the ways in which the work of Murdoch, Levertov and Dillard indicate their continuity with Julian.

Recovering Julian in Postmodernity

All three of our writers find inspiration in, and engage critically and extensively with, the writings of well-known mystics from a variety of historical and religious contexts.[59] Due to the remit of this study, I will restrict my investigation to how each of the three reads, interprets and re-imagines Julian in a postmodern context, because she is the one figure in whose work they all share more than a passing interest. I then provide an overview of the different ways that Murdoch, Levertov and Dillard engage with Julian in postmodernity. Murdoch 'reincarnates' her into the narratives of her plots, while Levertov attempts to imaginatively enter her life, and Dillard recreates her on an existential level in her own spiritual and working life.

58   James I. McClintock, *Nature's Kindred Spirits* (Wisconsin, USA: The University of Wisconsin Press, 1994), 102.
59   For example Murdoch; Meister Eckhart, Simone Weil; Levertov, Brother Lawrence, Martin Buber, Dillard, Abraham Herschel, Pierre de Chardin.

Murdoch positions herself as an anchoress in postmodernity through the character of the Abbess in *The Bell*. She also reincarnates Julian into a postmodern context and imagines how her 'visions' and the consequent reflection would differ. It is interesting to note that Jantzen surmises that the role of an anchoress in medieval England is closely comparable to that of a modern day psychotherapist or counsellor.[60] Lay people would come to an anchoress for spiritual advice. Indeed, Murdoch explores this idea through the character of the Abbess in *The Bell*, 'with whom she admitted a little to identifying'.[61] The Abbess encourages Michael Mead to set up a religious community for 'sick people, whose desire for God makes them unsatisfactory citizens'.[62] Michael Mead represents the masochistic side of mysticism. Despite having chosen the life of a religious contemplative, the Abbess real- ises that such a disciplined life is not the answer for the majority of people. Neither is it possible for those living the cloistered life to pro- vide salvation for those on the outside. Rather, Bajaj notes, the Abbess 'in her detached wisdom exhorts to perform sincerely small generous acts and strive to make imperfect love perfect'.[63] Michael initially fails to do this, as represented by his inability to extend love to his brother Nick, who eventually commits suicide. After his brother's death and the disintegration of the community, he is depicted as moving from a world he had tried to organise and structure to 'a world which is muddled, unprotecting without the consoling image of God and the

60   Jantzen, *Julian of Norwich*, 47.
61   Conradi, *The Saint and Artist*, 145 cites *The Listener* (31/12/81) 817. Murdoch did feel attracted to Anglo-Catholicism at one point in her life, making several visits or retreats to Malling Abbey in Kent between 1946 and 1949. In fact, Conradi tells us that the lay community and enclosed religious order of Bene- dictine nuns was more or less recreated wholesale in *The Bell*. (Conradi, *The Saint and the Artist*, 247).
62   Murdoch, *The Bell*, 81.
63   Kum Kum Bajaj, *A Critical Study of Iris Murdoch's Fiction* (New Delhi: Atlan- tic Publishing, 2001), 69.

consolation of the redemption of self'.[64] But it is the real world that is here described. The 'detached wisdom' of the Abbess is ultimately Murdoch's.

While a parallel can be seen between Murdoch and the Abbess in *The Bell*, Conradi reminds us that she can be equally identified with an 'emotionally muddled, silly Nora'.[65] Indeed, she was sometimes referred to as 'The Abbess of North Oxford' who cut herself off from reality and invented a fantastical alternative.[66] This I suggest is only partially true in a manner more fitting with Jantzen's description of a 'part-time' anchoress in postmodernity. In the course of his research for Murdoch's biography, Conradi found evidence that she was a loyal and caring friend to many. She travelled often and was a keen observer of 'reality', whether people, art or things. Indeed it would be very hard to be a novelist without 'real' experiences. This belief is captured through an incident in *The Bell* where a nun under the spiritual guidance of the Abbess, who although cloistered and thus removed from such experiences by definition, does not hesitate to throw off her habit and dive into the lake to save the suicidal Catherine.

Along similar lines, the character of Anne Cavidge in *Nuns and Soldiers* has left a religious order to live a good life in the outside world. One day, she has an extraordinary experience:

> Jesus was standing beside the table, with one hand resting upon it. Not daring yet to raise her eyes to his face, she saw his hand pressed upon the scrubbed grainy wood of the table. His hand was pale and bony, the skin rough as if chapped. Then he said her name, 'Anne', and she raised her eyes and simultaneously fell on her knees on the floor.
> Jesus was leaning with one hand upon the table and gazing down at her. He had a strange elongated head and a strange pallor of something which had been long deprived of the light, a shadowed leaf, a deep sea fish, a grub inside a fruit. […] He wore plimsolls upon his feet with no socks.[67]

---

64   Ibid., This movement towards spiritual perfection has parallels in Plato's mysticism, Hindu philosophy and Buddhist thought.
65   Conradi, *The Saint and the Artist*, 250.
66   Ibid., xxii.
67   Iris Murdoch, *Nuns and Soldiers* (London: Chatto & Windus, 1980), 205. Conradi informs us that Anne's 'vision' is based on a real life dream experienced by

Later, like Julian, Anne reflects on the experience.

> He seemed to her at times like a sprite, a fairy thing, a lost vagrant spiritual being. Perhaps he was in some sense local, a little god left behind by a lost cult which even he had forgotten. Or was not his 'locality' determined rather by the whole universe beaming its radiance in upon the monad soul? She remained persuaded that he was *her* Christ, hers alone. He's all I've got she thought. Somehow it was a true showing.[68]

The reference to a 'showing' is a direct reference to Julian's '*Shewings*', her testimony of having experienced God directly as all-embracing love. But this is a personal, localised and mystical Christ, one that has been buried under layers of doctrine and unimaginative readings of the Gospels. Her vision is not redemptive because this Jesus does not come to save her but to show her that she is responsible for her own life and any good that comes of it. Dipple asserts the connection to Julian is ironic because Anne's 'showing' is the exact opposite of Julian's revelations. Julian's Christ is 'a being of action and responsibility' with a 'message of reassurance', while Anne's is 'quizzical and non-authoritative'.[69]

Levertov: An Empathetic Reading of Julian in Postmodernity

Although Levertov dismissed claims that she was a mystic, several critics have attributed such qualities to her. Diane Wakoski notices that, 'like all mystics, Levertov believes in a God or the knowledge of a God which is beyond doctrine and organized religion'.[70] Her approach to God is through a harmonisation of body and spirit – an embodied spirituality. This is what Levertov found so illuminating in the writings of Julian, for like the anchoress, she refuses to despair in the world. Levertov informs us that Julian's theology informed her poem

---

Murdoch of an encounter with a guru who gave her comfort and advice. Conradi, *The Saint and the Artist*, 554.

68   Murdoch, *Nuns and Soldiers*, 361.

69   Elizabeth Dipple, *Work for the Spirit* (London: Methuen, 1982), 328–29.

70   Diane Wakoski, 'Song of Herself', in Linda Wagner-Martin (ed), *Critical Essays on Denise Levertov* (Boston, Massachusetts: G. K. Hall, 1991), 56.

'The Task',[71] in which she enjoins a trust and hope that God will make all things right in the end, but for now, we turn to her empathetic reading of Julian's life.

In her poem entitled 'The Showings: Lady Julian of Norwich, 1342–1416',[72] Levertov tries to imagine the life and mind of the female mystic whose life and writings so obviously influenced her own thought and work. She reflects on her personal struggle with writing and faith, which includes her attempt to 'synthesise and to name all the stuff of reality' against a background of a 'black nothingness' that constantly undercut her sense of certainty in the world.[73] This poem represents a very real attempt on the part of the author to understand the mystical knowledge that Julian gained.

Julian's childhood, of which we know nothing, is fictionalised in this poem. Levertov paints an idyllic picture, a mix of images from nature and medieval art and architecture. Without doubt, it was a time when people had a greater perception of the material world being suffused with the Divine. She imagines that 'her mother might have given [her] a newlaid egg, warm from the hen' or her brother 'his delicate treasure, a sparrow's egg', which she would later develop theologically into the notion of 'the macrocosmic egg, sublime paradox, brown hazelnut of All that is'. The experience of her own mother 'pointing out' things and Julian's concept of God as a maternal creator appear to combine in Levertov's mind here.

She starts by contrasting the 'the dizzying multiplication of all language can name or fail to name' with the 'the earth […] with the grain of one particular scrap of carpentered wood […] one especial leaf [… the] beat of our hearts *now*'. She then wonders how the myriad possibilities for knowledge relate to the smallness of things: how can humans ever begin to make sense of these mysteries? Julian, she says, asks 'us to turn our gaze inside out, and see *a little thing, the size of a hazelnut*, and believe it is our world'. This 'medieval enigma'

---

71   Denise Levertov, 'Work that Enfaiths', in *New & Selected Essays* (New York: New Directions, 1992), 252.

72   Levertov, *Breathing the Water*, 75–82.

73   James Gallant, 'Entering no-man's land: the recent religious poetry of Denise Levertov', in *Renascence* 50:1–2 (1997/1998), 123.

requires the suspension of concepts of time and place, to achieve a mystical comprehension that defies the boundaries of logic.

Levertov also reflects with great attention on Julian's life: what events and circumstances contributed to this mystical awareness? She wonders whether she ever loved a man, although she concludes that whether she did or not is irrelevant as she would have 'long since travelled through and beyond it'. In the poem, Julian is associated with the wisdom of older women even though she was relatively young by today's standards, for 'Thirty was older than it is now'; she also recognises that an educated woman would not have been the norm so 'somehow, reading or read to, she'd spiralled up within tall towers of learning, steeples of discourse'. Levertov imagines that, while learning how to read and write, 'bells in [Julian's] spirit rang new changes'. Mystical vision, theology and intellectual pursuits are all on the same trajectory to realising spiritual insights in the here and now.

The fact of Julian's 'bodily sickness' is not interpreted with the hindsight of post-Freudian psychological analysis that would diagnose 'neurosis'. Rather, Levertov imagines the intensity of such longings from her own experience of living in a desiring, questing, female body. Spiritual desire in the context of medieval mystical experience is, Levertov suggests, the 'desire to enact metaphor, for flesh to make known to intellect'. After all, this is at the heart of 'God's agony'; a God who takes on human flesh. Jantzen notes that mystics such as Julian projected a more positive perspective on corporeality due to their reinterpretation of the doctrine of the Incarnation. They were, in fact, exceptional in that they 'developed a strand of spirituality whose principle of integration is a significant alternative to dualistic thinking which rendered spirituality in effect a male prerogative'.[74] This will prove to be important later in our discussion.

The Middle Ages were certainly not idyllic times, however; they were times of war and the Black Death, hunger, strife, torture and massacre. The mature Julian reflected deeply on the presence of evil and apparent absence of God, as Levertov herself did in relation to the horrors of the twentieth century. One of the most outstanding of Julian's accomplishments, especially from a woman's point of view,

74   Jantzen, *Power, Gender and Christian Mysticism*, 224.

is her insight on the nature of sin. Levertov imagines her laughing at the 'spirit of evil', whom she thought as 'silly as his horns and imaginary tail'. Levertov, as we shall see, does not deny the reality of evil, but like Murdoch, sees it as something that resides in the human heart. Levertov's reading of Julian's experiences throughout her life helps us to contextualise Julian's 'revelations'. In her understanding, they are a result of a unique set of circumstances.

Dillard: Following in Julian's Footsteps

More than Murdoch and Levertov, Dillard actively and persistently longs for experience of God. Like Julian, who prayed earnestly to receive three wounds, she actively longs for any contact with the sacred through her repeated forays into the natural world, where she describes herself as 'stalking the sacred'. She records a number of experiences throughout the body of her writing that would fit the accepted definition of a mystical experience,[75] but considering that the definition of mysticism here is more about an orientation of being or consciousness, this does not warrant extra consideration. It is in *Pilgrim at Tinker Creek* that Dillard first imitates the life of Julian through her 'anchorhold' by Tinker Creek, and she then follows this up later and more explicitly in *Holy the Firm*.

In the latter, she spends a year at Puget Sound, deliberately setting the scene to imitate Julian in her anchorhold so she can study 'hard things'.[76] Positioned in the far east of the American continent, her environment mirrors her theological standpoint – 'at the rim of the real […] where time and eternity spatter each other with foam'.[77] This is a metaphor for the possibility of eternity breaking through into temporal time, or what she often refers to as the 'fringe'. Julian, who lived betwixt the secular and sacred worlds, existed in such an in-between physical place as well – except of course hers was a vastly narrower

---

75   See in particular 'the tree with lights in it', in Dillard, *Pilgrim at Tinker Creek*, 36.
76   Dillard, *Holy the Firm*, 19.
77   Ibid., 20–21.

world than the one that Dillard knows. It is only by seeking such wild and solitary places that the postmodern anchoress can effectively recreate the conditions appropriate for comprehending the big questions. Solitude in the chaotic world of the contemporary writer requires an active physical removal of the self from society. Furthermore, Julian would have been a kind of spiritual employee, with her physical needs being met in return for prayer on behalf of her benefactors. In both contrast and comparison, today's independent woman in the West has to earn her living by participating in Capitalistic society. As an anchoress, Julian's right to privacy for contemplation and prayer was a foregone conclusion, but a contemporary woman has to be single-mindedly determined to mark out space and time for private thought and contemplation.

Dillard describes the room where she lives on this desolate spot as being 'plain as a skull, a firm setting for windows'.[78] In fact, she goes on to explain that one wall of her room is glass, thus providing her with a frame from which to view the world both literally and figuratively. This mirrors Julian's anchorhold, which had three windows, and Dillard specifically refers to the medieval belief that 'the idea of a thing which a man framed for himself was always more real to him than the actual thing itself'.[79] Whereas Julian was connected to the church through her window, Dillard connects to the landscape through hers, which she interprets symbolically as 'an illuminated manuscript whose leaves the wind takes, one by one, whose painted illuminations and halting words draw me'.[80] While Julian was steeped in the teachings of the church, Dillard comes as a 'hollow' person with the intent of 'reading' or 'seeing' the sacred in the landscape at Puget Sound. The landscape is her sacred text within which the word becomes incarnated.

Holy the Firm is divided into three chapters, and various theories have been offered as to Dillard's reason for this formal strategy: the three days of Christ's passion; the three days of Julian's sickness in which she received her revelations; the Creation, the Fall, and Re-

78   Ibid., 21.
79   Ibid., 22–23.
80   Ibid., 24.

demption;[81] 'the tripartite pattern of faith, doubt and faith renewed';[82] 'the three stages of the mystic way – illumination, purgation, and union'.[83] In keeping with Dillard's shifting patterns of thoughts and insights, it seems likely that it could be either one of these suggestions or a synthesis of all of them. What is certain is that trinities seem to be in play, which echoes the underlying theme of the Trinity in Julian's *Showings*. One such trinity that deserves some attention is that of the nun, the thinker and the artist that Dillard presents as three possible 'windows' on the sacred. Seemingly, Dillard is attempting a fusion of these three roles as perceived within herself. Additionally, there is the character of Julie Norwich, who obviously invokes the medieval Julian who appears in this text. Because she is horrifically burnt in an aeroplane accident, Dillard has to grapple with the notion of a God who can allow such suffering. Rather than focusing on the sufferings of Christ, Dillard focuses on human suffering. She does, however, have a 'vision' of Christ, but one that is more cosmic in scope than personal.

Anyone familiar with Julian's description of her vision of Christ will recognise similar use of graphic descriptive language in Dillard's description of a vision of Christ being baptised in the Sound:

> He lifts from the water. Water beads on his shoulders. I see the water in balls as heavy as planets, a billion beads of water as weighty as worlds, and he lifts them up on his back as he rises. He stands wet in the water. Each one bead is transparent, and each has a world, or the same world, light and alive and apparent inside the drop: it is all there ever could be, moving at once, past and future, and all the people.[84]

A comparison to Julian's vision of Christ's suffering on the cross reveals the same attention to detail:

81   McClintock, *Nature's Kindred Spirits*, 91.
82   Nancy Lucas, 'Annie Dillard', *Dictionary of Literary Biography Yearbook 1980* (Detroit: Gale Research Company, 1981), 187, cited in William J. Scheick, 'Annie Dillard, Narrative Fringe', in *Contemporary American Women Writers: Narrative Strategies*, Catherine Rainwater, and William Scheick (eds) (Lexington: University of Kentucky Press, 1985), 63.
83   Robert Paul Dunn, 'The Artist as Nun: Theme, Tone and Vision in the Writings of Annie Dillard', in *Studia Mystica* 1:4 (1978), 18.
84   Dillard, *Holy the Firm*, 66–68.

I saw the bodily vision of the copious bleeding of the head persist. The great drops of blood fell from beneath the crown like pellets, looking as if they came from the veins, as they issue they were a brownish red, for the blood was very thick, and as they spread they turned bright red. And as they reached the brows they vanished; and even so the bleeding continued until I had seen and understood many things. Nevertheless, the beauty and the vivacity persisted, beautiful and vivid without diminution. The copiousness resembles the drops of water which fall from the eaves of a house after a great shower of rain, falling so thick that no human ingenuity can count them. And in their roundness as they spread over the forehead they were like a herring's scales.[85]

Dillard sees the whole world in a drop of water as Julian is shown it in a small round thing the size of a hazelnut. For both these women, Christ is immanent in the world. Julian's imagery employs language that would have been familiar to her from the medieval town of Norwich; houses would have had overhanging thatched roofs and herrings were a local staple at that time. Dillard draws hers from the deserted landscape.

What is important to note about both Julian's and Dillard's mystical visions and Murdoch's character of Anne Cavidge is that 'revelations' or 'visions' are not just for their own personal benefit. They are interpreted as being intended for the whole community. In the case of Anne, her vision provides the impetus to go out into the world and be a secret anchoress hidden in the world.[86] For Julian, it means making her insights accessible for other people through writing down and reflecting on her experiences. This act would not have been without its dangers for Julian. A woman who took it upon herself to write a book of spiritual teaching was literally risking life and limb. Convinced that they should be 'for the profit of many others',[87] Julian went to great lengths to make her readers understand that her revelations were meant for all her fellow Christians. It is in much the same attitude that 'ordinary people' populate Dillard's vision. Both women understood themselves to be a vehicle for revealing the truth about the nature of God.

85   Julian, *Showings*, 187–88.
86   Murdoch, *Nuns and Soldiers*, 309.
87   Julian, *Showings*, 134.

The practice of an anchoress was to withdraw from the world but was, according to Jantzen, actually 'the very antithesis of privatized spirituality that turns away from the world to some safe and unengaged cocoon. The very withdrawal is, paradoxically, a commitment to engagement'.[88] Like Murdoch's Abbess, a postmodern anchoress needs to be able to stand back at times whilst being prepared to immerse herself in the suffering and messiness of the world around her.

Mystical Ways of Seeing

Lastly, I will focus on contemplation as a metaphor for seeing. Specifically I will focus on these three writers, distinct approaches to the dialectical relationship between microcosmic and macrocosmic ways of understanding themselves and the world, or more succinctly, the inner and outer modes in their mystical 'seeing'. As suggested in the introduction to this chapter, there are epistemological issues surrounding mystical vision as a source of knowledge. But Jantzen shows, through a close reading of Julian's texts, that rather than prioritising the interior experience, Julian has the ability to move easily between interior to exterior experiences.[89] In other words, her writing, like that of Murdoch, Levertov and Dillard, is a product of spiritual, intellectual and corporeal sight.

Most of us take the ability to see for granted, and moreover, it is common to use the metaphor of vision to refer to knowledge (for example, 'I see' indicates comprehension and understanding).[90] However, the word 'vision' also has another, broader definition connoting

---

88   Jantzen, *Julian of Norwich*, xxii.
89   Jantzen, *Becoming Divine*, 309.
90   There are a growing number of scientific hypotheses concerning the role of vision in acquiring knowledge. A good place to start is Richard L. Gregory's *Eye and Brain: The Psychology of Seeing* (Oxford University Press, 1997). For a more in-depth analysis, try Donald D. Hoffman's *Visual Intelligence: How We Create What We See* (W. W. Norton & Company Ltd, 2000).

that human beings have the ability to imagine and speculate outside of particular historical, geographical and social contexts. It seems reasonable then to expect that knowledge of the sacred must rely in part on both types of vision – looking as a physical act and seeing metaphorically.

The sensual perception of the divine is typical of classical Christian mysticism as captured in the writings of Bonaventure, who states:

> concerning the mirror of things perceived through sensation, we can see God not only through his vestiges, but also in them as he is in them by his essence, power and presence [...] by which we are led to contemplate God in all his creatures which enter our mind through our bodily senses.[91]

However, in both Platonic and later Christian mysticism, the senses are only a means towards an end. The senses, of which sight is perhaps the most important, are like stepping stones that lead towards beatific vision. Conversely, for the contemporary contemplative, physical sight and intuitive or mystical sight are complementary.

Roger Hazleton proposes that metaphors pertaining to vision allow clarity in that they often refer to 'moments of extraordinary insight', as suggested in the adage 'seeing more than meets the eye'.[92] According to this hypothesis, these metaphors allow us a harmonious relationship between the visual senses, cognitive thinking and imagination that transcends the dualism of mind and body. In order to investigate this further, I will concentrate on three key areas. The first is concerned with seeing with the 'inner' eye of imagination and the 'outer' eye of physical vision as a means to mystical insight. Secondly, I will explore how subjective experience feeds into global or communal insight and expression. Lastly, I will pursue Murdoch's understanding of this phenomenon as it is manifested in the phrase 'attention', Dillard's understanding in her phrase 'stalking', and Levertov's in the word 'inscape'.

91   Bonaventure, *Classics of Western Spirituality* (Mahwah, New Jersey: Paulist Press, 1978), 69.
92   Roger Hazleton, 'Believing is Seeing: Vision as Metaphor', in *Theology Today* 35:4 (1979), 405–6. The author refers here to the work done by Gestalt psychologists who demonstrate the connections between thought and vision, e.g., Rudolf Arnheim, *Visual Thinking* (Berkeley: University of California Press, 1969).

'Seeing' with the 'outer' eye is fundamental to the creative writer's task and represents the initial stage of the creative process, in which information and impressions are gathered. Seeing with the 'inner' eye is the point at which illumination occurs. This closely relates to Bonaventure's description of mystical perception, when he suggested that there were three ways of seeing the sacred. The first involves the 'outer' eye, which sees the corporeal, material world. The second is the eye of reason, which sees symbolically by 'drawing distinctions and making conceptual relationships', while the third sees the 'luminous transcendental realms'.[93] Bonaventure's sense of vision implied that outer sight was eventually replaced by inner sight. This is no longer acceptable in postmodernity.

Through the character of Bruno in *Bruno's Dream*, Murdoch ponders whether the contemplation of nature reveals something about God. The dying Bruno reflects on his knowledge and love of spiders:

> There is a spider called *amaurobius*, which lives in a burrow and has its young in late summer, and then it dies when the frosts begin, and the young spiders live through eating their mother's dead body. One can't believe that's an accident. I don't know that I imagined God as having thought it all out, but somehow He was connected with the pattern, He was the pattern, He *was* those spiders which I watched...[94]

This represents the integration of the inner and outer eye, or as Murdoch succinctly puts it, 'seeing of the invisible through the visible, the real through the apparent, the spiritual beyond the material'.[95] This echoes Julian, who refers to her 'eye of understanding' in her vision of a small round thing in her hand.

Levertov found inspiration in Gerald Manley Hopkins' word 'inscape', which 'denotes intrinsic form, the pattern of essential characteristics both in single objects and, what is more interesting, in objects

---

93   Alex Grey, *The Mission of Art* (Boston and London: Shambala, 2001), 73. Grey does not provide a reference, but I presume he is referring to Bonaventure, *The Journey into the Mind of God*, III.1.
94   Iris Murdoch, *Bruno's Dream* (London: Vintage, 2001), 98.
95   Murdoch, *Metaphysics as a Guide to Morals*, 475.

of relation to each other'.[96] She develops this notion of inscape by attaching the concept not only to living beings and nature but also to human experience. Inscape refers to the unity behind creation, 'the wholeness at the heart of things' hidden within matter. It is not something imposed on matter by the mind, but rather, something that matter gives up and is only accessible through contemplation. Again, this is metaphorical language relating to both the process of looking and more accurately to perception, which infers a poet's intuitive or mystical knowing. Levertov repeatedly uses the metaphor of one thing hidden in another throughout her work to convey her discovery of both natural and spiritual phenomena. In 'The Garden Wall',[97] she describes a wall that initially goes 'unnoticed' but on closer inspection reveals, unexpectedly,

A hazy red, a
Grain gold, a mauve
Of small shadows.
… [She imagines the wall as an]
Archetype
Of the world always a step
Beyond the world, that can't
Be looked for, only
As the eye wanders,
Found.

Here, the wall, as a human construction behind the abundance of flowers, represents a boundary to Mystery. Levertov imparts the sense that the world beyond is rarely glimpsed, and then only through an act of close attention.

One of Dillard's primary themes in *Pilgrim at Tinker Creek* is that of awareness and sight,[98] and Bruce Ronda suggests that her 'seeing career' should 'be considered part of the tradition of seers whose mode of life she evokes'.[99] In this work, as we have seen, there are

96   Levertov, *The Poet in the World*, 7.
97   Levertov, *Poems, 1960–1967*, 132.
98   Ronda, 'Annie Dillard and the Fire of God', 483.
99   Ibid., 484. By this he means the life of solitary contemplation favoured by mystics.

two corresponding ways of 'seeing' the sacred. One is active and the other passive. The former refers to cognition, the latter to spirit. It is interesting to note that, while she utilises both, she ranks, like Bonaventure, the spiritual way of seeing to be of a higher order. In order to see with the mind, she tells us: 'I analyze and pry. I hurl over logs and roll away stones; I study the bank a square foot at a time, probing and tilting my head.' The other, spiritual way 'involves a letting go. When I see this way I sway transfixed and emptied.'[100] The secret of seeing thus is what Dillard describes using the metaphor of 'the pearl of great price'.[101] The empty rapturous self relates to the way of the mystic. The ability to see through the literal meaning of the material world requires the passive or receptive mode to dominate. However, as this discussion has indicated, the inner and outer eye of understanding are of equal import along the *via contemplativa*, relating metaphorically and literally to the interior and exterior modes of mystical knowledge.

Seeing Both Ways at Once

Wendy Doniger O'Flaherty suggests there is a microscopic and telescopic way in which to view of the world.[102] The former represents the narrower perspective usually associated with personal, localised experience, and the latter alludes to the universal or general view, which represents the typical 'God's Eye' view adopted in theological and philosophical discussion. Broadly speaking, this is the same as the opposing positions of Plato and Aristotle. Plato sought knowledge of 'the Good' in the realm of ideas outside of the world, whereas Aristotle studied things in the concrete world and was more orientated towards praxis than abstract thought. However, the ability to 'see' both ways at once is integral to the mystic way as outlined here. Julian was a supreme example of 'a witness to the microcosm's revelation of

100   Dillard, *Pilgrim at Tinker Creek*, 33.
101   Ibid., 35.
102   Wendy Doniger O'Flaherty, *The Implied Spider: Politics & Theology in Myth* (New York: Columbia University Press, 1998), 2.

the macrocosm'.[103] In a similar manner, the writers under discussion here 'look' both ways to enable an individual to see the macrocosm within their own microcosmic particularity. Furthermore, whilst characters, plots or incidents spring from the concrete and spiritual familiarities of the author, they share a common pool of human experience.

Murdoch's metaphor for vision is derived from her concept of 'attention', a term she borrows from Simone Weil. She succinctly defines attention as a 'just and loving gaze directed upon an individual reality'.[104] In order to avoid lapsing into fantasy, the gaze is directed by an exertion of the will and inspired by love so 'that the quality of attention [...] determine[s] the nature of the act'.[105] She further recognises that 'contemplation is hard to understand and maintain in a world increasingly without sacraments and ritual [which provide] an external visible place for an internal invisible act of spirit'.[106] Despite her arguments against a personal God, Murdoch recognised the usefulness of prayer or meditation as a 'technique of religion'. She simply states, '[p]rayer is properly not petition, but simply attention to God which is a form of love'.[107] She could not, however, conceive of God as a person, and her interest in Buddhist doctrine and practice *(dharma)* is probably due in part to her anxieties about the Christian God. Within those Eastern traditions, the doctrine of selflessness *(anātman)* and the dedicated practice of meditation *(bhāvanā)* are seen as excellent ways to focus attention away from fantasy.

One of Levertov's basic assumptions was that modern society is affected by astigmatism or myopia, which affects the capacity to see clearly. Every aspect of experience is polarised and viewed with split vision.[108] Hence there are consequent divides such as those between subject and object, male and female, body and spirit, private and public, psychological and political, individual and community, particular

---

103 Linda Kinnahan, 'Denise Levertov: The Daughter's Voice', in *A Poetics of the Feminine: Authority and Literary Tradition* (Cambridge: Cambridge University Press, 1994), 179.
104 Murdoch, *The Sovereignty of Good*, 34.
105 Ibid., 67.
106 Ibid., 69.
107 Ibid., 55.
108 Gelpi, *Denise Levertov*, 3.

and universal, mind/matter, physical/metaphysical, inner/outer, and etc.[109] Significantly, the writers under discussion here all demonstrate the mystic-poets ability to 'see' such pairings as a whole. Three collections of Levertov's poems refer specifically to the notion of seeing double: *The Double Image*, *Here and Now* and *With Eyes in the Back of Our Heads*.

Double vision is not about contradiction, but rather, paradox and centeredness, a condition in which 'aspects of relationship are twinned in concentricity'.[110] Unity, or harmony, is sought whilst recognising the difference of things. Levertov's poem 'A Vision'[111] demonstrates this theme vividly. Angels are, of course, God's messengers that move between the divine and human realms. They exist in between worlds so as such are exemplars of difference within unity and double vision. This poem reveals not only harmony within duality but also indicates that not being able to see two things at the same time is the root cause of 'the Fall'. That is, prioritising one's individual importance over another's, or simply not being able to see the perfection in another, leads to egotism and evil. Levertov provides a sharp criticism of the liberal ideology of individualism here in a similar vein to that found in Murdoch's work, which will be developed in Chapter Seven in the context of an integrated theology.

The fact that Dillard devotes a whole chapter to 'seeing' in *Pilgrim at Tinker Creek* indicates her belief of its import for contemporary mysticism.[112] She believes that seeing is fundamental to all our experience, stating 'What you see is what you get.'[113] Interestingly, Dillard overtly practises what Wendy O'Flaherty terms the microscopic and telescopic method of seeing the world around her. Sometimes she 'slop[s] creek water in a jar', to take home and scrutinise amoebae, at others she recounts that she 'can see two million light-years to the Andromeda galaxy'.[114] She also links light that 'dazzles'

---

109   Ibid.
110   Ibid.
111   Levertov, *Poems 1960–1967*, 223–24.
112   Dillard, *Pilgrim at Tinker Creek*, 16–36.
113   Ibid., 17.
114   Ibid., 26.

with darkness that 'appals', metaphorically to the mystic way of the *via positiva* and the *via negativa*.[115] Certainly, 'seeing' is a mystical task that requires 'discipline' and a 'lifetime of dedicated struggle'. Dillard reflects:

> The world's spiritual geniuses seem to discover universally that the mind's muddy river, this ceaseless flow of trivia and trash, cannot be dammed, and that trying to dam it is a waste of effort that might lead to madness. Instead you must allow the muddy river to flow unheeded in the dim channels of consciousness; you raise your sights; you look along it, mildly, acknowledging its presence without interest and gazing beyond it into the realm of the real where subjects and objects act and rest purely without utterance [...]. The secret of seeing is, then the pearl of great price.[116]

In other words, we should not try to deny our embodiment, as living thinking beings. However, because the 'pearl of great price' 'may be found' but 'may not sought', she encourages us to remain alert to the possibilities and set our sights beyond what we can see with physical sight.[117]

Unequivocally, for Murdoch, Levertov and Dillard the mystical task is to *see*. Seeing is the primary way of knowing and perceiving the sacred. What's more, seeing in this sense is clearly an interpretative act, as the information the eye receives must be filtered through cognitive and imaginative processes. Whether it is another human being, a non-human being, or part of the landscape, attention to the realities of others are precious sources of continuing revelation and understanding. Perhaps this is the most radical concept to be gleaned from these writers' work, that the mysterious nature of the sacred remains, in Dillard's words, 'unfathomably secret and holy and fleet',[118] and consequently invisible. Despite this, but perhaps because of this, the longing to 'see' the sacred continues for writer and mystic alike.

---

115 Ibid., 25.
116 Ibid., 35.
117 Ibid.
118 Ibid., 270.

Seeing the Sacred From Where We Are

As De Certeau puts it, 'mystics do not reject the ruins that surround them. They remain there.'[119] A mystical vocation is definitely not about escapism. Neither is it about inventing a new-fangled religion or achieving some new pseudo-spirituality. Moreover, rather than contemplation representing a state in which the soul seeks to escape the body, meaning is found within the materiality of our lives. We can now conclude that the *via contemplativa* in postmodernity has a number of key features. Firstly, taking this path requires a willingness to be passive before the mysterious beyond and a willingness to act upon insights. Secondly, being on this path means to see ourselves within a continuing journey that includes the mystics from the past. Lastly and most importantly, being on this path means cultivating dynamic vision that includes physical and intuitive insight as well as the ability to see connections to the bigger picture. Our creativity is the site for both receiving mystical insight and creating forms by which it can be conveyed to others.

---

119   De Certeau, *The Mystic Fable*, 25.

Chapter Three
The *Via Creativa*: Starting from the Given

So far, we have established that the process of writing is inseparable from a mystical sensibility in the life and work of Murdoch, Levertov and Dillard. In particular, we have discovered that the ability to 'see' in both a literal and metaphorical or mystical sense is fundamental to the mystic way in postmodernity. Without creative input and interpretation, however, what we 'see' does not find tangible expression – creative writing is one way of enabling such expression and provides a resource for the readers to perceive mystically. In fact, art in all its forms may function as a mediator between the spiritual and material conditions of human existence. The Catholic monk Thomas Merton knew this when he wrote, 'Art enables us to find ourselves and lose ourselves at the same time.'[1] For the purposes of this study, however, the creative writing of these three writers is the chosen art form under scrutiny. Further, I will argue that creativity is foundational to theological expression in postmodernity.

Linda Huffaker aptly defines creativity as 'the ability to blend familiar, diverse materials together to produce something completely new'.[2] In other words, creativity starts with the given, what we have before us, in all its plurality. Humans do not create *ex nihilo*. Intrinsic to this concept for this discussion is the fact that religious traditions, both 'familiar' and 'diverse', add to the blend in order to renew our theological vision in postmodernity. As Nicholas Lash reminds us, 'the way we "see" or understand the world, its story and its destiny [is] shaped and structured by the stories that we tell'.[3] Further, there

1   Thomas Merton in T. P. McDonnell (ed), *A Thomas Merton Reader* (New York: Bantam Doubleday, 1996), 387.
2   Lucinda Huffaker, *Creative Dwelling: Empathy and Clarity in God and Self* (Atlanta, Georgia: Scholars Press, 1998), 17.
3   Nicholas Lash, *Holiness, Speech and Silence: Reflection on the Question of God* (Aldershot, England; Burlington, USA: Ashgate, 2004), 3–4.

are close existential links between the creative artist and the life of a mystic. Of note, is the heightened ability to withdraw to another level of consciousness and a readiness to transcend boundaries of accepted knowledge – to live a life that is perennially open to creative possibilities – which certainly means that the *via creativa* is integral to the theological task. This chapter seeks to develop the connections between the creative writer, the mystic and the theologian in their quest for self-expression and metaphysical 'truths'.

Finding our Wings

This section develops the links between the role of the creative writer and the mystic. The title of this section suggests that many in our age have forgotten how to use their imaginations to transcend the limits of rational and empirical knowledge, that there is a pressing need to reactivate the imaginative faculties once more. More importantly for our discussion, theological debate is better served if imagination is allowed to participate more fully in its interpretation and expression. Certainly, accepting the role of the imagination in mystical perception has deep implications for theology, which by definition would become 'creative' theology. It surely then follows that revelation is not a one time historical event but a continual process happening within the human imagination, where temporality and eternity meet.[4] In fact, it is largely through the imagination that the mystical encounter happens,[5] which inevitably involves being passively contemplative before the transcendent in order to receive illumination. However, to follow the path of the

4   Within Catholic theology, there is the possibility for both as theologians understand that their discipline is in a continuing and creative relationship to original revelation.
5   The Sufi mystic Ibn Arabi provides some useful insights on the role of the imagination in perceiving the sacred. See William Chittick's work *The Sufi Path of Knowledge* (New York: State University of New York Press, 1989) wherein he has provided a comprehensive overview of Ibn Arabi's metaphysics of the Imagination.

via creativa requires that a mystic in postmodernity also actively engage with the materials before them in a creative manner.

Creativity and Mystical Awareness

In Chapter One, O'Donoghue's argument that mysticism is 'an extension of imagination' shed light on the connection between mysticism and creativity. The word 'imagination' derives from the word 'image'. This implies that the mental or spiritual processes rely on images as opposed to words or concepts. O'Donoghue points out that part of the reason for treating the imagination with suspicion is the fact that it is harder to engage with the idiosyncratic nature of imaginative thinkers than with critical thinkers such as philosophers. There is no 'common world of mystical imagination as there is of perception and conceptual thought'.[6] Consequently, the irrational nature of the imagination has a reputation among more 'serious' thinkers as being secondary to analytical thought, but rather than seeing the imagination as the end of truth, what happens if we understand it to be the beginning? What if we agree with O'Donoghue that the mystical is 'an extension of the conceptual, as a kind of exalted thinking that tends to go beyond the range of words, that goes beyond metaphysical discourse yet is somehow continuous with it?'[7] In this view, a mystical imagination does not replace the conceptual and analytical, but rather, takes over when logical or rational means of understanding can go no further.

Before we go any further in our discussion, however, we need to be clear that there is a distinction between the imagination as the source of fantasy and the imagination as it is needed for mystical practice. Murdoch was acutely aware that Plato's hesitations over art were based on the sound realisation that art can easily deteriorate into 'bad art', which encourages fantasy and facilitates escapism. In opposition, Murdoch suggests through the narrator of *The Black Prince* that '[g]ood art speaks truth, indeed *is* truth, perhaps the only truth'.[8]

6   O'Donoghue, 'Mystical Imagination', 186.
7   Ibid., 187.
8   Iris Murdoch, *The Black Prince* (London: Penguin, 1973), 11.

111

Moreover, in the postmodern world of fast images, instant gratification, or alternatively, extreme forms of religious fundamentalism, art offers an alternative means of exploring spiritual and moral issues. This is never a simple matter, however, because 'we are completely enclosed in a fantasy world of our own into which we try to draw things from outside, not grasping their reality and independence, making them into dream objects of our own'.[9] Murdoch's fictional portrayal of Socrates in *Acastos*, who did not have such a pessimistic outlook on art as Plato, perhaps captures her views most accurately:

> good art tells us more truth about our lives and our world than any other kind of thinking or speculation – it certainly speaks to more people. And perhaps the language of art is the most universal and enduring kind of human thought. We are mixed beings [...] mixed of darkness and light, sense and intellect, flesh and spirit – the language of art is the highest native natural language of that condition. [...] We are all artists, we are all story-tellers. We all have to live by art, it is our daily bread – by what our language gives us, by what we invent for ourselves, by what we steal from others. And we should thank the gods for great artists who draw away the veil of anxiety and selfishness and show us, even for a moment, another world, a real world, and tell us a little bit of truth.[10]

Art, or specifically in our discussion, creative writing, then speaks of a 'greater truth [that] lies beyond and through the facts'[11] and provides 'the light by which human things can be mended'.[12] If we consider O'Donohue's assertions, this is essentially a mystical perception.

Due to this conviction, Murdoch parts company with Plato, who banished creative writers as 'non-truth tellers'. He further considered a love of poetry to be a 'form of madness'.[13] Creativity, for thinkers such as Plato, is associated with the irrational part of the human mind or soul, and as such, it is understood to be dangerous and subversive.

---

9   Iris Murdoch, 'The Sublime and the Good', in Conradi (ed), *Existentialists and Mystics*, 216.
10   Iris Murdoch, *Acastos* (London: Penguin, 1986), 63.
11   Jasper, *The Study of Literature and Religion*, 146.
12   Murdoch, *The Black Prince*, 416.
13   Martha C. Nussbaum, *The Fragility of Goodness: Luck and Ethics in Greek Tragedy and Philosophy*, Revised Edition (Cambridge: Cambridge University Press, 2001), 203. Ironically, Plato did have to resort to writing his own myths such as those found in *The Republic, Phaedo* and *Symposium*.

Plato concluded that an individual could gain a more authentic and greater wisdom by separating the intellect from the rest of the personality,[14] and he deemed the rational mind to be more capable of purer, more logical thought than the irrational feelings and emotions. The latter he felt have the potential to degenerate into manic, wild and uncontrolled behaviour. For Murdoch, however, the tension between philosophy and the creative imagination, or what Plato termed '[the] old quarrel between philosophy and poetry',[15] was a means by which to investigate the 'Good'.[16]

Of course, the truth may also refer to social and political issues. In this sense, creative art certainly does contain a subversive and radical element that can disrupt the *status quo*. As Murdoch points out, 'Tyrants always fear art because tyrants want to mystify while art tends to clarify.'[17] She suggests that the power of the state and the Church as keepers of the absolute truths might be replaced by 'obvious and unpretentious truths; truths that are often unconnected and unhallowed by the system'. She also states that '[the] great artist, like the great saint, calms us by a kind of unassuming simple lucidity, he speaks with the voice we hear in Homer, in Shakespeare and in the Gospels'.[18]

In Murdoch's thought, great art 'inspires truthfulness and humility […] and is able to display and discuss the central area of our reality, our actual consciousness, in a more exact way than science or even philosophy can'.[19] In fact, she sees the task of the creative writer to be of even greater importance in postmodernity in as much as

---

14   Ibid., 205.
15   *Republic* (607 B).
16   Iris Murdoch, 'Literature and Philosophy: A conversation with Bryan Magee', in Conradi (ed), *Existentialsts and Mystics*, 4–5, Murdoch makes it clear that literature and philosophy are two distinct disciplines. Among other aspects, art is more widely accessible while philosophy tends to be more elitist. Philosophy requires exactness and logical thinking while art can be ambiguous and appeals aesthetically.
17   Iris Murdoch, 'Salvation by Words', in Conradi (ed), *Existentialists and Mystics*, 235.
18   Ibid., 242.
19   Ibid., 240.

our ability to *be* through words is part of a battle for civilisation and justice and freedom, for clarity and truth, against vile fake-scientific jargon and spiritless slipshod journalese and tyrannical mystification. There is only one culture and words are its basis; words are where we live as human beings and as moral and spiritual agents.[20]

What constitutes 'good art' remains elusive. The boundaries of fantasy and reality continually blur. It is only through a continual cycle of looking, reflecting and recreating that we avoid fantasy and reality combining to form eternally unquestionable truths, such as the doctrines and symbols of Christianity, which Murdoch jettisons. Because the artist does this naturally in his/her work, artists are, in Murdoch's thought, the more reliable tellers of truth.

Levertov also views creativity as an essential part of human communication and identity. Poetry of course utilises primarily the medium of language, and in 'Witness: Incommunicado'[21] Levertov speaks of the 'loneliness of, the solitude of thought before language'. Language then is fundamental in the human process of becoming, in relation to both the sacred and other beings, a culmination of inwardness that bonds us to others. Related to this is Levertov's idea of 'testimony', which she defines as the need of all creatures to 'give expression to [their] being'. Levertov connects this to 'primordial musicality' in which 'the singing creature expresses itself in and for its world'.[22] Rather than an uncontrolled outburst, this represents affirmation of the self as it acknowledges its relation to the rest of the world. Without language, humans remain solitary beings who are unable to express their thoughts or enter into creative interaction with their world, but according to Levertov, the poet has a special gift to articulate what others feel as well. The ability to empathise with the sufferings of others is crucial in highlighting injustices and provoking readers out of their apathy. She argues that words have the power to

20   Ibid., 241–42.
21   Denise Levertov, *Sands of the Well* (Newcastle upon Tyne: Bloodaxe Books, 1998), 94.
22   Levertov, 'Great Possessions', in *New & Selected Essays*, 125.

114

'penetrate deep into us [where] they change the chemistry of the soul, of the imagination'.[23]

The poet also has a heightened ability to express that which is outside the boundaries of usual or everyday comprehension. Levertov describes this through her understanding of 'the organic form' as 'the concept that there is a form in all things (and our experience) which the poet can discover and reveal'.[24] Poetry that is written in the organic form 'is based on an intuition of an order, a form beyond forms, in which forms partake, and of which man's creative works are analogies, resemblances, natural allegories'.[25] The task of the poet is then to create a form or poem based on their insights, and indeed, overall the artistic efforts of human beings are attempts to perceive the unperceivable in metaphoric language and imagery.

For Levertov, the first words of a poem to come to the poet's mind are the natural consequence of mystical contemplation. It is then up to the poet to actively continue in the further development of the poem. Writing a poem from a mystical consciousness then requires the writer to be both passive and active in order to bring hidden forms to life in words. During the process of writing a poem, Levertov reveals that 'the various elements of a poet's being are in communion with each other, and heightened. Ear and eye, intellect and passion, interrelate more subtly than at other times.'[26] At this stage of her career, she appears to be engaging with the Platonic Forms but does not recognise the theological influence, although later Levertov would link human creativity to the Incarnation.

In *The Poet in the World*, Levertov puts forward her view that 'the music of poetry comes into being when thought and feeling remain unexpressed until they become Word, become Flesh [*sic*].'[27] This view, it should be noted, is espoused before her conversion to Roman Catholicism, so it was only later that she fully understood the 'Word' and 'Flesh' in terms of the Incarnation. At this point, she is

23   Levertov, 'The Poet in the Word', in *New & Selected Essays*, 136.
24   Levertov, 'Some Notes on Organic Form', in *The Poet in the World*, 7.
25   Ibid.
26   Ibid., 9.
27   Levertov, 'Notebook Pages', in *The Poet in the World*, 17.

reflecting on theories of poetic form and function. The notion of the poem as music that waits in 'passionate passivity' until thought and feeling summon them into being is behind the notion of all things having 'inscape'.[28] The capitalisation of 'Word' and 'Flesh' undoubtedly denotes some spiritual or transcendent quality, however, and at the least she recognises inspiration as a gift or experience of grace from some higher reality.

Related to the notion of inscape within experience and creativity is what she expressed as the 'unreleased potentiality' within humans, which Levertov believes to be the deeper meaning of the parable of the mustard seed.[29] In 'On the Parable of the Mustard Seed',[30] she imagines Christ to be 'talking of miracle, the seed / within us, so small / we take it for worthless, a mustard-seed, dust, nothing'. This is where the kingdom must begin, as an inner growth from within each and every person. We as a species are 'not present to ourselves and therefore not present to the divine' in her view.[31] 'Mountains remain unmoved' because 'glib generations mistake the metaphor, / not looking at fields and trees, not noticing paradox'. The *via creativa* requires a creative engagement with both texts and the world, and freedom of expression is balanced by responsibility to others.

Elsewhere, she employs the image of unused wings in order to encapsulate her theory that people are unaware of both their capacity for spiritual joy and their ability to make an impact in the world.[32] The vocation and drive to write poetry was for Levertov the principal force in her life, and she used her 'wings' to her full ability, even prioritising her creative quest over her role as wife, mother or homemaker.[33]

---

28 Ibid.
29 Levertov, 'Some Affinities of Content', in *New & Selected Essays*, 14. The parable of the mustard seed is found in Matthew 17:20, Mark 4:30–32 and Luke 13:18–19.
30 Denise Levertov, *Door in the Hive* (New York: New Directions, 1989), 83.
31 Levertov, 'Some Affinities of Content', in *New & Selected Essays*, 14.
32 See Denise Levertov 'The Sack Full of Wings', in *Tessarae* (Newcastle upon Tyne: Bloodaxe Books, 1997), 1–2.
33 Wagner-Martin, *Critical Essays*, 1. The editor gleans this information from studying Levertov's private correspondences between 1954 and 1961 held in the Washington University poetry archive in St Louis, Missouri.

Dillard succinctly expresses the all-encompassing undertaking of creative writing in similar terms:

> Fiction can deal with all the world's objects and ideas together, with the breadth of human experience in time and space; it can deal with things the limited disciplines of thought either ignore completely or destroy by methodological caution, our most pressing concerns; personality, family, death, love, time, spirit, goodness, evil, destiny, beauty, will.[34]

So everything, whether it is of a worldly, personal or spiritual nature is caught up in the creative act of writing. A true artist does more than merely imitate what is already there – a true artist presents the reader with possibilities beyond the already known.

'Writing' or 'literature' is all-encompassing term, which could include a wide variety of genres, but regardless, unlike philosophy and science, literature makes no pretence to ever arriving at exactitude. When dealing with the secrets of the cosmos, this strategy works best because the writer is laying no claim to ultimate knowledge. Dillard provides a vibrant metaphorical account of how this works:

> Fine writing […] can penetrate very deep, piling object upon object to build a tower from which to breach the sky; it can enter with courage or bravura those fearsome realms where the end products of thought, and where perfect clarity is not possible. Fine writing is not a mirror, not a window, not a document, not a surgical tool. It is an artefact and an achievement; it is at once an exploratory craft and the planet it attains; it is a testimony to the possibility of beauty and penetration of written language.[35]

The aim of the mystic/writer/artist is to enter those 'fearsome realms' where rational thought cannot go. The mystic way in postmodernity, by definition, must therefore include an element of creativity. But how does this match up to theological understanding of human nature?

34 Dillard, *Living by Fiction*, 12–13.
35 Ibid., 105–6.

The Implications for Creative or Imaginative Theology

Lucinda A. Stark Huffaker (1998) argues that creativity defines what it means to be human in relation both to the sacred and to others. If creativity is fundamental to the human condition, it would seem more than logical that theology, that discipline which deals with our ultimate concerns, would have creativity at the centre of all theological deliberations. Similarly Soelle, who was inspired by Matthew Fox, insists that

> creativity presupposes union with the Creator, whose power lives in the oneness with us. Today we understand creativity not only as transformation of an individual soul but of the world as a whole, in which humans could live together.[36]

In fact, Fox goes further by suggesting that the refusal to create is the 'original sin' and that redemption is the liberation of creativity:

> We would prefer to put our imaginations back in the box, to turn over our creativity to others […]. But then we would feel guilty also. The dilemma for humans is that we are guilty if we create *and* if we choose not to create. Masochism, the desire to turn our power over to others rather than become empowered and responsible, becomes a popular value in a culture built on ideologies. So does victimization. The original sin becomes our fear of our own originality, our powers of generativity, our origins, our birth, our genesis, our beginnings – even our generosity, which like so much else is God-like in its scope.[37]

In Fox's estimation then, human creativity is the route to personal redemption as well as social transformation.

In Genesis 1:26, God declares 'Let us make humankind in our image, according to our likeness', which is the pivotal text for understanding the relationship between the Divine Creator and human creativity in the Judeo-Christian tradition. Dorothy Sayers argued that it is the human ability to create that corresponds to God's 'image'. Sayers, writing from an Anglican perspective, recognises the metaphorical

---

36 Soelle, *The Silent Cry*, 89.
37 Matthew Fox, *Creativity: Where the Divine and Human Meet* (New York: J. P. Tarcher, 2002), 91.

nature of this statement by the writer of Genesis, most notably in the relationship between created and creator:

> We use the word 'create' to convey an extension and amplification of some-thing that we do know, and we limit the application of the metaphor precisely as we limit the application of the metaphor of fatherhood. We know a father and picture ourselves an ideal Father; similarly, we know a human 'maker' and pic-ture to ourselves the ideal 'Maker'. If the word 'Maker' does not mean some – thing related to our human experience of making, then it has no meaning at all.[38]

It can also be said that the 'likeness' between Creator and creature calls for analogical language, as the Genesis account implies that both share an 'image' or the ability to imagine. Therefore, all human lan-guage is related to the human experience and enables the connection to the transcendent realm through creative thinking.

Metaphorical language makes it possible to say that God is 'heard' in a thunderstorm or 'seen' in a sunset, and indeed, any con-cept or understanding about God must be applied to the materials af-forded us through the senses. Such creativity in the realm of art becomes visionary rather than merely representations of the material world. The difference between Plato and later thinkers such as Dorothy Sayers is that she sees an analogous connection between the human experience of creative activity and of God and his creatures.[39] Sayers believed that the human mind cannot help making 'verbal images of God'[40] – an assertion that correlates to Julian's ideas about the human relationship to God.

Christian theologians, and the Church in general, have at best not fully appreciated how creative artists can contribute to God's continu-ing involvement with his creation, and at worst they have displayed severe distrust of the imagination as the work of the devil. Only re-cently have theologians begun to accept once again that the imagin-ation is a tool to apprehend the sacred. Gordon Kaufman (1993) is one

38   Dorothy L. Sayers, *The Mind of the Maker* (London: Mowbray, 2002), 21.
39   I am indebted to Michael H. J. Hampel's unpublished MA thesis 'Dorothy L. Sayers: Creative Mind and the Holy Trinity' (2002) for drawing my attention to her reflection on the analogy between a writer and the Holy Trinity.
40   Sayers, *The Mind of the Maker*, 50.

theologian who believes that there needs to be a move away from the emphasis on revelation emanating from a transcendent God and towards perceiving the sacred as knowable, chiefly through the imagination. As such, God is present in our ideas, which more often than not form as pictures rather than words, especially when imagining things that are unknowable or imperceptible through the normal senses.[41] This may explain why poetry, which attempts to paint a picture with words, acts on such a deep level. Therefore, we can suggest that the religious or theological imagination is, in effect, a creative force that synthesises images, ideas, metaphors, and forms drawn from our experience of the finite that are nevertheless capable of revealing 'truths' about the sacred.

As someone who could not accept a personal God and sought to tell the truth in her artistic genre, it is inevitable that there is a clash of interests in Murdoch's thought between traditional theistic beliefs and the role of the storyteller to disclose truth. In her essay 'The Fire and the Sun', Murdoch summarises the artist's continuing dilemma concerning religion:

> To present the idea of God at all, even as a myth, is a consolation, since it is impossible to defend this image against the prettifying attentions of art. Art will mediate and adorn, and develop magical structures to conceal the absence of God or his distance. We live now amid the collapse of many such structures, and as religion and metaphysics in the West withdraw from the embraces, we are it might seem forced to become mystics through lack of any imagery which could satisfy the mind.[42]

Because the Church, in her view, can no longer provide consolation in a plausible or realistic manner, the work of the artist takes on a more central role. The Protestant iconoclastic movement in the West has exacerbated the lack of imagery historically, but in more recent times, the proliferation of information technologies and mass-produced objects, or what Murdoch refers to as 'sub-art', has left a void in the reli-

---

41   Gordon Kaufman *In Face of Mystery: A Constructive Theology* (Cambridge, Massachusetts: Harvard University Press, 1993).
42   Murdoch, 'The Fire and the Sun', in Conradi (ed), *Existentialists and Mystics*, 463.

gious sensibilities that may benefit from 'good art'. Art then is essential for our spiritual well-being.

Levertov has a much clearer understanding of the importance of recovering the imagination as a tool to perceive theologically. In *Tesserae*, a book that contains snippets from her life, she begins with 'A Sack Full of Wings', a childhood memory of her father's stories lovingly remembered and written down. She recalls the story of a peddler who passed through her father's village in Russia from time to time. Apparently he always carried a large sack on his back, which Levertov's father imagined to contain wings, 'which would enable people to fly like birds'.[43] Through the common metaphor of flight, there is a reference here to the twin themes evident in Levertov's life and work: the ambition to create and the quest for transcendence.

The link between literary endeavours and theological insight is made clearer by George Steiner, who is persuaded that

> any serious attempt at this licentious genius in language [...] any serious grammatology and semantic mapping will conduct inquiry towards a valuation, positive or negative, of the theological [... as all written and oral communication is] inextricably enmeshed in the metaphysical and theological or anti-theological question of unbounded saying.[44]

Here Steiner suggests that creative writing, and the language it employs, is always, by its very nature, theological. This contrasts sharply with the approach taken by theologians who apply theological concepts to individual texts in order to explore their own faith.[45] In short, what Steiner is suggesting is that the human condition is itself an ongoing theological project, and therefore, by extension, any literal or dogmatic adherence to received doctrine in is merely misinformed. Moreover, the individual quest in this regard is part of the larger dynamic whole.

---

43   Denise Levertov, *Tesserae* (Newcastle upon Tyne: Bloodaxe Books, 1997), 1.
44   George Steiner, *Real Presences* (Chicago: Chicago University Press, 1991), 59.
45   See for example David S. Cunningham's *Reading is Believing* (Brazos Press, 2002), wherein he explores the Christian faith within the framework of the Apostle's Creed by delving into various films and books. He refers to works by Murdoch in a confessional way that the author herself did not intend.

In the context of postmodern mysticism, I argue that epiphany is a concept that bridges the gap between literary and theological use of the imagination. Epiphanies are moments of illumination, more specifically, such moments that relate to how an individual experiences truth rather than merely relaying an idea of it. One of the main assertions within the current discussion is that such epiphanic experiences can happen through creative and imaginative engagement with the natural world, other people or texts. Some may actively seek after such moments, while for others, they may come unbidden.

Epiphanies can be both manifestations of the divine, as in Anne Cavidge's vision of Christ, or they may be small seemingly insignificant moments of illumination such as that experienced by Stuart in *The Good Apprentice* when he sees a small mouse in the London Underground and realises his role in life as being significant through his day to day living in relationship with others as opposed to a self-imposed asceticism. Dillard often refers to them as 'incursions of the Divine' and confesses that she lives for such experiences, 'the moment when the mountains open and a new light roars in spate through the crack, and the mountains slam'.[46]

Theologically speaking, it could be argued that God, the Good, or the Divine needs human thought and feeling to become manifest in the world. Dillard writes,

> God's being immanent, said Abraham Joshua Heschel, depends on us. Our hearts, minds, and souls impel our spines to lift or dig, our arms to take or give, our lips to speak good words or bad ones. God needs man; kenotically or not, he places himself in our hands.[47]

Heschel reminds us that without humans to experience and express divinity as immanence, transcendence does not exist. In this light, the cosmos and the sacred are mutually dependent on each other; each one gives expression to the other. The human imagination or soul is the place where these two opposites meet in a dynamic of expressive creation and interchange of love. Historically, I will assert, these con-

46   Dillard, *Pilgrim at Tinker Creek*, 36.
47   Annie Dillard, *For the Time Being* (New York: Vintage Books, 1999), 200.

nections are more evident in female mystics and more recently likely to materialise in literature written by women.

Women and Creativity

Again, a more creative use of language is important for mystical theology to counteract the language of theology itself. As Soelle quite rightly points out, although women's mystical experience and writing are the subject of theology, the theories used to categorise and conceptualise said experiences tend to derive from more 'scientific' or objective approaches, which drowns out any hope of empathy or holistic thinking.[48] Soelle further posits that the conventional language of theology does not attain 'living speech' as it

> usually expresses itself in a language void of consciousness because it is empty of emotion, insensitive to human experience, ghostlike, neutral, uninteresting, unappealing, flat. It admits of no doubt, which is to say it represses the shadow side of faith and does not lift it into consciousness.[49]

So here is a reminder that theological language represses those elements of life and faith that it would prefer to forget into the unconscious. However, if it is ever to achieve anything akin to popular appeal, theological language must relate to human experience whilst maintaining the ability to reach the innermost parts of the human soul. This is what Dillard meant by words that can 'penetrate'. I will discuss women's special contribution to the *via creativa* in two key areas. First, there will be an overview of the need to detach from stereotypical perceptions of gender roles in order to create space and claim a mystic identity. Second, I will introduce the possibility that women's words might balance out the voice of 'male' reason.

48   Soelle, *The Strength of the Weak*.
49   Ibid., 84.

Jantzen argues that mystics like Julian have historically been those who engage in 'creative and courageous efforts at pushing back the boundaries of thought and action so that liberation could be achieved'.[50] Yet, paradoxically, in the contemporary world it is apparent that a privatisation of mysticism

> keeps God (and women) safely out of politics and the public realm; it allows mysticism to flourish as a secret inner life, while those who nurture the inner life can generally be counted on to prop up rather than challenge the status quo of their workplaces, their gender roles, and the political systems by which they are governed, since their anxieties and angers will be allayed in the privacy of their own hearts' search for peace and tranquillity.[51]

For female mystics such as Julian, and novelists such as the Brontës, George Eliot and Jane Austen, writing has been a means to transgress the limitations of their enclosed existence.

Although Julian lived in the premodern era, she nevertheless provides a suitable role model for contemporary female writers and theologians because of her popularity and willingness to transcend theological boundaries and to challenge people both intellectually and spiritually. In medieval England during the fourteenth century, the only route to an education would have been through the Church. It would have been extremely rare for a woman to penetrate this male world of privilege. It would have been rarer still for her to produce writings that contained theological teachings and articulated sophisticated arguments. Moreover, Julian deserves special recognition for writing in vernacular English – the language of the people as opposed to the language of the Church, which was Latin. Julian believed in exposing people to religion – not excluding them from it.[52]

As a woman, she would certainly have put herself in an exceptionally precarious position by daring to offer spiritual counselling and theological education through her writing. Perhaps this is why she re-

---

50   Jantzen, 'Feminist Philosophers and Mystics', in *Hypatia*, 9 (1994), 13.
51   Jantzen, *Power, Gender and Christian Mysticism*, 346.
52   Jantzen, *Julian of Norwich*, 14.

fers to herself as 'the wretched worm, the sinful creature to whom it was shown'.[53] As if to reinforce this, she places a great emphasis on the fact that she does not intend any reward or recognition for herself when she writes: 'it was not revealed to me because God loves me better than the humblest soul who is in a state of grace'.[54] The infamous injunction in Timothy 2:11–14 that women cannot teach was the acceptable state of affairs in the fourteenth century. In line with this ruling, she stresses her own humility before God and her community: 'but God forbid that you should say or assume that I am a teacher, for that is not and never will be my intention; for I am a woman, ignorant, weak and frail.'[55]

This cautious approach reflects the attitudes towards women and the power of the Church in the fourteenth century. Indeed, a diplomatic approach such as this would not only have been necessary to be received seriously but also reflects her sensitivity to the potential outrage a woman could be met with if she were too outspoken. The Church would certainly have dismissed anything that opposed its teaching as heretical. Besides, she would have been all too aware that the Church was burning Lollards just down the road from her anchorhold in Norwich.

Notwithstanding this need for safety, there is a marked increase in her confidence from the Short Text to the Long Text. Yet, categorically, it was the norm for a male scribe to censor the texts of female mystics, so we cannot be sure if there are other voices in Julian's *Shewings*, and scholars continue to speculate about the extent to which Julian's manuscripts remained her own words.[56] But there would seem to be a tone of protest against the patriarchal church when she asks whether it would be right for her to keep silent and 'not tell you of the

---

53   Julian, *Showings*, 133.
54   Ibid., 134.
55   Ibid., 135.
56   Lynn Johnson argues that Julian maintained a good deal of authority in 'The Trophe of the Scribe and the Questions of Literary Authority in the Works of Julian and Margery Kempe', in *Speculum*, 66:4 (1991), 820–38. For the view that Julian had limited control over her texts, see Louis Dupré & James A. Wiseman (eds), *Light from Light: An Anthology of Christian Mysticism* (New Jersey: Paulist Press, 2001), 229–46.

goodness of God' just because she is a woman.[57] Despite these gaps in our knowledge about her life, she has become a role model for women who seek to transcend their gender roles in the Church.

Writing in the twentieth century under the values of Western democracy, Murdoch, Levertov and Dillard have more freedom of speech, especially as they maintained some control over the editing process. However, Virginia Woolf's (1921) plea that, in order for women to write, they need 'a room of their own' is no less true in postmodernity than in previous eras. Janet Martin Soskice makes a valid point about the practicalities of women following a spiritual path:

> despite markers that could lead elsewhere, Christian 'received spirituality' is still shaped by particular views of contemplation, contemplative prayer and religious ecstasy that disenfranchise many people, and perhaps especially women.[58]

Many women get so caught up with the day-to-day business of working, running a home and bringing up children that there is no time left to nurture a spiritual life. Mystics like Julian and writers like Murdoch, Dillard and Levertov can only practise their art or pursue the mystical life through finding opportunities for solitude. After all, even humble figures like Muhammad, Gandhi and Christ had an entourage of female helpers. In a similar manner, Julian would have had servants who provided domestic services, allowing her to devote her life to spiritual matters. Traditionally, the archetypal roles of Mary and Martha do not mix. In postmodernity, however, the boundaries between contemplation and work are not so clear-cut.

It is evident that Murdoch was not ignorant of the constricted life of many women. This is borne out by the fact that, in many of her novels, women are more likely to have to break free of domestic or social bonds in order to achieve some level of fulfilment. Male characters, on the other hand, are more likely to be grappling with their

---

57   Julian, *Showings*, 135.
58   Janet Martin Soskice, 'Love and Attention', in Michael McGhee, *Philosophy, Religion and the Spiritual Life* (Cambridge: Cambridge University Press, 1992), 62. By 'received spirituality', Soskice is referring to the traditional Christian notion of mystical visions or a contemplative life such as that in religious orders where the hassles of ordinary life do not impose.

inflated egos. However, problematically, the only definably good figure in Murdoch's oeuvre is Ann Peronnet in *An Unofficial Rose*, who does her duty as a wife without complaint and puts other people's needs before her own.

> Ann had never really had the conception of doing what she wanted. The idea of doing what she ought, early and deeply implanted in her soul, and sedulously ever since cultivated, had by now almost removed from her the possibility, even as something *prima facie*, of a pure self-regarding movement of will.[59]

She does not react with anger to her husband's unfaithfulness; she waits passively for him to return to her. She cannot even imagine the possibility of leaving her husband for a much more promising relationship with Felix. Ann is emblematic of *agapic* or selfless Christian love, and indeed, this novel contains one of Murdoch's favourite topics – the tension between the artist and the saint. Ann is devoid of creative capabilities because she is too bound to duty. Murdoch in her own life displayed none of these qualities and ruthlessly pursued her writing vocation with scant regard to conventions concerning the role and status of women within marriage.

While reading John Bayley's account of his life with Murdoch, one of the most striking revelations is the fact that his wife kept her own space. She steadfastly maintained both a physical and intellectual distance from her husband whilst living and working in close proximity to him all of their married life. As Bayley comments, they 'grew closer and closer apart'. [60] Peter Conradi informs us that, 'While in Steeple Aston she worked in isolation, hardly emerging except to go to the village shop'.[61] Bayley speculates whether she would have been so prolific if, like Woolfe's imaginary sister of Shakespeare whose talents never came to fruition, she had married someone else and become bogged down in domesticity. After the publication of *The Green Knight* in 1993, Murdoch herself commented that, had she had a brother, her own education would have suffered due to the fact that a

---

59   Iris Murdoch, *An Unoffical Rose* (London: Vintage, 1962), 240.
60   Audio tape, *Iris: A Memory*.
61   Conradi, *Iris Murdoch*, 537. From 1970, she also rented a flat in South Kensington.

male sibling would have been given priority.[62] It seems that Murdoch was indebted to both her father for insisting she have an education and her husband for providing a stable, yet liberating base from which to work.

Despite Levertov's insistence on gender not being an important issue in her work, several poems illustrate the inner conflicts of living in a woman's body in her experience. We saw in the last chapter how quite a few of Levertov's poems reflect upon the inevitable existential tensions between being a mother, a political activist and a prolific poet. To be a poet and a mother inescapably means having to choose between offspring of the mind and offspring of the body. Yet the artist in Levertov's opinion cannot exist and work in isolation from the world. As she states in 'Decipherings',[63] 'When I lose my center / of gravity / I can't fly ...' In short, balance is the key to a fruitful life as a poet, but it is a constant struggle to hold differing loyalties in tension.

The poem 'In Mind'[64] also encapsulates more of this sense of a divided self. Here Levertov juxtaposes two different types of women: one who 'is kind and very clean without / ostentation'. The other 'is not kind'. One wears 'a utopian smock or shift' and the other is dressed in 'opals and rags, feathers / and torn taffeta'. Dianne F. Sadoff argues that Levertov depicts here that 'one woman is nature, the other imagination; the poem structures a paradox within a dualism [where] all are contained in the complex paradoxical imagination of the poet who creates herself'.[65]

Later in her life, writing after her divorce in a poem entitled 'A Woman Alone',[66] Levertov reflects on her solitude in a positive light.

...a kind of sober euphoria makes her believe
in her future as an old woman, a wanderer,
seamed and brown,

---

62   Ibid., 49. As it was her parents had to borrow money from the bank in order to give Iris an education.
63   Levertov, *Oblique Prayers*, 9.
64   Levertov, *Poems, 1960–1967*, 143.
65   Dianne F. Sadoff, 'Mythopoeia, the Moon, and Contemporary Women's Poetry', in Wagner-Martin, *Critical Essays* (1991), 250.
66   Denise Levertov, *Poems 1972–1982* (New York: New Directions, 2001), 91.

little luxuries of the middle of life all gone,
watching cities and rivers, people and mountains,
without being watched; not grim or sad,
an old winedrinking woman, who knows
the old roads, grass-grown, and laughs to herself ...
no one can walk the world any more,
a world of fumes and decibels.
But she thinks maybe
she could get to be tough and wise, some way,
anyway. Now at least
she is past the time of mourning,
now she can say without shame or deceit,
O blessed Solitude.

It seems that Levertov had concluded that the solitary life has its advantages despite feelings of isolation.

In *The Writing Life*, Dillard imaginatively portrays the arduous and solitary existence of the writer. She too seems to spend extended periods of time in seclusion in order to write. Whilst writing *Pilgrim at Tinker's Creek*, she became so absorbed that she would spend fifteen to sixteen hours a day writing in complete solitude, living on chocolate milk, Coke, coffee and cigarettes as well as managing to kill off her plants by forgetting to water them.[67] Not many women would have either the financial resources or support to undertake such an experience, and obviously, the ability to experience solitude closely correlates to independence and freedom. But Dillard recounts another annoying problem associated with being a female writer.

Following the publicity from receiving the Pulitzer prize for *Pilgrim*, Dillard tells us in the 'Afterward to the Twenty-Fifth Anniversary Edition' that she was asked to model clothes for *Vogue* and to appear on television.[68] One literary critic remarked at the time, Parrish tells us, that Dillard was 'extremely good looking'.[69] In retrospect, Dillard writes that she believes her decision to avoid such publicity

---

67   Annie Dillard, *The Writing Life* (New York: Harper, 1990), 27, 37.
68   Dillard, *Pilgrim at Tinker Creek*, 281.
69   Nancy Parrish, *Lee Smith, Annie Dillard and the Hollins Group* (Baton Rouge, LA: Louisiana State University Press, 1998), 124. Parrish doesn't name this critic but it is evident from photos of the sixties that she did appear to conform (unintentionally I would imagine) to the prevailing notion of female beauty.

'saved my neck'.[70] Before the publication of *Pilgrim at Tinker Creek*, she was acutely aware of the fact that being a woman could seriously affect the book's reception. In fact, she did try to get it published without a picture of herself and under the non-gender specific pseudonym of A. Dillard because she recognised that 'a great number of admirable men do not read books that American women write'.[71] So, in a manner similar to Murdoch, she deliberately subverts her own identity. It is perhaps more surprising in Dillard's work, however, as she mostly writes in the first person and yet regrets being persuaded to write under her own name by her publishers.[72]

Rosemary Gordon argues that, for the creative act to begin, the actual process of writing requires psychic and personal balance of self:

> Creativity involves play and paradox and depends on a person's capacity to tolerate contradictory – yet also complementary – qualities or processes, such as, for instance, activity and passivity; receptivity and productivity; consciousness and unconsciousness; masculinity and femininity. It might also involve the capacity to balance surrender and control, effort and passivity, waiting and forging ahead, solitude and communication.[73]

It is at such moments as these described by Gordon that the self is poised between 'passivity and activity', 'consciousness and unconsciousness', and 'receptivity and productivity'. Immediately, there is a sense of the woman writer who exists between the traditional gender binary oppositions such as 'active' and 'passive' and 'male and female'. Overwhelmingly, there is recognition of creativity occurring in between the conscious and unconscious mind.

---

70   Dillard, *Pilgrim at Tinker Creek*, 281.
71   Ibid., 280.
72   The dependent and exploitative relationship writers are forced into with publishers is a continuing area of personal conflict for many writers.
73   Rosemary Gordon, *Bridges: Psychic Structures, Functions and Processes* (London: Karmac Books, 1993), 339.

While not wishing to make any claims that women have the monopoly on drawing on the unconscious for creative and mystical insight, they are perhaps less likely to cordon it off from the conscious mind.[74] In her depiction of Anne Cavidge's vision of Christ, Murdoch carefully and deliberately blurs the distinction between the world of the dreaming unconscious and the waking conscious by virtue of depicting the vision as happening immediately upon waking. A key example of this is, as Mark Hederman speculates, evidenced in *Jackson's Dilemma*, Murdoch's last novel, which must have been written 'largely from the unconscious' due to her oncoming Alzheimer's.[75] Sadly, she was also at this point beginning to, as she described it, 'sail away into the darkness'.[76] It comes as no surprise that Levertov as a poet takes the unconscious aspect of her practice as writer the most seriously – and we have already noted her warning about distinguishing between fantasy and reality. Dillard is more disposed to 'daydreaming' – her subconscious invades her waking consciousness in order to perceive mystically.

Levertov often refers to the unconscious in terms of the 'inner eye'. In 'The Hymn',[77] she praises the insights that come to her in her dream life. Whether such insights are born of experiences that are part memory or part the power of imagination, she is thankful for them. The detailed landscape she depicts where 'each leaf / rippling, gleaming, / visible almost to vein and serration' causes her to weep 'tears of gratitude' is not allegory or parable – 'it is clear *seeing*'.[78] The suggestion in this poem is that the power of such insight is as 'the well in

---

74   See for example, Hélène Cixous, *Three Steps on the Ladder of Writing*, trans. Sarah Cornell and Susan Sellars (New York: Columbia University Press, 1993).
75   Mark P. Hederman, *The Haunted Inkwell* (Dublin: The Columba Press, 2001), 94.
76   Conradi, *Iris Murdoch*, 589.
77   Levertov, *Sands of the Well* (Newcastle upon Tyne: Bloodaxe Books, 1998), 97.
78   Paul A. Lacey, 'Wanderer and Pilgrim; Poet and Person', in Little & Paul, *Denise Levertov*, 250.

which / we forget to dip our cups' and is an overlooked resource of human potential to find meaning.

She wrote more explicitly about the function of dreams in her poetry in *Light up the Cave*, wherein she says that the trick is to make the reader feel that they are themselves experiencing the dream.[79] As she remarks, dreams are actually about 'the *clearness* of its terms' and 'powerful clarity'.[80] In dreams, 'we effortlessly receive images and often their double significance',[81] which implies that dream images are passively received – they cannot be forced by an act of will. Most importantly, the implication here is also that the dream must contain some significance to warrant a poetic rendition – 'The double significance' refers to the individual and the universal significance as well as concrete experience and the symbolic or psycho-spiritual.

In her poem 'Writing in the Dark', Levertov shows just how important the ideas are to writers that come between the awake and dreaming self:

> Keep writing in the dark:
> a record of the night, or
> words that pulled you from the depth of unknowing,
> words that flew through your mind, strange birds
> crying their urgency with human voices.[82]

Levertov acknowledges that 'words that may have the power to make the sun shine again' mostly arise at such moments – and then 'only once in a lifetime'. That is, those exact same words will never come to the poet again. Creative inspiration for Levertov is something received (passive) but also something that must be written down (active), and in the physical act of writing, there is a conjoining of the material and spiritual 'kingdoms'.

Dillard recounts one particular experience of this nature in *Pilgrim at Tinker Creek*:

79   Denise Levertov, *Light up the Cave* (New York: New Directions, 1981), 34.
80   Ibid., 35.
81   Ibid., 39.
82   Levertov, *Poems 1972–1982*, 261.

132

I was dead, I guess, in a deep black space high up among many white stars. My own consciousness had been disclosed to me, and I was happy. Then I saw far below me a long, curved band of color. As I came closer, I saw that it stretched endlessly in either direction, and I understood that I was seeing all the time of the planet where I had lived. It looked like a woman's tweed scarf; the longer I studied any one spot, the more dots of color I saw. There was no end to the deepness and variety of the dots.[83]

Dillard imagines the mystery of creation through the simple symbolism of 'a woman's tweed scarf'. The scarf is a comforting image, and near to the end of the dream, Dillard recalls seeing 'the earth as a globe in space' and 'being filled with deep affection of nostalgia' just before she opens her eyes. This closely resembles Julian's vision of the small thing held in her palm recounted in Chapter One. Dillard suggests that 'we all ought to be able to conjure up sights like this' in order to go ever deeper into the very fabric of life.[84] The complex nature of symbolism, creative imagination and the ability of the mind to transcend the body found in the dream world offer the possibility of mystical insight. This is not to say that, like Julian's visions, it does not need to be filtered through the rational mind, however.

Women's Words

Jantzen demonstrates that Augustine, taking his cue from Platonic antibody ideas, argued that 'the mind has no sex' but still asserts that males are closer to God than females, whom he associated predominantly with materiality and reproduction.[85] The same masculinisation of reason continued in the thought of influential philosophers such as Kant and Hegel. Feminist philosopher Pamela Anderson believes that this now means 'the modern philosopher [...] can imagine himself as disembodied'.[86]

---

83   Dillard, *Pilgrim at Tinker Creek*, 142.
84   Ibid., 143.
85   Jantzen, *Becoming Divine*, 31.
86   Pamela Sue Anderson, 'Myth, Mimesis and Multiple Identities: Feminist Tools for Transforming Theology', in *Literature and Theology*, 10:2 (1996), 113.

Murdoch, Levertov and Dillard articulate the same principles but in non-gendered terms. Murdoch, for example, provides a picture of the Kantian man of reason:

How recognizable, how familiar to us, is the man so beautifully portrayed in the *Grundlegung*, who confronted even with Christ turns away to consider the judgment of his own conscience and to hear the voice of his own reason. [...] This man is with us still, free, independent, lonely, powerful, rational, responsible, brave, the hero of so many novels and books of moral philosophy. The *raison d'être* of this attractive but misleading creature is not far to seek. He is the offspring of the age of science, confidently rational and yet increasingly aware of his alienation from the material universe which his discoveries reveal.[87]

It is impossible not to catch Murdoch's tone of sarcasm here. She even goes as far as ascribing to this 'man' the name of Lucifer as found in Milton's *Paradise Lost*.[88] We are likely to ask after reading this passage if she was associating evil with a lack of creativity. For her, the worst aspect of the man of reason is that the will, his ability to choose, is now the creator of value. The ways that rationality and the emphasis on the power of the mind or will have contributed to oppressive structures and spiritual malaise is immediately recognisable from Murdoch's 'picture'.

In 'Abel's Bride',[89] Levertov deals more specifically with the roles of the sexes and utilises the Biblical character of 'Abel's Bride' as an archetypal image for a wife. In an interview with Michael Andre, Levertov expresses her opinion that, in 'the character of man as I know him, there is a certain vulnerability that is greater than woman's vulnerability'.[90] She is saying in effect that women are the stronger sex and that a man 'goes out alone to his labours. [...] His sex hangs unhidden / or rises before him / blind and questing'. On the other hand, Levertov assumes that women are more aware of themselves because '[w]hen she goes out / she looks in the glass, she remembers / herself'. Levertov often uses the image of looking in a mirror to repre-

87 Murdoch, *The Sovereignty of Good*, 80. Murdoch refers to Kant's work *Grundlegung zur Metaphysik der Sitten*, 1785.
88 Ibid.
89 Levertov, *Poems 1960–1967*, 163.
90 Brooker, *Conversations with Denise Levertov*, 63.

sent looking at and defining the self. Man by contrast has 'no mirror / nest[ing] in his pocket'.

Additionally, the archetypal man in this poem represents, according to Levertov, man's consciousness, which 'has gone out so much towards the abstract'.[91] Most interestingly, she also writes: 'Stones, coal / the hiss of water upon the kindled / branches – her being / is a cave, there are bones in the hearth'. Levertov (still in the interview with Andre) informs us that she was here

> harking back to the times in the ancient world. [...] Babylon [perhaps] where woman was dominant and where Isis was worshipped, and any time in society where women were not oppressed as they have been in most societies in the modern world, where they were actually a sort of dominating figure. I was thinking of that part of the unconscious layer of the woman's psyche too.[92]

In other words, Levertov is convinced that women contain within themselves a latent and lost power. The reference to 'bones in the hearth' relates to the loss of woman's true psychic and sexual self, which has been sacrificed on the altar of the male ego. Women as bodily-incarcerated beings are in a paradoxical position of experiencing the obliteration of the authentic, sensual, thinking body.

Dillard speaks in less gendered terms but feels that both Christianity and science have

> cut down on the fun. Everywhere Christianity and science hushed the bushes and gagged the rocks. They razed the sacred groves, killed the priests, and drained the flow of meaning right off the planet. They built schools; they taught people to measure and add, to write, and to pray to an absent God. The direction of recent history is towards desacralization, the unhinging of materials from meaning. The function of Western knowledge is to 'de-spookify'. [93]

However, for Dillard, a creative use of words can help to reverse this trend of desacralisation, yet she recognises that 'art is a terrible interpreter' because 'art cares not if it truly knows the world'.[94] It is a fine

---

91   Ibid.
92   Ibid.
93   Dillard, *Living by Fiction*, 136.
94   Ibid., 149.

line, but if art does not claim to be the last word, art can be interpretative, a 'subtle pedagogy'.[95] However, this only works if the author conceals meanings strategically within the text in such a way that the reader can find them. Dillard imagines the writer's words as probes that search space – 'The line of words feels for cracks in the firmament. The line of words is heading out past Jupiter this morning' – and the writer as analogous to the person in Houston, Texas watching the monitor:

> Now you watch the symbols move on your monitor; you stare at the signals the probe sends back; transmits in your own tongue, numbers. Maybe later you can guess what they mean – what they might mean about space at the edge of the solar system, or about your instruments. Right now, you are flying. Right now, your job is to hold your breath.[96]

Humble Johnson sums up Dillard's thinking about the writing process in *The Writing Life* as 'strain[ing] to capture in language a concept that outruns language [where] words become entities that take on a life outside of the writer. [...] Language sails into space finding its destination, the single planet in a universe with no walls'.[97]

As far as theology is concerned, creative literature and poetry has provided women with the opportunity to return from the margins where they have historically been 'silent outsider[s] to official revelation'.[98] More than this, I would suggest that women become the space for divine transformation, the site of gestation of new paradigms. We now turn to our theological conversation partners to make sense of the *via creativa* as a theological task.

95   Ibid., 155.
96   Dillard, *The Writing Life*, 20–21.
97   Humble Johnson, *The Spaces Between*, 21.
98   Mary Grey, *The Wisdom of Fools?* (London: SPCK Ltd, 1993), 14.

Creating the Future

Here we will explore Jantzen's idea of 'natality' in conjunction with McFague's notion of humans as co-creators to establish the creative writer's role in theological transformation. Julian's phrase 'being endlessly born' will be taken to represent the creative possibilities latent in human effort, or what Jantzen terms 'natality'. This perspective evokes a mystical calling for humans to become what McFague describes as co-creators with God.[99]

'Being endlessly born'

Drawing on the work of Jewish philosopher Hannah Arendt and the psychoanalytical theories of Luce Irigaray, Julia Kristeva and Jacques Lacan, Jantzen argues for a symbol of the feminine based on 'natality', which focuses on 'life *before* death' as opposed to life *after* death.[100] Ideally, the concept of natality celebrates embodiment in the here and now over an emphasis on the immortal soul's survival in a realm that exists beyond death. Her proposal has received mixed reactions. For example, Tina Beattie argues that, although commendable in many ways, Jantzen's theories are flawed in that they offer 'a disembodied and idealized discourse of natality, remote from the bloody passions of motherhood, birth and death'.[101] While Nancy Frankenberry, on the other hand, shows concern that Jantzen never fully explains or develops a feminist religious symbolism and asks the thought-provoking question: Do we actually need one at all?[102] However, I think that Beattie and Frankenberry both misunderstand the

99 I am aware that this is not exclusive to McFague. See for example Catherine Keller, *Face of the Deep: a Theology of Becoming* (London: Routledge, 2003).

100 Jantzen, *Becoming Divine*, 141. My italics.

101 Tina Beattie, Review of *Becoming Divine: Towards a Feminist Philosophy of Religion*, 1998 by Grace M. Jantzen, in *Reviews in Religion and Theology* 7:3 (2000), 308–10.

102 Nancy Frankenberry, Review of *Becoming Divine: Towards a Feminist Philosophy of Religion, 1998* by Grace M. Jantzen, in *Hypatia*, 16:1 (2001), 98–100.

metaphorical meaning of Jantzen's theory – she herself would emphasise that she is not trying to disavow the realities of death and suffering. Moreover, Jantzen's utilisation of the concept of 'natality' preempts the creation of symbols that have the potential to replace one concretised metaphor with another.

Jantzen specifically picks up on Julian's' notion of being 'endlessly born', which she interprets as 'a natality that is concerned with this present life'.[103] Translating this concept into the modern world, Jantzen notes that in

> [t]he deadly material and discursive practices of a thought-world in which violence is taken for granted and expresses itself through every sort of battle, literal and metaphorical, as the taken-for-granted response to a situation is deemed undesirable. [...] It is urgent that there should be those who step back and ponder the mind-set and heart-hurt that is acted out in such violence, greed and destructiveness, the cultural symbolic of the West that if it continues to be acted out will certainly destroy the planet through pollution if not through warfare.[104]

To this end, Jantzen proposes a symbolic natality in the process of *Becoming Divine* as a new way of thinking and acting. Hannah Arendt depicted natality as a fundamental dimension of the human condition and experience, and she concluded that, therefore, it is entirely appropriate to identify it as a central category of thought.[105] Furthermore, the metaphor of natality is essentially about the possibility of new beginnings and therefore correlates agreeably with creativity. Jantzen argues that

> taking natality seriously has direct and immediate consequences for a shift in the imaginary. It affirms the concreteness and embodied nature of human lives and experience, the material and discursive conditions within which subjects are formed and out of which religious symbols must emerge. [...] It is only within our gendered embodiment that the source and criteria of religious imagination can be drawn.[106]

103 Jantzen, *Julian of Norwich*, xix.
104 Ibid., xx.
105 Jantzen, *Becoming Divine*, 144. Arendt's concerns arose specifically out of her experiences of totalitarian regimes such as National Socialism, which emerged from standard Western thought that she understood to be deeply problematic.
106 Ibid., 146.

Jantzen argues that 'natality' radically opposes both Heidegger's notion of 'Being-towards-death' as a way towards freedom and authentic life and the 'self confident universal rational ego' with its 'view from nowhere'.[107] Arendt's vision is based on her perceived need for a new world order based on mutual understanding and partnership brought about by what Jantzen terms 'a transformation of the necrophilic imaginary'.[108] Arendt's thought is a radical shift from the ideal of a disembodied mind as an authentic and free self, such as Plato envisaged. In *The Life of the Mind* she writes:

> The very capacity for beginning is rooted in *natality*, and by no means in creativity not in a gift but in the fact that human beings, new men, again and again appear in the world by virtue of birth.[109]

Therefore, both Arendt and Jantzen consider natality as an ongoing process that has been repressed in favour of 'the view from nowhere', which has dominated philosophical and theological formulations of human nature and our place in the world. While the metaphor of birth is evident in Western philosophy it has become an abstraction only, too far removed from the actual biological process of birth that inspired it. This is damaging as it reinforces the separation between body and mind.

Metaphors of Birth

Plato held firm opinions about the priority of the spiritual birth of wisdom and virtue over giving birth in a physical sense.[110] Likewise, Simone de Beauvoir made the distinction between what Sara Ruddick describes as a 'merely physical procreativity and the worthier cre-

---

107   Ibid., 37, 133. 'The view from nowhere' is a phrase Jantzen uses repeatedly and is taken from the title of Thomas Nagel's book, *The View from Nowhere* (Oxford: Oxford University Press, 1986) which argues that we perceive the world in a detached way.

108   Jantzen, *Becoming Divine*, 147.

109   Hannah Arendt, *The Life of the Mind* (San Diego, New York and London: Harcourt, Inc, 1978), 217.

110   Plato, *Symposium*, 11, 208e–9a, 209d, cited in Ruddick, 193.

ations of artists and intellectuals'.[111] Both these positions prioritise 'brain-children' over 'children after the flesh'. I do not advocate the either/or approach of Plato and de Beauvoir, but would suggest that the possibility of new beginnings inherent in the metaphor of birth needs to be re-established.

Murdoch espoused the view that life consists of doing our best to be good and to keep trying to achieve the good despite continual setbacks. In *The Nice and the Good*, Willy states,

> We are not good people […]. All we can do is constantly to notice when we begin to act badly, to check ourselves, to go back, to coax our weakness and inspire our strength, to call upon the names of virtues of which we know perhaps only the names. We are not good people, and the best we can hope for is to be gentle, to forgive each other and to forgive the past, to be forgiven ourselves and to accept this forgiveness and to return again to the beautiful unexpected strangeness of the world.[112]

So the quest for goodness is never realised. But the possibility of new beginnings means we can get nearer to our goals with each small step.

Levertov uses the metaphor of birth both in relation to her own personal creativity and in the broader theological sense. In her poem 'Ascension'[113] for example, Levertov explores the duality of matter and spirit as she imagined Christ would have experienced it. Using the metaphors of birth and the germination of seeds, Levertov discusses the mystery of faith: 'He again / Fathering himself. / Seed-case / splitting. / He again / Mothering His birth: / torture and bliss'. In this one poem Levertov fuses male and female as well as nature and spirit. She also refers to the paradox of human joy and suffering that being alive entails, but with a focus on natality as opposed to necrophilia.

Levertov also describes the creative art of writing poetry in terms of giving birth:

111   Sara Ruddick, *Maternal Thinking: Towards a Politics of Peace* (London: The Women's Press Ltd, 1989), 193. This refers to Simone de Beauvoir's *The Second Sex*.
112   Iris Murdoch, *The Nice and the Good* (London: Penguin, 1968), 198–99.
113   Denise Levertov, *Evening Train* (New York: New Directions, 1992), 115.

The poet is in labor. She has been told that it will not hurt but it has hurt so much that pain and struggle seem, just now, the only reality. But at the very moment when she feels she will die, or that she is already in hell, she hears the doctor saying, 'Those are the shoulders you are feeling now' – and she knows the head is out then, and the child is pushing and sliding out of her, insistent, a poem.[114]

Similarly, Dillard refers to closing off a piece of work as 't[ying] off the umbilical cord'.[115] This does not denote an ending however but the potential for becoming.

Non-closure

The resistance to closure in literary pursuits is related metaphorically to the mystical notion of continual departure and to the optimism regarding new beginnings just outlined. This is not essentially a problem for Murdoch, owing to the 'compelling but unreachable spiritual goal' of the Good.[116] Murdoch's novels remain incomplete and imperfect as a means of subverting the traditional closure of the questing male hero that dominates Western fiction. The former structure and metaphorical meanings of the novel disappear before the horizon of possible futures. The ending of *The Time of Angels* is a case in point. Following the suicide of his brother and sinister happenings at the rectory, Marcus emerges from 'the vacant shell whose significant spaces would soon be merged into the empty air',[117] into 'the feeble sunshine and [...] the big bustling scene of men at work [...] the gay din of ringing voices and babbling transistor sets'.[118] Marcus has gone (literally) through the dark labyrinth of doubt to rejoin the world – a world that is still in the making. Ultimately, Murdoch does not resort to nihilistic notions of despair but instead suggests that hope and the prevalence of the Good is cause for optimism.

114 Levertov, 'The Poet in the World', in *The Poet in the World*, 107.
115 Dillard, *The Writing Life*, 7.
116 David J. Gordon, *Iris Murdoch's Fables of Unselfing* (Columbia and London: University of Missouri Press, 1995), 38.
117 Iris Murdoch, *The Time of Angels* (London: Chatto & Windus, 1966), 244.
118 Ibid., 249.

The refusal of closure, while not peculiar to women's writing or feminist literary endeavours, does seem opposed to what might be described as a masculinist approach to finality. This is suggested most aptly through the open structure of *The Sea, The Sea.* The book ends with Charles Arrowby asking 'what next I wonder?'[119] It is only by accepting the impossibility of closure and the quest for certainty that the future remains open to change and transformation. Murdoch herself emphasises that a work of art is only ever an attempt to create a 'formal unity and statement, [which] carries a built-in self-critical recognition of its incompleteness'.[120] Levertov's epic poem 'Staying Alive' contains her reflections of the victims of Vietnam War and her personal protest, and there she writes, 'O holy innocents! I have / no virtue but to praise / you who believe / life is possible [...].' In short, the poem tells us that we have affirmation but not final resolution. The poem remains open-ended, like the life that it celebrates.[121] Ironically, it is the horrors of the world, war in particular, that can blunt or prevent creative endeavours. Dillard, by contrast, is characteristically direct. She ends *Living By Fiction* by asking,

> Do art's complex and balanced relationships among all parts, its purpose, significance, and harmony, exist in nature? Is nature whole, like a completed thought? Is history purposeful? Is the universe of matter significant? I am sorry I do not know.[122]

Co-Creators

In order to revolt against prevailing paradigms of violence and domination we need to create a different future. The driving thesis of McFague's work to date is based on the belief that no metaphor or model relating to God is final. The fact that we have 'stuck' with male metaphors of a dominating God has allowed human beings to domin-

---

119 Murdoch, *The Sea, The Sea* (London: Vintage, 1999), 502.
120 Murdoch, 'Salvation by Words', in Conradi (ed), *Existentialists and Mystics*, 240.
121 Paul Lacey, 'The Poetry of Political Anguish', in Gelpi, *Denise Levertov*, 161.
122 Dillard, *Living by Fiction*, 185.

ate nature instead of seeing themselves as responsible stewards or co-creators. To be a co-creator is to recognise our intimate connection with mystery, but also to recognise our responsibility to create a sustainable and just future world. This emphasises a model for theology wherein, firstly, 'our novel constructions offer new possibilities in place of others. In this sense we create the reality in which we live; we do not copy it, or to put it more pointedly, there are no copies, only creations'.[123]

The second point concerns the belief that the new replacements are better than what they replace. It is of course impossible to judge this empirically – all we can do, she suggests, is '"to live within" testing it for its disclosive power, its ability to address and cope with the most pressing issues of one's day'.[124] Murdoch, Levertov and Dillard demonstrate that art has a crucial role in the creation of these new paradigms. For example, the closing sentence from *The Black Prince* encapsulates Murdoch's theory that art is an essential truth-teller:

> Art is not cosy and is not mocked. Art tells the only truth that ultimately matters. It is the light by which human beings can be mended. And after art there is, let me assure you all, nothing.[125]

So, in postmodernity, the role of the writer (or artist) takes on a more serious role as possibly the only mediator of 'truth'. The tension between fiction and truth is a basic component of the discussion in Chapter Six.

Levertov affirms that humans have the potential to create in an unexpected twist in 'Life at War',[126] where she finds it difficult to imagine that humankind,

> whose music excels the music of birds,
> whose laughter matches the laughter of dogs,
> whose understanding manifests designs
> fairer than the spider's most intricate web

123   McFague, *Models of God*, 26.
124   Ibid., 27.
125   Murdoch, *The Black Prince*, 416.
126   Levertov, *Poems, 1960–1967*, 229–30.

– that 'humans, men who make;
whose language imagines mercy, lovingkindness',

have the latent ability to destroy and create according to whim.
On a more cosmological scale, Dillard speculates

> that imaginative acts actually weigh in the balance of physical processes.
> Imaginative acts – even purely mental combinations, like the thought that a cer-
> tain cloud resembles a top hat – carry real weight in the universe [and thus acts
> of the imagination are] doing something which counts in the universe's reckon-
> ing of order and decay – which counts just as those mighty explosions and
> strippings of electrons do inside those selfsame stars.[127]

Dillard cannot rationalise this viewpoint and dismisses it as a 'crack-
pot notion', but she intuitively feels that acts involving the creative
imagination are stopping the world from falling apart, 'saving the
universe'.[128] Later in *For the Time Being*, she develops this through
the Kabbalistic notion of *Tikkun Olam*, or Holy restoration. This is a
Jewish idea that human beings are co-creators with God, corresponding to McFague's theology, which will be discussed further in the
final chapter.

Creativity Starts with the Given

I have argued in this chapter that creativity is integral to the mystic
way in postmodernity, and I have drawn on theological insights that
articulate the benefits of creativity in such terms as natality and co-
creation. In the process, there has been an exploration of the key
challenges and benefits of women's contributions in this regard in
particular. This marks the conclusion to part one of this book, which
has outlined the conceptual and methodological underpinnings of the
mystic way in postmodernity by drawing on insights of Murdoch,

127 Dillard, *Living by Fiction*, 174.
128 Ibid.

Levertov and Dillard alongside theologians who share a similar sensibility. The second part is concerned with the process of discerning,
describing and interpreting mystically in postmodernity. The starting
place must be our experience and the language used to express it – or
the *via positiva*. It is only by starting from what we know that we can
hope to create new futures.

Part Two

Chapter Four
The *Via Positiva*: Love and Life

In the first part of this book, I examined the theoretical and conceptual foundations of the mystic way in postmodernity, and in particular, relative to Murdoch, Levertov and Dillard as creative writers. In order to demonstrate how literary texts provide a means for this shift in consciousness, the second part will examine the process of the mystic way through the well-known mystical categories of the *via positiva* and the *via negativa* – but with a postmodern twist.

This chapter specifically interrogates the *via positiva* as the starting place for the mystic way in postmodernity as expressed by our literary writers. As noted previously, the *via positiva* as the affirmative or cataphatic way in mystical discourse traditionally represents all that we can say about God. Consequently, this path favours 'images, sensory impressions, visions, voices – a mysticism mediated through the senses, through symbols, through concrete objects, and through human relationships'.[1] Turner describes cataphatic language as 'a kind of riot, an anarchy of discourse in which anything goes'.[2] And herein lies, by a kind of paradox, its *apophatic* quality – cataphatic language 'names' God as inevitably indefinable precisely through the very 'anarchy of discourse'.

The use of cataphatic language in mystical discourse highlights the creative potential of language for theology, but it also alerts us to the fact that it might also threaten the discourse of 'truth' by virtue of being difficult to control conceptually. Typically, in the writings of mystics such as Julian, we find a constant gush of elaborate metaphors to describe the experience and comprehension of God. As Matthews reminds us, an 'outpouring of creation' is at the heart of the mystical

1   Ruffing (ed), *Mysticism and Social Transformation*, 5.
2   Turner, *The Darkness of God*, 20.

life, which is more properly expressed as Eros or erotic love.[3] Nevertheless, reason or intellectual reflection is not abandoned. As Jantzen writes, 'if we suspend the question of truth we are left with no criteria with which to assess the projections of the imagination'.[4] The *via positiva* is then but the first stage of what Louth calls an 'on the way' form of theology.[5]

The first aspect of the *via positiva* to be discussed is an engagement with the here and now through the cultivation of 'amazement'. Mystical insight that surfaces within ordinary experience, such as wonder in the natural world, is crucial if mysticism is to be democratised. Second, the spotlight will turn to love, including *eros*, as a way to grasp and to express mystical insights. In the final part of this chapter, we will turn our attention to the darker side of human existence. As Soelle reminds us, wonderment in the face of the created world has 'its bleak side of terror and hopelessness that renders one mute' as well.[6] It is not possible to embrace fully the sheer wonder of being without accepting the unexplainable mysteries of pain, suffering, and death. Murdoch, Levertov and Dillard help us to face these realities in a pragmatic way, and indeed, the need to engage with both aspects of the *via positiva* is a necessary dimension of postmodern theology.

The Here and Now

Our writers realise, as does Soelle that the quest for meaning begins by 'consenting to one's being here, being today, being now'.[7] Experience of the particular can occur in nature, in relationships with other beings, or simply in an individual's experience of living in a human

---

3   Matthews, *Both Alike to Thee*, 106–7.
4   Jantzen, *Becoming Divine*, 192.
5   See Chapter 2.
6   Soelle, *The Silent Cry*, 90.
7   Ibid., 91.

body. The notion that wisdom resides in the natural world is an ancient one, as is the belief that encounters with others offer moments of illumination, and we saw in Chapter One that the value placed on ordinary experience is central to the mystic way in postmodernity. Plato, in Murdoch's imagined dialogue, states that religion

> must be everything, it must be proved by loving people and learning things and looking at things. It's not abstract, it's all here. It's not retiring from the world, it's knowing the world, the real world, this world as it really is, in all its details.[8]

In other words, the *via positiva* means to pay attention to ordinary events and phenomena that people encounter in their lives.

Audrey Rogers notes that Levertov adopts this stance, describing her as a poet for whom 'all her experience [...] became the raw material for poetry: a woman awakening to the world of men, the act of being and staying alive, burgeoning nature, the city and its people'.[9] In her early poem 'Illustrious Ancestors'[10] Levertov refers to her Hasidic forebears who understood 'the language of birds; and used what was at hand'. 'The language of birds' is a metaphor for mystical language. Levertov notices that her Hasidic ancestors derived mystical language and meaning from attending to their immediate surroundings, a concept that is affirmed by McFague, who cites Paul Lacey's comment that 'One *puts off* the habitual but does not repudiate it; when the habitual is seen afresh, it testifies to the holy'. McFague also suggests that this practice bears testimony to the fact that 'the ordinary is the bearer of the miraculous'.[11] In fact, Levertov further believed that intense experiences, whether they are awe, love, anger or joy, demand to be '*brought to speech*'.[12]

---

8   Iris Murdoch, 'Above the Gods', in Conradi (ed), *Existentialists and Mystics*, 516.
9   Rodgers, *Denise Levertov*, 17.
10 Levertov, *Collected Poems 1940–1960*, 77.
11 McFague, *Speaking in Parables*, 102 cites Paul Lacey *The Inner War: Forms and Themes in Recent American Poetry* (Philadelphia: Fortress Press, 1972), 114.
12 Denise Levertov, 'Some Notes on Organic Form', in *The Poet in the World*, 8.

Dillard fully epitomises this need to attend to 'the world's abounding objects, its rampant variety of people, its exuberant, destructive, and unguessible changes'[13] and provides an alternative perspective in this regard by asserting her own awareness of being a created person in a world of other created beings:

> I salt my breakfast eggs. All day long I feel created. I can see the blown dust on the skin on the back of my hand, the tiny trapezoids of chipped clay, moistened and breathed alive. There are some created sheep in the pasture below me, sheep set down here precisely, just touching their blue shadows hoof to hoof on the grass. Created gulls pock the air, rip great curved seams in the settled air: I greet my created meal amazed.[14]

This is Dillard grounded in the created world. Her words possibly reflect Heschel (whom Dillard respects as a great religious thinker) and his notion that wisdom is to be found in such moments of awe. However, this passage does not suggest that nature has wisdom concealed within itself, but rather, that revelation occurs through developing a mystical awareness of our own bodily existence as part of nature.

Radical Amazement

The first stage of the *via positiva* in Soelle's vision is the mystical development of amazement and wonder, and like Dillard, she finds inspiration in this regard in the writings of the Jewish theologian Abraham Heschel. Attention to mystery and wonder at the heart of reality links contemplation (prayer), creativity (imagination), and the apprehension of beauty (amazement) as expressed by Heschel:

> To pray is to take notice of the wonder, to regain a sense of the mystery that animates all beings, the divine margin in all attainments. Prayer is our humble answer to the inconceivable surprise of living. It is all we can offer in return for the mystery by which we live. Who is worthy to be present at the constant unfolding of time? Amidst meditations of mountains, the humility of flowers – wiser than all alphabets – clouds that die constantly for the sake of His glory,

13   Dillard, *Living by Fiction*, 78.
14   Dillard, *Holy The Firm*, 25.

we are hating, hunting, hurting. Suddenly we feel ashamed of our clashes and complaints in the face of the tacit glory of nature. It is so embarrassing to live! How strange we are in the world, and how presumptuous our doings! Only one response can maintain us: gratefulness for witnessing the wonder, for the gift of our unearned right to serve, to adore, and to fulfil. It is the gratefulness which makes the soul great.[15]

Borrowing and elaborating upon Heschel's term 'radical amazement', Soelle suggests that we need to relearn a child's ability to wonder.[16] Heschel himself argues that we are able to look at the world though two faculties – reason and wonder.[17] To prioritise the latter means, instead of adapting the world to our concepts, we need to adjust our minds to the world. Mary Grey cites Dillard's *Pilgrim at Tinker Creek* as a good example of someone who has resisted the urge to dominate and impose meaning on the created world. Grey points to the experiences and reflections recorded there as being wholly 'embedded' in the seasons of nature and thus providing 'an account of the sacred, of evil, of ambiguity [that] is wrested from the struggle to find a language for events, and not vice versa'.[18] This viewpoint takes nothing for granted, and in Heschel's words, acknowledges that 'we are amazed at seeing anything at all; amazed not only at particular values and things but at the unexpectedness of being as such, at the fact that there is being at all'.[19] In short, Soelle does not see the possibility of starting anything new unless we rekindle a zest for life.

As a novelist, Murdoch created exuberance and abundance whilst her philosopher's voice sought precision and clarity. The critics were keen to point out Murdoch's 'excesses, her torrents of adjectives and heedless sentences',[20] together with the complexities associated with her large cast of characters in her novels. One reader sees this in a

15   Abraham Joshua Heschel, *Man's Quest for God* (Santa Fe: Aurora Press, 1998), 5.
16   Soelle, *The Silent Cry*, 88–89.
17   Abraham Joshua Heschel, *Man is Not Alone: A Philosophy of Religion* (New York: Farrar, Straus and Giroux, 1951), 11.
18   Grey, *The Wisdom of Fools?* 79.
19   Heschel, *Man is Not Alone*, 12.
20   'Closing the book on a literary lion', at http://www.suntimes.co.za/1999/02/14/news/news53.htm

positive light, pointing to the fact that her stories 'richly imply [...] an invisible fecundity beyond our imagining'.[21] An example from *A Fairly Honourable Defeat* illustrates how a novel can explore both wonder and fear in the face of contingent reality. Morgan, Tallis' estranged wife, has been caught between two men, the demonic Julius and the 'good' figure of Tallis. This scene depicts the reactions of a chance encounter with nature during a car journey when they stop:

> She seemed to see the expanse of green floor between the high flowering banks and it was alive with movement and huge forms. The great ray from afar was pinning her down. [...] Was it [...] disgust, fear, horror as at some dreadfulness, some unspeakable filth of the universe?'[22]

Later, after recovering from a dizzy spell, her mood changes:

> The scene was there before her again, the yellow grass of the slopes alive with flowers, the green grass of the track, wiry and short as if it had been cut, as if the place were a garden, as if it were a still small road, but a road not trodden by human feet. The hot air was thick with flowery scents and subtle dry emanations. The insects were hissing and murmuring in the honeyed forest of the grass. But now it was suddenly more beautiful to her, more intensely coloured and more absolutely here, under a sky which had resumed its blue. It was as if she had passed through a screen into some more primitive and lovely world, as if she were millennia away in the past or the future in some paradise of undimmed experience and unblurred vision. 'How beautiful it all is', she said. 'How infinitely beautiful. I worship it.'[23]

This depicts a movement from the dark aspect of eros to an understanding that 'happiness is free innocent love'.[24] This description parallels Dillard's account of looking for 'the pearl of great price' referred to in the last chapter. Whether or not this reflects Murdoch's personal experience is pure speculation but it would certainly be difficult to recreate this without some prior similar epiphanic moment.

21   D. Milburn, 'Iris Murdoch: Fragments of a Re-cognition'. http://www.Texas chapbookpress.com/magellanslog35/murdochfecundity.htm
22   Iris Murdoch, *A Fairly Honourable Defeat* (London: Penguin, 1970), 187.
23   Ibid., 192.
24   Ibid., 193.

But what comes first – the language or the experience of wonder? In *Sands of the Well*, Levertov declares her belief in a 'Primal Speech'[25] or an 'Ur-language', which can still be 'discovered in ocean's grottoes', which connects to the human desire to affirm and name things – 'anything'. Levertov describes this as the 'infant utterance, "This! This!"' whilst 'showing and proffering the thing'. This closely resembles Soelle's remark that amazement means to behold the world as if for the first time, like God on the sixth day of creation, with the 'radical wonderment of the child' and say, 'Look! How very good it all is!'[26] Levertov echoes the same sentiment when recounting a childhood memory in 'First Love',[27] wherein she recalls noticing a flower through the innocent eyes of a very young child:

> It looked at me, I looked
> back, delight
> filled me as if
> I, not the flower
> were a flower and were brimful of rain.
> *And there was endlessness*
> Perhaps through a lifetime what I've desired
> has always been to return
> to that endless giving and receiving, the wholeness
> of that attention,
> that once-in-a-lifetime
> secret communion.

This 'once-in-a-lifetime' feeling of connection is at the heart of the life of the mystic. It is an experience of amazement and childlike wonder instigated in this instance by close attention to a small snapshot of nature. It must be noted that this is not the same as James' notion of preconceptual ineffable experience, which 'defies expression' so that 'no adequate report of its contents can be given'.[28] Within

---

25   Levertov, *Sands of the Well*, 95.
26   Soelle, *The Silent Cry*, 90–91.
27   Levertov, *This Great Unknowing*, 14.
28   James, *The Varieties of Religious Experience*, 414–15. James also identifies transience, passivity and a noetic quality as characteristic of mysticism. The latter refers to states of knowledge which could be argued as contradicting his notion of ineffability.

the experientialist model of understanding, experience is primary to mysticism, and it is only after the event that language tries to capture it. In adults, as Cupitt notes, there is 'no such thing as "experience" outside of or prior to language'.[29] In effect, this means that experience and interpretation are simultaneous and mutually supporting. However, Levertov and Soelle point to a time in human life before language is fully developed when wonder and amazement are more present.[30] This is not to deny the power of language but to infuse it with fresh insight. Levertov explains how this has continued into her adult life. Levertov replied in response to the question, 'What does the word "religious" mean to you?'

> The impulse to kneel in wonder... The impulse to kiss the ground... The sense of awe. The felt presence of some mysterious force, whether it be what one calls beauty, or perhaps just the sense of the unknown – I don't mean 'unknown' in the sense of we don't know what the future will bring. I mean the sense of the numinous, whether it's in a small stone, or a large mountain.[31]

In other words, for Levertov, the sacred is an all-pervading 'mysterious force'.

A passage from Dillard's *Pilgrim at Tinker Creek* helps demonstrate the connection between 'radical amazement' in the face of this mystery and cataphatic language in much the same way:

> It's a good place to live; there's a lot to think about. The creeks – Tinker and Carvin's – are an active mystery, fresh every minute. Theirs is the mystery of the continuous creation and all that providence implies: the uncertainty of vision, the horror of the fixed, the dissolution of the present, the intricacy of beauty, the pressure of fecundity, the elusiveness of the free, and the flawed nature of perfection. The mountains – Tinker and Brushy, McAfee's Knob and Dead Man – are a passive mystery, the oldest of all. Theirs is the one simple mystery of creation from nothing, of matter itself, anything at all, the given [...]. The creeks are the world with all its stimulus and beauty; I live there.[32]

---

29   Cupitt, *Mysticism After Modernity*, 74.
30   This is different from William James' idea of religious experience prior to language in adults.
31   William Packard, 'Craft Interview with Denise Levertov', in Brooker, *Conversations with Denise Levertov*, 49.
32   Dillard, *Pilgrim at Tinker Creek*, 4–5.

It is clear that Dillard's experience of living by Tinker Creek is both a mystical and intellectual mystery. Language is of great import for Dillard as a writer, but like nature, language has the capacity to both reveal and conceal. Although it 'selects, abstracts, exaggerates, and orders', Dillard reminds us of the fact that 'language is a fabricated grid someone stuck in a river'.[33] Language, Dillard reminds us, is wholly inadequate for expressing the complexities of reality and any attempt is always contextualised and personalised by an individual writer.

For most of us, this non-questioning acceptance of reality is a very hard state to achieve, but if we place too much emphasis on the role of the intellect, we miss out spiritually. Dillard defines innocence as 'the spirit's unselfconscious state at any moment of pure devotion to any object. It is at once a receptiveness and total concentration.'[34] Being passive is a state of 'receptiveness', but observation is also active in the requirement for 'total concentration' that is only achieved through directing the attention by an act of will. If this state of active passivity is achieved, Dillard promises 'a higher innocence, a new in-nocence: the redemption of knowledge, the rough merger of the com-plex products of thought with the simple and received sensations of life in time'.[35] The *via positiva* is primarily devoted to the sensory world of particulars.

Finding the Sacred in Nature

Although Murdoch does not endorse an overt ecological agenda, she does suggest that nature provides opportunities for unselfing – occasions that promote 'a pure delight in the independent existence of what is excellent [...] and inspires love in the highest part of the soul'.[36] The 'independent existence' of nature is essentially uncorrupted by

33   Dillard, *Living by Fiction*, 70.
34   Karla M. Hammond, 'Drawing the Curtains: An Interview with Annie Dillard', in *Bennington Review* 10 (1981), 38.
35   Ibid.
36   Murdoch, *The Sovereignty of Good*, 84.

human desires, whereas art can fall prey to personal desires and self-delusion.[37] While such moments 'inspire love' and 'pure delight', they include the risk of being isolated romantic or sentimental incidents. In short, such moments need productive expression to enable a change of consciousness.

The phenomena of nature permeated Levertov's poetry throughout her long career. As we have already seen, it is partly through her keen sense of sight that she is able to draw on this vast resource. In an interview with Ed Block, she attributes her ability to notice things to her mother, whom she portrays as 'something of an artist' and a great 'pointer-outer', who would point out such things as clouds and flowers as well as naming them.[38] This seems to have been of immense importance to Levertov, for it provided the groundwork for the development of a poet who sees and describes the world. Levertov was to take on the same role with her students, whom she thought had become too 'book' and analytically-orientated. On occasions, she would hold her class by the lake on the Vassar campus where she taught, so that students could look up from their books for a moment to see the beauty of nature.[39] Although the ability to name things is valuable, it is always secondary to looking or being attentive to the wonder and beauty of the world.

In an interview with Gary Pacernick, Levertov recounts her conviction that poems can serve to remind people of many things they otherwise fail to notice, and to reveal the extraordinary within the ordinary, and to stimulate imagination and intuitive knowledge by

---

37   Some would disagree with Murdoch here. Simon Schama, for example, argues in *Landscape and Memory* (London: Harper Collins, 1995) that nature is an interpreted concept and criticises the notion of pure nature in as much as most spaces and landscapes have been subjected to the human imagination. Indeed there can hardly be any part of our landscape which has not been shaped by human hands. For the purposes of this argument the focus is on human experience within nature and I would wish to avoid the somewhat romantic idea that nature is pure because it detracts from ethical considerations and the human effort to grasp transcendent meaning.

38   Block, 'Interview with Denise Levertov', in *Renascence* 50 (1997) http://www. questia.com/PM.qst?a= o&d=5001524879

39   Ibid.

being beautiful, moving and powerful – just as poems have always done. At the beginning of the twenty-first century, one of the things about which poetry can nudge people is ecological consciousness and conscience. Because poetry has traditionally dealt with 'Nature' anyway (especially poetry in English), it is well placed to do so.[40]

Indeed, nature provides the raw materials of Dillard's mysticism. In *Holy the Firm*, Dillard deliberately employs the structure of the mystical way through her meditations on landscape. The first day represents the *via positiva*. She commences the book in what can be described as standard cataphatic language:

> Every day is a god, each day is a god, and holiness holds forth in time. I worship each god, I praise each day splintered down, splintered down and wrapped in time like a husk, a husk of many colors spreading, at dawn fast over the mountains split. [...] The god lifts from the water. His head fills the bay. He is Puget Sound, the Pacific; his breast rises from the pastures; his fingers are firs; islands slide wet down his shoulders. Islands slip blue from his shoulders and glide over the water...[41]

This passage conveys the pantheistic view of god as being everywhere. In the next chapter, we will see how Dillard has to negate this and moves from describing God with a small 'g' to God with a capital 'g' once his presence becomes all pervading.

As the book progresses, Dillard continues to pile up details of her encounter with nature on the fringe of the American landmass. Later, she experiences a 'deepening of wonder' when she sees a new island out of her window on Puget Sound that she cannot name.[42] William Schreik interprets this to signify 'more than another temporal solidity; it becomes a metaphorical index to a pervasive continuum within creation that evokes wonder'.[43] Echoing Soelle's interpretation of God's

40   Gary Pasternick, 'Interview with Denise Levertov', in Little & Paul, *Denise Levertov*, 85.
41   Dillard, *Holy the Firm*, 11–12.
42   Ibid., 25–26.
43   William J. Schreick, 'Annie Dillard, Narrative Fringe', in Catherine Rainwater, and William J, Scheick (eds), *Contemporary American Women Writers: Narrative Strategies* (Lexington: University of Kentucky Press, 1985), 56.

declaration at creation, Dillard exclaims, 'I see it! I see it all!'[44] Seeking God in nature seems logical enough, considering the mystery of creation, but Dillard reminds us that Westerners no longer see meaning in the natural world as the ancients once did. She suggests that

> [w]e commonly (if tacitly) agree that the human world has human meaning which we can discover, and the given natural world does not. [...] Doodles, Shakespeare, and Nepalese altars are human; we can interpret their human significance. Puddles, frost cracks, clouds, and chemical compounds are not human and have no human significance.[45]

Surprising as it may seem, especially coming from someone who has spent so long seeking the sacred in the natural world, Dillard concludes that it is only within human experience that meaning resides. Nature tells us nothing on its own – it is only our experience of it that counts.

Finding the Sacred in Ordinary Experience

How can an individual experience contribute towards the religious symbolic? Jantzen suggests that poets (and other artists) can only offer their work and insights to the community and then stand back, as it is 'only within the larger social and historical context that it could find resonance and be taken up into the symbolic'.[46] Literary writers and theologians, or postmodern mystics can only write through their own experience of living and thinking in their specific contexts and hope to engage their readers through a shared humanity as opposed to an overarching ideology.

Our discussion will concentrate on the character of Anne Cavidge in *Nuns and Soldiers* and the Irish rebels in *The Red and the Green* to demonstrate how it is possible to gain insight by reflecting on personal experiences. Collectively, these characters represent Murdoch's interpretation of Plato's concept of spiritual progression as

44   Dillard, *Holy the Firm*, 28.
45   Dillard, *Living by Fiction*, 138–39.
46   Jantzen, *Becoming Divine*, 115.

entailing a movement from 'appearance to reality'. In both cases, Murdoch suggests that religious, political and/or national ideologies are not real and involve an illusionary obsession with the self that eclipses true insight.

Anne originally escaped the messiness of life to live within the confines of a convent only to realise that she can only achieve true spiritual fulfilment by immersion in as opposed to escape from the world. Murdoch deploys some interesting phrases to depict this realisation. For example, at one point Anne imagines herself to be 'a secret anchoress hidden in the world'.[47] Her friend Gertrude describes her as a 'Mary Magdalene in reverse!' And later in the novel, she declares, 'Anne's Martha and I'm Mary!' As a 'postmodern anchoress', Anne realises she needs to be embedded within the real world, which means she must live as a woman in a woman's body. Historically, women who chose the life of a nun have renounced and repressed sexuality. Although Anne does not become sexually active, she is nevertheless aware of her sexual desires around the opposite sex through her obsessive love for the Count. Above all, Anne as Martha recognises that to follow her vocation fully she must be attentive to the needs of others. Gertrude, as Mary, is the more egotistical of the two. We saw in Chapter Two that Anne's 'vision' of Christ helped her to realise the futility of seeking salvation in the supernatural realm. Caroline Geurin succinctly sums up Murdoch's 'theology' here:

> Salvation is a matter of very mundane elements combining in a manner that empowers the most ordinary beings. [...] In a world without God, salvation is the ability to confront the inevitability of death without searching for some kind of magical loophole.[48]

In other words, salvation comes about by accepting the realities of the human condition and part of that condition that must be accepted are human failings and weaknesses. In a wider context, Murdoch believed

---

47   Murdoch, *Nuns and Soldiers*, 309.
48   Caroline Guerin, 'Iris Murdoch – A Revisionist Theology? A Comparative Study of Iris Murdoch's *Nuns and Soldiers* and Sara Maitland's *Virgin Territory*', in *Journal of Literature and Theology*, 6:2 (1992) 166.

that the moral task was to make sure that we do not become responsible for the oppression of others.[49]

The Red and the Green is the only novel set in Murdoch's native land of Ireland. It is also her only attempt at an historical novel. The narrative pivots around the 1916 Easter Uprising in support of Home Rule in Dublin. In what contains chilling similarities with our own times post 9/11 and 7/7, Murdoch attempts to uncover the misguided view of heroism and bravery in the name of religion. Whilst attending Mass in a Dominican Chapel, Barney has a moment of revelation concerning the futility and self-deceptive nature of his and his comrades' actions:

> Barney could see plainly, as if a surgical light had been shone within him, that the machinery of his virtuous intent was simply not attached to the living animal that he really was. Nothing that moved here touched the great powerful thing underneath which went its way regardless. It was the strength of the thing, its fat strength, which made him despair. He had thought himself a man haunted at least by goodness, but these hauntings were merely the bog fires of his own psyche.[50]

He comes to realise that his perception of 'good' is a false one, nothing compared to the larger pulse of life. After falling asleep, he wakes up alone in the darkness:

> He stared at the sanctuary light and felt the certain almost bodily presence of perfect Goodness. And with this he felt, as he had not felt before, an absolute certainty of his own existence. He existed and God, opposite to him, existed too. And if he was not, by that juxtaposition, simply dissolved into nothing it could only be because God was love.[51]

This is an experience of union or of an oneness with being, that perceives a heightened awareness of both self and all that exists. This is Murdoch's perennial answer to the meaning of life: love. Unfortunately, Barney soon forgets his moment of illumination and therefore

49   Ibid., 170.
50   Iris Murdoch, *The Red and the Green* (London: Penguin, 1965), 173.
51   Ibid., 176.

does not progress spiritually or morally. Such epiphanic experiences can be only isolated moments of reverie unless they are acted upon.

As a poet, Levertov never failed to notice the mystical importance of every seemingly insignificant event. Rudolph L. Nelson depicts Levertov as a poet 'at the threshold of the transcendent', a poet who helps us to realise that 'one reaches eternity by going deeper into today'.[52] Joy, if it is to be found anywhere, arises within real everyday experience throughout much of Levertov's poetry. In 'Matins',[53] for example, she writes, '[t]he authentic! I said / rising from the toilet seat'. Levertov appears here to invoke Julian's oft-quoted phrase praising human bodily functions: 'A man walks upright, and the food in his body is shut in as if in a well-made purse. When the time of his necessity comes, the purse is opened and then shut again, in most seemly fashion.'[54] Levertov continues to find the sacred in 'Matins', this time whilst preparing a child's breakfast: 'Stir the holy grains, / set the bowls on the table and / call the child to eat.' Sandra Gilbert suggests that Levertov makes the reader aware of 'the awesome, eternal delight – which is always in some sense, waiting to illuminate and transfigure the façade of the ordinary'[55] in moments such as these. That is, the materiality of her life, like Julian's, contains symbols and signs of deeper truth.[56] She makes the ordinary extraordinary. For Levertov, immanence is the key to transcendence and is typical of the 'transcendental mysticism' found in Romantic poetry generally.[57] Rather than acting as a veil that hides the sacred, the 'authentic' is the medium through which the transcendent shines, an insight which affects her approach to writing poetry.

Levertov mostly writes in what she describes as 'the organic form'. In her essay 'Some Notes on Organic Form', she defines her approach as 'the concept that there is a form in all things (and our

52 Rudolph. L. Nelson, 'The Edge of the Transcendent', in Wagner-Martin, *Critical Essays*, 234–35.
53 Levertov, *Poems 1960–1967*, 59–62.
54 Julian, *Showings*, 186.
55 Sandra M. Gilbert, 'Revolutionary Love', in Gelpi, *Denise Levertov*, 202.
56 Ibid., 203.
57 Gelpi, *Denise Levertov*, 3.

experience) which the poet can discover and reveal'.[58] As noted previously, she uses Gerard Manley Hopkins' term of 'inscape' to further explore this idea, which she attaches not just to living beings and nature but also to experience. So, poetry that is written in the organic form 'is based on an intuition of an order, a form beyond forms, in which forms partake, and of which man's creative works are analogies, resemblances, natural allegories'.[59]

Gelpi suggests that, when writing poetry, Levertov

> sought to be organic so as to enact verbally the psychological, moral and spiritual effort to realise – in landscape, cityscape, human relationships, marriage, motherhood – that essentializing sense of individual wholeness and of individual participation in the whole.[60]

It is through depicting the particularities of life that Levertov is able convey how the individual participates in the whole, in everything that is.

Dillard's writing abounds with attention to the details of nature while at the same time displaying a disregard for literal truth. In this regard, her writing embodies a dialectical tension between the material and the spiritual, the natural and the transcendent so that her vision is always contradictory.[61] Her descriptions of watching the eclipse, patting the puppy, and the tree with the lights in it are but three examples of her ability to blend realism with fiction for the sake of mystical vision and her art. In short, the reader never really knows what Dillard sees with her eyes or where temporal reality ends and the eternal breaks through. This is largely due to her conviction that nature is a 'trick' of God that both conceals and reveals.[62] In fact, she tells us in *The Writing Life* that she deliberately shut out the natural world by enclosing herself in a study carrel when she wrote the second half of

58   Levertov, 'Some Notes on Organic Form', in *The Poet in the World*, 7.
59   Ibid.
60   Gelpi, *Denise Levertov*, 4. This distinctly Platonic perspective shows a correlation with Murdoch's notion of the Good as the idea of perfection.
61   McClintock, 'Annie Dillard: Ritualist', 93.
62   Lorraine Schaub, 'Tricks of Eye and Spirit: Invisibility and Illusion in Annie Dillard's *Pilgrim at Tinker Creek*'. http://www.hoardeordinaries.com/lori/research/tricks.html

Pilgrim at Tinker Creek.[63] She deliberately blotted out the reality of nature and continued to write from just her notes and imagination. This quality of other-worldliness in Dillard's writing contrasts sharply with the stereotypical image of the nature writer. Patricia Ward calls Dillard '*a voyant* – a seer whose imaginary eye transforms the prosaic details of this world into another universe'.[64] Nevertheless, these erratic and unruly images still derive from her individual everyday experiences.

This brief survey of Murdoch's, Levertov's and Dillard's writing reveals that salvation, if it is to be found at all, is to be sought within the here and now. In postmodernity, the *via positiva* must be entrenched in our particular lives as we live them within nature and alongside our fellow human and non-human creatures. In other words, mystical awareness is the ability to see the extraordinary in the ordinary. For humans to achieve this awareness, however, they must strive to nurture their ability for passion and erotic love.

Recovery of Love and Eros

Throughout much of the Christian tradition, the virtues of love as *agape*, generally defined as self-sacrificing love, have been extolled over those of the lower *eros*. The former is associated with divine love and the latter with human physical love. The exception has been within the mystical tradition where erotic language has provided a means to communicate the mystic's desire for God. Mysticism, as defined by Soelle, must seek to recapture the language of eros in order to reconcile bodily and spiritual concepts of love. She imagines an erotic relationship between humans and the sacred as well as with each other

63   Dillard, *The Writing Life*, 27–28.
64   Patricia Ward, 'Annie Dillard's Way of Seeing', in *Christianity Today*, 22 (1978), 974.

and nature as being essential in postmodernity.[65] It should be noted, however, that eros is not just about sexual love but also includes energy, passion and desire in all aspects of life. Specifically, this section will interrogate the ways in which Murdoch understands the term eros as love, Levertov's exhortation to live life to the full, and Dillard's observations concerning 'extravagance'.

Murdoch on Love and Eros

McFague, whose chief concern in *Super, Natural Christians* is to construct a Christian spirituality based on nature, draws on Murdoch's work to propose that we have to see the world as it is in order to love it. Knowledge and love go hand in hand.[66] Murdoch stated that 'Love is the extremely difficult realisation that something other than oneself is real. Love [...] is the discovery of reality'. McFague elaborates on this by stating:

> Love is being objective, the recognition that reality is made up of others. The relational self can feel a close connection with others as subjects who live in their own worlds with their own interests (as I do), without wanting to fuse with them. Rather the relational self desires to know these others, to understand and appreciate them.[67]

This implies that love and knowledge of both human and non-human life forms in what McFague calls a 'subject-subject model' corrects an anthropocentric view.

Morality, Murdoch suggests, is in a perpetual state of flux by virtue of the fact humans have to contend with 'impulses of love, rational reflection, new scenery, conscious and deliberate formation of new attachments'.[68] Moreover, the pursuit of goodness and ethical

65 Soelle, *The Silent Cry*, see Chapter 6. This is discussed in more detail in Chapter Six.
66 Sallie McFague, *Super, Natural Christians* (Minneapolis: Fortress Press, 1997), 29.
67 Ibid., 106. McFague quotes from Murdoch's essay 'The Sublime and the Good', in Conradi (ed), *Existentialists and Mystics*, 215.
68 Murdoch, *Metaphysics as a Guide to Morals*, 300.

values inevitably involves tensions between 'axioms, duties and Eros'.[69] 'Axioms' are those general or universal beliefs concerning rights and a sense of justice. 'Duties' relate to the moral force that most people recognise as doing the right thing in their daily lives. 'Eros' represents

> the continuous operation of spiritual energy, desire, intellect, love, as it moves among and responds to particular objects of attention, the force of magnetism and attraction which joins us to the world, making it a better or worse world.[70]

Murdoch interrogates, rejoices and reflects upon the vagaries of human love in her novels. Primarily she exposes false notions of love that are possessive or narcissistic; 'almost all [lovers] are shown to be travellers lured by the enchantment of a mirage'.[71] Further, Murdoch exposes many of her male characters' egotistical concerns. Typically, their obsessions with female characters derive from their own needs and desires devoid of any awareness of the woman's (or sometimes young boy's) subjectivity. Men enclose female characters ideologically, psychologically, emotionally and physically. Charles' obsession with Hartley and her subsequent incarceration in *The Sea, The Sea* is an obvious example. A central concern for Murdoch in her novels is that individuals can only love truly through unselfish attention.

Consequently, Murdoch addresses the tension between the imperfections of human love and the desire for the perfection of the Good that exists beyond the human realm. While she openly explores these themes in her fiction, however, she tends to mask them in her philosophical writings. In the plots of her novels, misplaced love is the source of evil while rightly directed love moves towards affirmation of the Good. The intrusion of the ego blocks the journey of the soul towards the Good. Cato's spiritual progression is thwarted through his unruly passions and self-delusion in *Henry and Cato*. Falling hopelessly in love with the young Joe and his romantic notions of living a good life ensure that he is doomed as a priest because his intentions are ultimately egotistical. The fact that he ends up murdering Joe is

69   Ibid., 492.
70   Ibid., 496.
71   Griffen, 'The Influence of the Writings of Simone Weil', 15.

emblematic of love that seeks to fulfil selfish desires and has no real concern for the being of the other person. In brief, Murdoch's view of love is not sentimental; she is aware that love can at worst be violent, is mostly ambiguous and not altogether the route to happiness. Nevertheless, it would appear that she believes in love as the means with which to achieve an authentic spirituality and morality. Eros, or the life instinct in Freudian terminology, is the driver on the path towards the Good. Murdoch defines Eros as

> sexual energy as spiritual energy [and] our life problem is one of the transformation of energy. [...] We must transform base egoist energy and vision (low Eros) into high spiritual vision (high Eros).[72]

Taking her cue from Plato, Murdoch sees a parallel between physical desire for another and the soul's desire for the Good. Eros is thus paradoxically the best and worst of human consciousness because it is both 'the place of most fundamental insight'[73] as well as 'the source of our greatest errors'.[74] Nussbaum is dismayed that Murdoch appears to lean towards Dante's vision of sexual love in *Purgatorio* as 'an impediment and source of delusion' as opposed to Plato's view in *Phaedrus* that 'sexual ferment [...] is a valuable [and necessary] part of the search for truth'.[75] However, although graphic sex scenes are absent in Murdoch's novels, there are occasions when the consummation of sexual desire clarifies a situation.[76] Further, Conradi's biography reveals that Murdoch did experiment with her own sexuality. However, perhaps based on her experiences of the sexual power that Elias Canetti had over her, it seems that she relegated sexual desire to the status of low eros. Her approach to sexuality was generally of a more pragmatic nature, comically illustrated through the character of

72   Murdoch, *Metaphysics as a Guide to Morals*, 24.
73   Murdoch, *The Sovereignty of Good*, 73.
74   Ibid., 103.
75   Martha C. Nussbaum, 'Love and Vision: Iris Murdoch on Eros and the Individual', in Maria Antonaccio & William Schweiker (eds), *Iris Murdoch and the Search for Human Goodness* (Chicago: Chicago University Press, 1996), 36–37.
76   Bradley's consummation of his love for Julian in *The Black Prince* is one obvious example. This is the pivotal moment where he begins to move towards the Good through love.

Leonard Browne, Tallis' father, in *A Fairly Honorable Defeat*, who declares, '[w]hat a rubbishy arrangement sex is [where] a projection upon one body is laboriously inserted into the hole in another'.[77] Murdoch does not deny the embodied nature of eros, but rather, recognises the need to exercise restraint and to direct eros through the will, towards the Good.

Levertov on the Lived Life

A passionate response to life corresponds to the urge to write for both mystics and creative writers. Levertov was of the opinion that much of academic writing (literary criticism in particular) was too 'narrow' as if it 'had been developed from a thesis'. She prefers writers who 'love the work and plunge into it for their own pleasure' – writers who 'open doors for the reader'.[78] And, despite the atrocities and evil she saw in the world, she continued to believe that life was still a cause for celebration. The journey through life was something to enjoy, not merely endure. One of her favourite phrases comes from the poet Rainer Maria Rilke: 'the unlived life, of which one can die'.[79]

Whether in her personal life or in her work, Levertov was a woman fully engaged with the world. Her poem 'O Taste and See'[80] testifies to her belief that, for a fully lived life, people need to savour all that life has to offer by making use of all the senses. Here she reverses Wordsworth's line '[t]he world is too much with us; late and soon'.[81] Levertov felt that humans needed to be awakened and aware of the world with all their senses. The whole gambit of human experience – 'grief, mercy, language, tangerine, weather' – is symbolised as fruit that should be hungered after, plucked and tasted to the full. This appeal to the senses is a stark contrast and radical departure from male

77   Murdoch, *A Fairly Honourable Defeat*, 63.
78   Block, Ed, 'Interview with Denise Levertov'. http://www.questia.com/PM.qst?a=o&d=5001524879
79   Levertov, *Light up the Cave*, 98.
80   Levertov, *Poems, 1960–1967*, 125.
81   This is the first line of William Wordsworth's poem 'The World is Too Much With Us', which appeared in *Poems in Two Volumes* (1807).

Western mystical traditions. For example, Bonaventure, although he starts his mystical journey in the material world in which 'we are led to behold God in vestiges', moves to an understanding that it is only through the soul that God is finally reached by 'reentering into ourselves [and] leaving the outer court'.[82] For Levertov, leaving 'the outer court' would have meant to ignore suffering and injustices she saw all around her.

Paul Lacey notes that one poem in particular, 'Conversion of Brother Lawrence',[83] aptly conveys Levertov's attempt to reconcile religious faith with the lived life.[84] She finds in this man an example of an uncomplicated life of contemplation. In particular, it is Brother Lawrence's ability to make his whole life a life of prayer lived in the presence of God. He does not 'exalt nor / avoid the Adamic legacy', but simply makes it 'irrelevant'. Levertov imagines him as being continually open to the presence of God so that within his being 'there life was, and abundantly; it touched your dullest task' so that every task was 'easy / Joyful, absorbed'. Levertov refers to him as someone who 'practised the presence of God'.[85] Lacey concludes that by projecting herself into Brother Lawrence's life, Levertov is able to envisage how 'our fullest identity' embodies itself in life and work.[86] For Levertov, of course, this life and work is that of a poet, which she obviously equates with the life of a religious mystic.

---

82 Bonaventure, 'The Soul's Journey into God', in *Bonaventure: Classics in Western Spirituality* (Mahwah, New Jersey: Paulist Press, 1978), 3.

83 Levertov, *Sands of the Well*, 113–14. Brother Lawrence was born in 1610 in France, served his country as a soldier, and joined a new monastery near Paris in mid-life where he spent most of his forty years serving the community as a cook and later as a sandal maker.

84 Paul A. Lacey, 'To Mediate a Saving Strategy: Denise Levertov's Religious Poetry'. *Renascence* 50 (1997) http://www.questia.com/PM.qst?a=o&d=5001524883

85 'Practising the Presence of God' was the title of a publication that circulated following the death of Brother Lawrence in 1691.

86 Paul A. Lacey, 'Denise Levertov: Testimonies of a Lived Life', in *Renascence* 53 (2001). http://www.questia.com/PM.qst?a=o&d=5001050780

Dillard on Extravagance

In *Pilgrim at Tinker Creek*, Dillard encourages her readers to 'take a wide view, look at the whole landscape, really see it, and describe what's going on here'.[87] From early on, she notes, 'If the landscape reveals one certainty, it is that the extravagant gesture is the very stuff of creation'.[88] Later she reflects, 'that there are so many details seems to be the most important fact about creation',[89] which she takes as evidence that 'the creator goes off on one wild, specific tangent after another, or millions simultaneously, with an exuberance that would seem unwarranted'.[90] The proliferation of species is itself a perennial mystery and a wonder. The word 'extravagance' epitomises Dillard's perception of the Creator. In return, she suggests that humans should respond similarly.

When advising aspiring writers, Dillard counsels, '[w]rite as if you were dying. At the same time, assume you write for an audience consisting solely of terminal patients'.[91] In *Holy the Firm* she makes the more overt claim that the urge to write is paralleled to a nun's passion for mystical experience through the metaphor of the moth that cannot resist the flame and is consequently subsumed within it.[92] A passion devoid of ego or the will-to-power renders itself metaphorically in the image of someone who bathes in the 'fires of the spirit'. Obviously, Dillard sees her role as synonymous to that of Julian's in the fourteenth century, and the type of the nun and the artist entwine in her new understanding. The artist must be in touch with the Absolute at base, which she called *Holy the Firm*:

> His face is aflame like a seraph's, lighting the kingdom of God for the people to see, his life goes up in the works; his feet are waxen and salt. He is holy and he is firm, spanning the long gap with the length of his love, in flawed imitation of

87   Dillard, *Pilgrim at Tinker Creek*, 11.
88   Ibid.
89   Ibid., 130.
90   Ibid., 138.
91   Annie Dillard, 'Write Till You Drop'. At the end of this essay, she refers to the dying words of Michelangelo: 'Draw Antonio, draw and do not waste time'.
92   Dillard, *Holy the Firm*, 16–17.

Christ on the cross stretched both ways unbroken and unthorned. So must the work be also, in touch with […]; spanning the gap, from here to eternity home.[93]

In *Holy the Firm* 'burning' is the dominant metaphor for all of creation yearning for the sacred, but burning equally represents the passionate urge to write.

On a more theological note, much of contemporary Christianity in Dillard's view has become blasé, suggesting that churchgoers 'seem like brainless tourists on a packaged tour of the Absolute'.[94] She thinks the eighteenth-century Hasidic Jews 'had more sense' as they lived and prayed in the realisation that life was short and unpredictable.[95] Likewise, the early Christians lived with the constant knowledge of possible persecution or death and the belief in imminent divine intervention. As it was for these early believers, for Dillard God is a wildly unpredictable God so that life must be lived at the edge.

The *via positiva* for Murdoch, Levertov and Dillard pivots around the cultivation of *eros* or passion. Eros is characterised by Murdoch as either high or low eros. Levertov on the other hand, exemplifies a passion for life that invokes plunging wholeheartedly into the tangible world. And Dillard revels in excess, embraces extravagance in the world as she sees it, and expects humans to respond similarly. Regardless of the specific perception, it would seem that it is only as embodied and passionate individuals that we can immerse ourselves in the *via positiva*, but this practice will inevitably incorporate the darker aspects of human life as well.

93 Ibid., 72. The reference to 'waxen' and 'salt' refers to the idea of a created being, as when she salts her breakfast eggs, and waxen is a reference to the moth in the flame that represents the mystic's desire to suffer in order to gain mystical insight.
94 Annie Dillard, *Teaching a Stone to Talk* (New York: Harper, 1993), 52.
95 Ibid., 53.

The Dark Side of Human Existence

Postmodern theologian Mark C. Taylor conceptualises the postmodern self as being both 'rootless and homeless', as someone who is 'always suspicious of stopping, staying and dwelling'.[96] Yet, the contingent is all we have, and the postmodern human is often reluctant to dwell upon the nastier aspects of existence, but we need to see it all. To explore this aspect of the *via positiva*, in this section we will examine the horrors found in the contingent, facets of suffering and injustice, and the fact of our own mortality from the perspective of the three writers under discussion.

Horror of the Contingent

Ultimately, we cannot pass by the darker side of existence that includes the 'natural' horrors found in nature, the fact of suffering and pain, and death itself. As faithful observers of their surroundings, Murdoch, Levertov and Dillard represent the horrors of contingency alongside its beauty, often piling up detail concerning certain events, which invokes feelings of revulsion and horror in the reader. Ultimately, they all aim to portray reality as it is, with no sentimental gloss. As Gatens-Robinson notes, 'The Western theological tradition has often found the natural world deeply puzzling [and] an embarrassment [...] with all its untidy intricacy, its fecund excesses, its apparent gratuitous cruelty.'[97] Somehow, too acute an observation of nature does not fit in with the idea of God as wholly good, just and loving as there is pain and suffering alongside beauty. Furthermore, feminist religious thinkers tend to romanticise nature, which Gatens-Robinson notes can leave us with 'a version of the problem of evil that is as

---

96   Mark C. Taylor, *Erring: A Postmodern Theology* (Chicago & London: The University of Chicago Press, 1984), 156.
97   Eugene Gatens-Robinson, 'Finding our feminist ways in natural philosophy and religious thought', in *Hypatia* 9:4 (1994), 207–22.

unworkable as that of traditional theology'.[98] By incorporating Murdoch and Dillard's representations of the world into theological reflection, however, a more realistic account of the human condition emerges. Levertov focuses more on the human influence on suffering so will not be included in this section.

Donna Gerstenberger outlines Murdoch's novels as dealing with 'the irrational in its various manifestations. The terrors of existence', which are 'rendered comic, pathetic and ridiculous all at once'.[99] The absurdity and randomness of human existence haunts the various plots. For example, the religious community at Imber Court in *The Bell* represents an attempt to keep such chaos at bay through an ordered life. By imposing strict regulations and boundaries, they hope to keep the darker side of life outside. An individual character who tries similar tactics is Effingham in Murdoch's novel *The Unicorn*, who as an 'intelligent hedonist' and 'happy egoist'[100] cannot face such reality:

> Effingham looked at the big struggling fish with pity and revulsion. It was dreadfully alive. Pip took it by the head, pulling it out of the net. He disengaged the line, and before Effingham could look away he had killed the trout, putting a thumb in its mouth and breaking its back by a quick pressure of his hand. Such a rapid passage, such an appalling mystery. Effingham sat down on a rock feeling slightly sick.[101]

Later, he faces a near death experience in a bog, which becomes for him an epiphanic moment. By facing reality, a reality shorn of its illusions, especially the fact of one's own mortality, where he realises:

> Since he was mortal he was nothing and since he was nothing all that was not himself was filled to the brim with being and it was from this that the light streamed. This then was love to look and look until one exists no more, *this* was the love which was the same as death. He looked, and knew with a clarity which was one with the increasing light, that with the death of the self the world becomes quite automatically the object of a perfect love.[102]

98   Ibid.
99   Donna Gerstenberger, *Iris Murdoch* (New Jersey: Associated University Press, 1975), 15.
100 Conradi, *The Saint and the Artist*, 163,
101 Iris Murdoch, *The Unicorn* (London: Penguin, 1966), 108.
102 Ibid., 167.

Such encounters are not always so positive, however. Moy has an encounter with a swan in *The Green Knight* that makes her realise that humans cannot hope to understand the processes of nature, which may seem alien to our altruistic sensibilities. Upon seeing a swan attacking a small black duck in the park, she sets out to save the smaller bird:

> Moy stepped into the water, waving her arms and shouting. She stumbled, trying to lift her feet from the mud, and blundered forward. The water splashed about her [...]. In an instant the duck became free [...]. Then as Moy steadied herself the swan was upon her, she saw the great wings, unfolded and in the surface water the big black webbed feet trailing like claws, as the swan fell upon her, pressing her down with its descending weight as it had pressed down the little struggling duck. Moy lost her balance and slipped backward seeing the heavy curving breast above her, the snake-neck like a rope of greying fur and for an instant, as if in a dream, eyes glaring in a mad face.[103]

Until this experience, Moy had maintained a sentimental view of nature, but this incident shocks her into facing the horror of the contingent. A creature with mythological renown as a symbol of grace and beauty is here portrayed with features such as 'claws' and a 'mad face', features more easily associated with beasts of terror. Effingham, however, does not learn from his encounter and carries on as before while Moy develops morally and spiritually through this sharp reality check.

Dillard's contemplation of nature takes this recognition of the horror within the beauty of nature to the extreme. She learns from the anomalies or absurdities as well as the wonder and beauty. The scandal of particularity is that things happen that appear to indicate a cosmic indifference to suffering, thus making our inevitable mortality all too obvious. Dillard observes this most keenly in the natural world. Whilst out on a summer walk, with her keen eye attuned to her surroundings, Dillard recounts an episode in which she stumbles across 'a very small frog with wide, dull eyes' and observed that

> he slowly crumpled and began to sag. The spirit vanished from his eyes as if snuffed. His skin emptied and drooped; his very small skull seemed to collapse and settle like a kicked tent. He was shrinking before my eyes like a deflating

103   Iris Murdoch, *The Green Knight* (London: Penguin, 1993), 175.

football. I watched the taut, glistening skin on his shoulders ruck, and rumple, and fall. Soon part of his skin, formless as a pricked balloon, lay in floating fold like bright scum on top of the water: it was a monstrous and terrifying thing. I gaped bewildered, appalled. An oval shadow hung in the water behind the drained frog; then the shadow glided away. The frog skin bag started to sink.[104]

The 'thing' she saw was a giant water bug that literally pulverised and sucked out the insides of its prey. For Dillard, this event is an enduring and potent symbol of the mystery of cruelty in nature, one to which she often returns. This encounter with seemingly pointless waste and the fact that every living being appears to be eating some other being becomes a centre-point of her engagement with a God who allows such horror amid beauty. She cannot help but see life reduced to what she terms the 'universal chomp'.[105]

This demonstrates that Dillard fully immerses herself not just in the beauty of nature but also in the tragedy. She does not observe the whole of nature in the hope of finding evidence of God – in fact the more she observes the more confused she becomes:

> Fish gotta swim and birds gotta fly; insects, it seems, gotta do one horrible thing after another. I never ask why of a vulture or shark, but I ask why of almost every insect I see. More than one insect – the possibility of fertile reproduction – is an assault on all human value, all hope of a reasonable god.[106]

Therefore, the realities of nature are at odds with much of theological doctrine and dogma. Nevertheless, the facts are inescapable. Dillard wrote a paper on Job early in her writing career so we know that she has an ongoing engagement with the purpose of suffering, but she does not pretend to have any answers for the dichotomy she perceives within creation.

Later in her career, she focuses more on the human plight in *For The Time Being*. She offers a profusion of random facts about our world throughout the book, and in Chapter One she starts with a catalogue of human birth defects: 'the bird headed dwarfs', children born with various bits of anatomy missing or grossly deformed. As it is

104 Dillard, *Pilgrim at Tinker Creek*, 7–8.
105 Ibid., 170.
106 Ibid., 64.

possible to give and receive love from these children and the fact that they are undeniably part of the mysterious creator's plan – who are we to question the God that allows such grotesque manipulations of the human form? In the same vein, she continues to recount natural disasters such as earthquakes, floods, famines and bubonic plague that kill people by the thousands. Equally, she refers to human evil in the form of the annihilation of species and mass genocides. She challenges her readers to think about how we should react to all this. It seems that Dillard herself reacts with a mix of wonder, lament and horror, but she also wonders where God is in all this. From her observations, she concludes that 'mostly God is out of the physical loop. Or the loop is the spinning hole in his side'.[107] In the end, she readily admits, 'I don't know beans about God'.[108]

Suffering and injustice

Soelle makes a clear distinction between 'natural' suffering as part of nature and suffering caused by oppression and domination of unjust systems. Further to this, in *The Unicorn*,[109] Murdoch clearly questions whether self-inflicted suffering can be redemptive. Through the disassociation of her mind from her body, Hannah voluntarily casts herself into the female role of an instrument through which the spirit speaks.[110] There seems to be a desire to repress femaleness and sexuality in Murdoch's characterisation of Hannah. In fact, through the character of Hannah, Murdoch evokes the strict enclosure of women religious mystics and the function they fulfilled for the Church. Conradi further suggests that this character's room represents a 'half Platonic Cave, half ascetic's cell'.[111] In any event, it is a tale about the distant Good. Hannah chooses the suffering of isolation in an attempt

107 Dillard, *For the Time Being*, 168.
108 Ibid., 169.
109 Gabriele Griffen informs us that this novel was based on Simone Weil's idea of the 'transfer of evil', in *The Influence of the Writings of Simone Weil on the Fiction of Iris Murdoch*, 60.
110 Ibid., 71.
111 Conradi, *The Saint and The Artist*, 162.

to satiate feelings of guilt for adultery, and others are only too happy for her to become a hapless scapegoat or quasi-mystical figure. Bajaj concludes that Hannah's self-imposed suffering can be interpreted on many theoretical levels, but at its core, it is based on egoism and is therefore not pure or vicarious suffering.[112] The unicorn is a symbol linking Hannah to Christ and Mary, but it ultimately becomes a redundant or false correlation.

As part of her demythologising of Christianity, Murdoch decentralises suffering as a means of atonement. This is most evident in her portrayal of the mystical Christ who appears to Anne Cavidge in *Nuns and Soldiers*. I turn to Siguna Ramanathan's concise analysis of this in *Iris Murdoch: Figures of Good* (1990) in which she closely compares the incident with Julian's account of encountering Christ in her *Shewings*. Anne was 'filled with a thrilling passionate joyful feeling that passed through her like an electric current',[113] and although, as Ramanathan notices, the apparition must have come from Anne's passions, but we cannot rule out emotions which can be unreliable.[114] Whereas Julian ponders every detail of Christ's suffering and physical wounds, when the suffering of Anne's Christ is mentioned, he curtly replies, 'I have no wounds. My wounds are imaginary.'[115] The reason behind this is Murdoch's belief that suffering has become sentimentalised in the Judaeo-Christian tradition. In *The Sovereignty of Good* she makes this explicit: 'It is very difficult to concentrate attention upon suffering and sin, in others or in oneself, without falsifying the picture in some way while making it bearable.'[116] Ramananthan interprets this to mean that, although moral improvement must inevitably involve suffering, Murdoch is reminding us 'that suffering must be the by-product of a new orientation and not an end in itself'. It is significant in this regard that Murdoch's Christ discourages sentimental feelings. The point of Anne's Christ is *love*, suggesting 'a practical,

112 Bajaj, *A Critical Study of Iris Murdoch's Fiction*, 108–9.
113 Murdoch, *Nuns and Soldiers*, 295.
114 Ramanathan, *Figures of the Good*, 108.
115 Murdoch, *Nuns and Soldiers*, 296.
116 Murdoch, *The Sovereignty of Good*, 73.

ethical Christianity divested of all its supremely beautiful consolatory imagery'.[117]

In short, for Murdoch, it is important to see pain and suffering for what it is. This is what happens to Anne:

> She was amazed to find her imagination flinching from his sufferings upon the cross as from an abominable, hardly conceivable torture. It was now like something she had read about in the newspapers, terrible things which gangsters or terrorists did to their victims. [...] How there were no angels, no Father, only a man hanging up in an unspeakable anguish, of which for the first time she was able to grasp the details. She felt appalled and sick...[118]

Rather than suggesting that Murdoch is misreading Julian, Ramananthan deduces that Murdoch, in fact, presents the core of the anchoress' understanding, as Julian ultimately moves beyond the suffering to the 'endless love' that Christ represents.[119]

Murdoch does not see suffering and pain as a means to achieving the good as affirmed within the Christian doctrine of redemption, but neither does she endorse an illusionary attitude that ignores its reality. Rather, she exemplifies the importance of acknowledging that suffering for some, such as for those who endured the Holocaust, is a part of reality that needs, on the one hand, to be overcome, but on the other, that must not be idealised. Furthermore, the roles of chance and individual responsibility are equal partners in events that life throws at us.

The central themes of Levertov's poetry spring from the conflicts between her 'capacity for joy as well as her anguish over suffering', presenting a duality of vision.[120] How to address this duality poetically (i.e., how can the poet feel and write about personal joy and the pain of others at the same time?) informed much of her work. This conflict also relates to the theological question: How can a just and loving God allow suffering to exist? The search for a unifying solution to these 'temporal' and 'eternal' questions is the underlying motivation of Levertov's life work.

---

117 Ramanathan, *Figures of the Good*, 110.
118 Murdoch, *Nuns and Soldiers*, 36–62.
119 Ramanathan, *Figures of the Good*, 112–13.
120 Little, Margaret Olivia, 'Seeing and caring: the role and affect in feminist moral epistemology', in *Hypatia* 10:3 (1995), 117–38.

Nelson argues that Levertov ultimately fails to produce 'a poetic world in which love is the goal; she would create a poetic world in which love is the greater power, but she cannot'.[121] She cannot redeem the harsh realities of war through poetic nostalgia. Levertov continually grappled with the problem of how to find personal meaning against the backdrop of human indifference to suffering, and ultimately, the most she can do is to incite the reader to take action. By the time she wrote *The Freeing of the Dust*, she is able to express the Vietnamese suffering without sacrificing her own *joie de vivre*. The turning point came during a visit to Vietnam where she witnessed the indomitable spirit of the Vietnamese people, and thereafter she is able to juxtapose joy and suffering. She indicates this balance in the poem 'In Thai Binh (Peace) Providence'[122] where she witnesses 'yet another child with its feet blown off' but also 'a boy and small bird both / perched, relaxed, on a quietly grazing / buffalo' as suggestive of 'peace within the long war'.

Dillard's most acute meditation on suffering materialises in *Holy the Firm* through her account of Julie Norwich, whose face is burnt off as a result of a plane crash. Dillard kept a newspaper cutting of a man who suffered burns by her mirror for two years to remind her of the pain that others experience. Human suffering, such as that experienced by burns victims, represents senseless suffering. However, the fact that creatures kill other creatures (thereby causing suffering) in order to survive is an entirely different matter. The fact that everything is eating everything else is a continual puzzlement to Dillard, and as Pamela Smith notices, in Dillard's experience, 'the story of nature […] is a story of eating'.[123] Earlier, in *Pilgrim at Tinker Creek*, she writes that survival is a matter of chance and circumstance, within which species must either 'chomp or fast'.[124] Such things remain perennial mysteries: the cruelty in nature, the suffering of people that continues despite our prayers and praise. Perhaps, Dillard speculates,

121   Cary Nelson, 'Levertov's Political Poetry', in Gelpi, *Denise Levertov*, 164.
122   Levertov, *Poems 1972–1982*, 22–23.
123   Pamela A. Smith, 'The Ecotheology of Annie Dillard: A Study in Ambivalence', *Cross Currents* 45:3 (1995), 341–59.
124   Dillard, *Pilgrim at Tinker Creek*, 240.

'beauty itself [is] an intricately fashioned lure, the cruellest hoax of all?'[125] Finally, however, casting doubt and despair aside, she concludes that 'beauty is not a hoax... Beauty is real.'[126] A wind borne maple key that crosses her path towards the end of *Pilgrim at Tinker Creek* provides the sign of hope, something that is 'blown by a generous unending breath'.[127]

The *Via Positiva* Leads to the *Via Negativa*

This chapter has argued that the *via positiva* employs cataphatic language and cultivation of amazement in the attention to reality, which Soelle affirms is tantamount to praise that is

> an aesthetic activity in which something is perceived, seen and made visible, extolled, celebrated, and sung about. It is loved out of darkness into light. [...] The oft-lamented spiritual impoverishment of today has to be recognized above all in this inability to praise life. People may see the clouds chasing along, feel the wind, and notice the fish playing in the water. Yet they may not see, feel, and notice because they are not amazed by it. Instead, they are caught up in themselves. Giving praise does not come on its own; to name what has been inflicted on life is something that suggests itself much more readily. Praise has no easy task because it has to be read into things, thereby getting close to the productive aesthetic state.[128]

This awe and wonder in the created world also spills over into ordinary experience within which the sacred is likely to break through at any moment. This chapter has shown that the world of particulars also includes suffering pain and inevitable death – something that these writers acknowledge exists alongside the beauty of the world. Rather than trying to make sense of these things, all three writers conclude that the most appropriate thing to do is to accept them as mysteries.

125 Ibid., 270.
126 Ibid., 271.
127 Ibid., 273.
128 Soelle, *The Silent Cry*, 185–86.

Unburdening theology from the necessity of explaining the dark side of existence allows a passionate, even erotic response to life in the here and now. Despite the horrors that Dillard witnesses during her encounters with nature, she can still end her book with an acclamation that depicts her as 'exultant, in a daze, dancing, to the twin silver trumpets of praise'.[129] However, as Soelle points out, 'to praise God is the first prompting of the journey, thus to miss God is another unavoidable dimension of it'.[130] It is therefore at the edge of the *via positiva* that the mystic is led towards the *via negativa*.

129   Dillard, *Pilgrim at Tinker Creek*, 277.
130   Soelle, *The Silent Cry*, 90–91.

Chapter Five
The *Via Negativa*: Living on the Edge

The Judeo-Christian model of a personal, predominantly male God who resides 'up there' has not satisfied a range of thinkers for several centuries. As a result, throughout the twentieth and into the twenty-first centuries, theological formulations concerning the nature of God have become increasingly vague and ambiguous. John A. T. Robinson captured these shifting perceptions in 1963 in his controversial book *Honest to God*:

> There are depths of revelation, intimations of eternity, judgements of the holy and the sacred, awareness of the unconditional, the numinous and the ecstatic, which cannot be explained in purely naturalistic categories without being reduced to something else. [...] The question of God is the *question whether this depth of being is a reality or an illusion*, not whether *a* Being exists beyond the bright blue sky, or anywhere else.[1]

There is a distinct mystical edge to what is otherwise a basic theological statement, and considering that this publication was a million-copy bestseller, it must have appealed to the public imagination. Robinson's assertion here and the interest his book generated was representative of an emerging concept of faith as encompassing the experiential, as opposed to that which is merely hieratic and passively received. In fact, at the time of writing, the present Archbishop of Canterbury, Rowan Williams, is promoting the mystical aspect of

---

1   John Robinson, *Honest to God* (London: Westminster John Knox Press, 1963) 55. John Robinson (ca. 1919–1983) was an Anglican New Testament scholar and at one time Bishop of Woolwich, who utilised and made palatable for the general public the best insights of theologians Paul Tillich, Rudolf Bultmann and Dietrich Bonhoeffer. He is seen as the founder of the progressive or liberal Christian movement in Britain. To more conservative Christians, Robinson's secularised Christianity had more in common with secular humanism than the traditional understanding of Christianity.

Christianity.[2] Archbishop Williams began his address for a remembrance service for those who had died in Iraq at St Paul's cathedral by quoting from the French Catholic poet Charles Péguy: 'Everything begins with mysticism and ends with politics'.[3] Much discussion has ensued as to what he meant by this, but for the purposes of this study, it is assumed that his quotation encapsulates the mystic way in postmodernity. Both Robinson and Williams recognise that humans exist in a tension between a tangible world of beauty and suffering and an eternally mysterious or unfathomable intuition of something 'out there'.

According to Louth, the classical understanding of mystical theology as found in Denys the Aeropagite states that the *via negativa* in classical mystical discourse represents the fact that

> [w]ith our understanding we can grasp God's manifestation of Himself in creation, but in the very act of understanding God's manifestation of Himself we realise that the One thus manifested transcends His manifestation.[4]

Writing at the beginning of the twenty-first century, the *via negativa* is characterised by Soelle in phrases such as 'being apart', 'letting go of possessions, violence and ego', 'missing God' and 'the dark night'.[5] The last two phrases readily equate with the classical mystical perception of a God who remains perennially beyond any human grasp, but in the postmodern world of Western capitalism and consumerism, Soelle promotes an additional political dimension consisting of resistance, personal renunciation of cultural norms, and a willingness to estrange oneself from prevailing ideologies and notions of the autonomous, individual self. She specifically defines this through the idea of 'unforming', which captures her determined belief that we need to let

2   Rowan Williams' insights in *Teresa of Avila* (London: Continuum, 2000) reflect Denys Turner's view that the self-understanding of mystics was not about a paranormal change in consciousness, but rather, represented incarnational or life-changing wisdom. Williams also recognises the role of artistic imagination in Christian spirituality. See his recent book *Grace and Necessity* (Morehouse: Harrisburg, PA, 2005).
3   http://news.bbc.co.uk/1/hi/uk/3181220.stm 27/10/05.
4   Louth, *The Origins of the Christian Mystical Tradition*, 172.
5   Soelle, *The Silent Cry*, 93.

go of our false desires and dependency on consumerism.[6] Accordingly, the third part of *The Silent Cry* is devoted to her revisionist reading of mystical sources, and in it she argues that mystical contemplation in postmodernity must move towards the *via activa* or just actions that confront oppressive systems of power, whether they be in society or religious organisations such as the Church.

Consequently, a position of resistance requires a radical self-questioning, and the first part of this chapter will explore ways in which the mystic in postmodernity must develop an ego that is un-attached to prevailing cultural norms and values that promote material possessions and violence. Soelle's notion of 'resistance' is the next topic to be discussed as an added gloss on medieval mysticism. The fourth section utilises the phrase 'the dark night of the soul' as coined by St John of the Cross, which is most popularly associated with the *via negativa* and refers to an inevitable stage of doubt and despair in which the seeker must grapple with questions such as the purpose of pain and suffering and the inevitability of our death. In fact, the writers we are discussing interrogate the dark side of the human soul to such an extent that the reader cannot help but feel implicated in the misfortunes of others. In postmodernity, this calls for an additional awareness of the darkness in each and every human soul and its potential for evil. The fifth and final section engages with what I have termed 'The Apophatic Edge'. Apophatic theology 'is concerned with our understanding of God, when, in the presence of God, thought and speech fail us and we are reduced to silence'.[7] Metaphors of silence, absence and nothingness are revitalised in the writings of contemporary literary writers despite the inadequacies of human language and concepts to capture mystery. However, in the end, these metaphors are insufficient to quench our desire to continue to find that unknowable mystery which Soelle links to 'missing God'.

6   Ibid., 92.
7   Louth, *The Origins of Christian Mystical Tradition*, 165.

Negation of the Self in Postmodernity

What is commonly termed 'postmodern angst' or 'fear of the abyss' manifests from the absence of the Good and/or the loss of belief in a God who will save us. In order to situate the *via negativa* within postmodernity, this section explores the ways in which the end of absolutes and the 'death of God' have contributed to a sense of meaninglessness that humans try to overcome through various means. In this regard, underpinning Murdoch, Levertov and Dillard's critique of both modernism and postmodernism is a critique of notions about the autonomous self (modernism) and the dangers of relativism (postmodernism) – which will also be discussed.

Postmodern Emptiness

Fox perceptively proposes in *Original Blessing* that the Enlightenment 'has rendered all of us who live in Western civilization citizens of light' and thus 'we have become afraid of the dark. Afraid of no light. Of silence'. He relates this specifically to our desire for 'more images, more light, more profits, more goodies', suggesting that a 'light orientated spirituality is superficial, surface-like', and a bid to flee from our own mortality and unavoidable deaths.[8] The legacy of the Enlightenment, especially in post-Kantian thought, has resulted in an exaggerated and somewhat distorted notion of the human subject. According to Lakeland's summation,

> [t]he freedom of the individual from all constraints upon thought means that the subject can become an object to itself, and can thus come to know itself ultimately as a transcendental subject over and against the world as a whole.[9]

---

8   Matthew Fox, *Original Blessing* (New York: Tarcher, 2000), 134–35.
9   Paul Lakeland, *Postmodernity: Christian Identity in a Fragmented Age* (Minneapolis: Fortress Press, 1997), 14.

Lacking a transcendental Other, autonomous selves have an unlimited sense of the their own intellect and power, which has a corollary in Murdoch's observation that

> we live in a scientific and anti-metaphysical age in which the dogmas, images, and precepts of religion have lost much of their power. We are also heirs to the Enlightenment, Romanticism, and the Liberal tradition. These are the elements of our dilemma: whose chief feature, in my view, is that we have been left with far too shallow and flimsy idea of human personality.[10]

Overarching this 'transcendent' yet 'flimsy idea' of the human subject is the steadfast confidence that Truth is obtainable through human reason alone. The way of negation in the mystical tradition robustly contradicts this in three key areas. Firstly, the goal is to lose the self or ego in order to find the self. Freedom is not achieved through the operation of rational thought but by letting go of false desires and empty dreams. Secondly, as Soelle asserts, the mystic acknowledges the need 'to continually seek new concepts, words, and images only to discard them as inadequate'.[11] Lastly, both in Platonic and religious mysticism, there is a transcendental Other, either God or the Form of Good, to which an individual orientates his/her soul or mind, whereas in existentialist or Kantian thought, for example, the human mind or self is all that there is.

Arguably, the eradication of transcendental absolutes in the socio-political world by 'The Man of Reason'[12] underpins a culture of dominance over marginalised peoples and the earth's ecology and has a detrimental effect on the human psyche. Soelle offers a portrayal of the world reduced to a huge supermarket where 'absent-mindedly yet at the same time absorbed in what we are doing, we push our shopping-carts up one aisle and down the other, while death and alienation

---

10   Iris Murdoch 'Against Dryness', in Conradi (ed), *Existentialists and Mystics*, 287.

11   Soelle, *The Silent Cry*, 67.

12   The title of Genevieve Lloyd's book, *The Man of Reason: 'Male' & 'Female' in Western Philosophy* (London: Methuen & Co. Ltd, 1995). She uses the term 'man' and 'male' in a metaphorical sense to refer to what she sees as an over-emphasis on 'male' attributes of logic and reason, especially the pretence to neutrality.

have the run of the place'.[13] In short, our postmodern existence would appear to encourage social and spiritual disengagement through lack of religious meaning and moral absolutes.

Drawing on Victor Frankl's theories, Lakeland suggests that the sense of meaninglessness that pervades society means that people opt for either 'one of two ersatz absolutes, the will to power or the will to pleasure'.[14] Individuals do either what everyone else does or what somebody tells them. In order to cope with this postmodern emptiness and the potential threats posed by moral relativism, we are witnessing an increase in fundamentalist ideologies globally. Soelle suggests that this represents a clinging to the God of our childhood through an inability to let go. Instead, she insists, we 'must leave God for the sake of God'.[15]

Murdoch's treatise on morality makes it clear that she was suspicious of individualistic thinking:

> The chief enemy of excellence in morality (and also in art) is personal fantasy – the tissue of self-aggrandizing and consoling wishes and dreams that prevents one from seeing what there is outside one.[16]

Central to her theory of moral realism is the relation of the individual to the Good that challenges existentialists, such as Sartre, who argue for the autonomy of the individual will as well as expressing a rejection of human liberalism. Two of Murdoch's novels, *A Fairly Honourable Defeat* and *The Time of Angels*, explicitly explore the possible dangers of a pervading sense of meaninglessness following the loss of transcendent absolutes in the postmodern world. Both refer to a common theme in Murdoch's work, that humans are 'essentially finders of substitutes'.[17] In all her works, most efforts to fill the void left by religious belief fall short of either finding happiness or being good.

13   Dorothee Soelle, *Death By Bread Alone: Texts and Reflections on Religious Experiences* (Philadelphia: Fortress Press, 1978), 8.
14   Lakeland, *Postmodernity*, 10.
15   Soelle, *The Silent Cry*, 68. Soelle draws on Eckhart's phrase: 'And so I ask God to rid me of God' here.
16   Murdoch, *The Sovereignty of Good*, 59.
17   Murdoch, *A Fairly Honourable Defeat*, 233.

A Fairly Honourable Defeat creates a plot within which a battle ensues between the will-to-power in the demonic (Murdoch's term for someone who displays characteristics of both the will-to-power and the will-to-pleasure) figure of Julius King and the will-to-love in the Christ figure of Tallis Browne.[18] In a similar manner to many Shakespearean comedies, there is an attempt by 'evil' (Julius) to conquer 'good' by disrupting the relationship between two homosexual men, Simon and Axel, or what Conradi terms as 'this quarrel between love and cynicism'.[19] Evil does defeat good – but only just. In the process, there is an underlying critique of political power and capitalism, which Murdoch understood to be a corruption based on the will-to-power or the elevation of reason.

Carel Fisher, as a representation of the demonic in *The Time of Angels*, functions as a prophetic warning of the possible dangers posed by an autonomous individual who loses the fear of holy retribution when belief in God ends. Through Murdoch's fictional portrayal of a priest who loses his faith, she suggests that human beings who no longer have a focus of attention on God present an opportunity for moral chaos to ensue. In this case, he asserts his power over others, turning his ward into a sexual slave and attempting to do the same with Pattie, the house servant. Due to the fact that Murdoch's demonic figures are universally men, she also seems to be implying that the male ego is particularly susceptible to this form of moral perversion. Women, on the other hand, are more likely to suffer from forms of self-negation, which is equally injurious to their spiritual and moral well-being.

Likewise, Levertov delves into the causes of violence within a Western society. In 'The Youth Program',[20] she addresses an issue that should concern everyone: what are we raising our children to be? The fact that they habitually spend vast amounts of time 'before their screens, playing a million missions a week' and have cast aside their 'teddybears, cuddly tigers, unicorns, [...] Arthurian picture books, [...]

---

18   In fact, it is a secular form of the Trinity with Leonard Browne as the Father to complete the triad.
19   Conradi, *The Saint and the Artist*, 215.
20   Levertov, *Evening Train*, 77.

cardboard theatres' are evidence, she argues, that children are not suf-ficiently feeding their imaginations. They are not experiencing the joys typically associated with childhood. Instead, they are growing up surrounded by a culture of war and destruction. Viewed as an inter-rogative, Levertov's provocative suggestion that someone should 'turn off the power' is an ethical question posed to all parents and Western society in general. Much of the postmodern emptiness experienced in today's society is, in Levertov's opinion, down to the plain fact that many of us have forgotten how to use our imaginations.

Dillard's main objective, her passionate wish to make people acknowledge the supernatural in the midst of a materialistic culture, is not that far removed from Levertov's conviction. Writing in an essay entitled 'Winter Melons', she explains the current state of affairs:

> Once again Gnosticism prevails in the West, but this time the creed is reversed. We are newly 'in the know', and what we 'know' is that no spiritual order or realm obtains whatever, and no god lives. We know that in the past men be-lieved in miracles, and thought the world was flat and wild geese wintered on the moon. Oh, they were a credulous bunch back then.[21]

The fact that farmers can grow melons in the winter is emblematic of how far our understanding and ability to manipulate creation has ad-vanced. Mysteries and miracles are on the wane and the function of Western knowledge, she states, is to 'de-spookify'. The Church has contributed to this trend, particularly with the notion of private prayer so that it was 'but a single, natural step' to secular existentialism. Indeed, it is possible to trace human progression throughout history from the point where everything had meaning to postmodernity where nothing has any meaning.[22]

The lack of a transcendent referent has the potential to create a relativistic notion of what it means to be moral. Or in colloquial terms, there is a pervading sense that 'anything goes' along with the accom-panying fear of anarchy and chaos. The question is how do we reclaim the mystical in our postmodern situation thus defined? Soelle finds Plotinus' statement apt for the contemporary world:

---

21   Annie Dillard, 'Winter Melons', in *Harpers* 248 (1974), 89.
22   Dillard, *Living By Fiction*, 136.

Man as he now is has ceased to be All. But when he ceases to be an individual, he raises himself again and penetrates the whole world. Then becoming one with the All, he creates the All.[23]

In short, in order 'to be all' the mystic must, paradoxically, find and lose the self at the same time in order to experience the epiphanic moment.

Mystical Moments

In Chapter Two, the concept of contemplation was discussed in part through the concept of 'seeing' and 'attention'. We also explored how an 'epiphany' is an event that links the mystic and the poet in chapter three. Here I want to concentrate on those brief, elusive, sometimes unexpected occasions wherein an opportunity for an epiphany or mystical illumination presents itself. With some practice, this can happen at punctuated moments throughout anyone's day – although the mystic has to be in a constant state of attentive preparation. Colloquially, busy people talk about 'taking time out', but for the mystically attuned person, these moments are where eternity can break through at any moment. My conjecture is that Murdoch, Levertov and Dillard help us to understand Soelle's push for the revival of 'the mystic sensibility that's within all of us'.[24]

Murdoch suggests that contemplation of nature and art can help us to detach from self-centred concerns. The following describes her experience of one such 'mystical moment':

I am looking out of my window in an anxious and resentful state of mind, oblivious of my surroundings, brooding perhaps on some damage done to my prestige. Then suddenly I observe a hovering kestrel. In a moment everything is altered. The brooding self with its hurt vanity has disappeared. There is nothing

23   Soelle, *The Silent Cry*, 213 cites Rudolf Otto, *Mysticism East and West: A Comparative Analysis of the Nature of Mysticism*, trans., Bertha L. Bracey and Richenda C. Payne (New York: Macmillan, 1962), 225.

24   Soelle, *The Silent Cry*, 301.

now but the kestrel. And when I return to thinking of the other matter it seems less important.[25]

So the apprehension of beauty in nature has the ability to suspend ego-tistical concerns. By focusing on some other self, 'consciousness has been altered by attention to an object outside its previous range'.[26] For Murdoch, this temporary loss of the sense of self operates psychically in the development of a moral sensibility, because 'when clear vision has been achieved, self is a correspondingly smaller and less interest-ing object'.[27] Such a moment is characterised by a movement of love towards others rather than the classical sense of the annihilation of the soul into God. In Chapter Two, we discussed how this movement of love is akin to Murdoch's notion of prayer.

In Murdoch's novels, this mystical moment is more often than not likely to manifest itself as a renewed awareness of, or reorientation of, moral consciousness. In *The Book and the Brotherhood*, for ex-ample, Gerard has a moment when he realises that his attention has been on stroking his own ego through his intellectual pursuits and that he has ignored the moral worth of others in the process:

> The thought that Grey [his pet parrot] might have starved to death was so terrible to Gerard that he suddenly sat bolt upright, and [...] there flowed into him, as into a clear vessel, a sudden sense of [...] all the agony and helpless suffering of created things. He felt the planet turning, and felt its pain, oh the planet, oh the poor poor planet.[28]

For Levertov, such moments similarly appear in sporadic, random and isolated events. In 'Sojourns in the Parallel World'[29] she recounts how it is possible to take a respite from 'our lives of human passions' through a response to 'Nature' with its 'insouciant life':

25   Murdoch, *The Sovereignty of Good*, 84.
26   Maria Antonaccio, *Picturing the Human: The Moral Thought of Iris Murdoch* (New York: Oxford University Press 2000), 136.
27   Murdoch, *The Sovereignty of Good*, 67–68.
28   Iris Murdoch, *The Book and the Brotherhood* (London: Penguin, 1987), 584.
29   Levertov, *Sands of the Well*, 49.

Cloud, bird, fox, the flow of light, the dancing
pilgrimage of water, vast stillness
of spellbound ephemerae on a lit windowpane,
animal voices, mineral hum, wind
conversing with rain, ocean with rock...

In such contemplation, it becomes possible to lose the self, 'because we drift for a minute'. Such experiences are, in Levertov's view, life changing because 'we lose track of our obsessions'. These brief moments represent the immersion of oneself in the whole,[30] a time to reconnect with the All as described by Plotinus.

Dillard has a similar sense of the dialectical nature of such occurrences. On the one hand, she states that '[i]t's all a matter of keeping my eyes open. [...] I watch every sunset in hopes of seeing the green ray.'[31] At other times, however, she describes herself as 'letting go' so that she 'sway[s] transfixed and emptied'.[32] These latter moments are the precursors to the 'mystic vision of a fusion which obliterates time and space'.[33] Dillard refers to these moments of 'seeing' as a 'pearl of great price' that 'may be found' but not sought – such illumination is a gift.[34] The most profound of these moments that sustained Dillard's spiritual life is the famous 'tree with the lights in it' incident in *Pilgrim at Tinker Creek*:

> [O]ne day I was walking along Tinker Creek thinking of nothing at all and I saw the tree with the lights in it. I saw the backyard cedar where the mourning doves roost charged and transfigured, each cell buzzing with flame. I stood on the grass with the lights in it, grass that was wholly fire, utterly focused and

30   Levertov 'Some Affinities of Content', in *New & Selected Essays*, 6. Levertov speaks of the influence of the Northwestern poets on her thought here that takes inspiration from Chinese and Japanese poetry as well as Buddhism, wherein people are more attuned to their living in relation to a landscape. She also acknowledges Native American spirituality and its concept of the spiritual presence in landscape.

31   Dillard, *Pilgrim at Tinker Creek*, 19. The green ray Dillard refers to is a natural phenomenon that occurs at sunset.

32   Ibid., 33.

33   Joseph, Keller, 'The Function of Paradox in Mystical Discourse', in *Studia Mystica* 6:3 (1983), 14.

34   Dillard, *Pilgrim at Tinker Creek*, 35.

utterly dreamed. It was less like seeing than like being for the first time seen, knocked breathless by a powerful glance.[35]

Dillard's 'vision' here represents the possibility of rare and precious moments when eternity breaks through into the temporal. Furthermore, the 'tree with the lights in it' is a metaphor for God's presence filtered into the world. This was to be developed more fully in *For The Time Being* through her use of Gnostic, Kabbalist and Hasidic sources.[36] The *via negativa* inevitably requires the loss or negation of self in order for the subject-object melding of classical mysticism; however, in Soelle's mystical vision, this loss itself becomes ego-ridden if it does not manifest as active resistance.

Resistance

That is, Soelle argues that the *via negativa* as a mystical praxis must also be a way of resistance:

> Concepts like asceticism, renunciation of consumerism, and using less and simpler ways of living make it apparent that the way of conscious resistance has to lead from ego-fixation (that globalized production requires a partner) to ego-lessness. What is missing is a reflection that shows more clearly how complicit we are ourselves in the consumerist ego that the economy desires.[37]

Essentially this means a willingness to jettison the will-to-power and the will-to-pleasure in favour of the will-to-love, which requires by definition that people put the needs and well-being of others before personal success or gratification.

---

35   Ibid., 36.
36   Dillard, *For The Time Being*, 48–49; 135–39.
37   Soelle, *The Silent Cry*, 229–30.

Political Resistance

As a dedicated political activist, Levertov embodied Soelle's ideal of resistance, and as we have already noted, many of her poems raise issues related to injustice and violence. Her areas of concern were vast: the environment, non-human species, and marginalized or oppressed peoples. But there is the reoccurring theme of awakening people to the moral responsibility that being human entails. Political activism was not her passion in the same way that poetry was, but rather, she instinctively felt that 'if one is an articulate person, who makes certain statements, one has an obligation as a human being to back them up with one's actions'.[38] Her anti-war stance in her political poems and appearances at demonstrations characterised her life and work of the sixties and seventies. She also addressed the social and environmental ills of modern society in her poetry. In particular, the section 'Witnessing from Afar' in *Evening Train* deals with issues pertinent to the anguish of contemporary society: environmental degradation, homophobia, domestic violence and – as we have already seen – children who are saturated in technology.

The first poem, 'The Reminder',[39] is a call to wake up from apathy. We may think 'that the malady we know the earth endures seems in remission', but the fact that swimming in lakes is ill advised shows that 'deep underneath remission's fragile peace, the misshapen cells remain'. In 'Tragic Error'[40] she delves deeper into the theological underpinnings of humans who have 'looted and pillaged' the earth's natural resources. She suggests that the charge in Genesis to 'subdue' the earth is 'miswritten, misread' and that our task should have been 'to love the earth, to dress and keep it like Eden's garden'. As Soelle rightly points out, it is only by beginning with amazement and wonder that 'makes the horror about destruction of wonder so radical'.[41]

Levertov was just as passionate about the atrocities of war and the absence of peace. She was, for example, a dedicated campaigner

---

38   Brooker, *Conversations with Denise Levertov*, 30.
39   Levertov, *Evening Train*, 67.
40   Ibid., 69.
41   Soelle, *The Silent Cry*, 92.

against the brutalities in Latin America, such as the death squads, which the American government, to her horror, supported. Therefore, she felt implicated in the suffering of others and her sense of guilt surfaces in many of her poems. In 'Thinking about El Salvador',[42] she refers to silence – the silence of those who cannot voice the violence and mayhem inflicted on them because of the countless heads that have been 'chopped off'. The other side of silence then is darkness. It is remaining silent despite being aware of various injustices to people in those countries dependent on the first world: 'my voice hides in its throat-cave ashamed to sound into that silence of raped women, of priests and peasants, teachers and children [...].' This form of silence that results from ignoring the sufferings of others is not that far removed from evil latent in the human soul.

Resisting Evil in the Human Soul

Murdoch, Levertov and Dillard display a keen perception of the latent evil in the human psyche. Their interpretations offer fresh insight, and Levertov and Murdoch incite their readers to become politically and morally aware of their part in the suffering of others. For Dillard, suffering in general remains more of a mystery. The fact that Dillard fails to act upon her observations of suffering could be where she falls short of the definition of a mystic in postmodernity, but this will be challenged in the last chapter. Mystics in postmodernity must shift their attention from the beatific vision imagined in life after death towards the suffering and injustices within the real world and the potential for evil within themselves.

Murdoch wrote several novels in the Gothic genre: *The Flight from the Enchanter*, *The Time of Angels*, and *The Unicorn*. It was within the Romantic Gothic that she was able to connect with her belief that 'in modern literature [there are] so few convincing pictures of evil'.[43] Within the closed structure of these narratives, Murdoch examines the perennial theme of good struggling against evil in a variety

42   Levertov, *Oblique Prayers*, 32.
43   Murdoch, 'Against Dryness', in Conradi (ed), *Existentialists and Mystics*, 294.

196

of disguises, but overall, love is associated with good and power is associated with evil. Additionally, however, she can fully develop her theory that fantasy is the opposite of reality as these two elements coalesce within this kind of novel. A demonic male figure, Mischa Fox in *The Flight from the Enchanter*, demonstrates this conception. In the words of the critic Zohreh Sullivan:

> Man's capacity to impose restricting patterns, fantasies, and myths on external reality is seen not only in his gods and leaders but in the ineffectual organizations he creates that also serve as unwitting accomplices of power and instruments of evil.[44]

Set in an isolated spot on the west coast of Ireland, *The Unicorn* deliberately recalls 'the Romantic sublime, with a plot borrowed from Victorian Gothic'.[45] The murky interior of Gaze castle and the imagery of light and dark form the sinister background for Murdoch to portray 'the idealisation of Hannah's sorrowing beauty among persons who are drawn to feel for her a love that enhances their own image of self'.[46] She is in fact a symbol of Murdoch's contention that people are enclosed 'in a fantasy world of our own into which we try to draw things from the outside, not grasping their reality and independence, making them into dream objects of our own'.[47] It is this failure that allows the baser side of human nature to surface. That is, the world as it really is becomes distorted as it is passed through the individual's ego, allowing that individual to rationalise and carry out the most terrible acts because they fit neatly into a fantasised worldview.

Levertov's vision of harmony and 'sacredness, even the sacramentality of temporal existence'[48] becomes increasingly blurred after 'O Taste and See' as she has come to realise that human beings are on

44   Zohreh T. Sullivan. 'The Contracting Universe of Iris Murdoch's Gothic Novels', in Lindsey T. Tucker, *Critical Essays on Iris Murdoch* (New York: G. K. Hall & Co. 1992), 65.

45   Conradi, *The Saint and the Artist*, 113.

46   David J. Gordon, *Iris Murdoch's Fables of Unselfing* (Columbia and London: University of Missouri Press, 1995), 130.

47   Murdoch, 'The Sublime and the Good', in Conradi (ed), *Existentialists and Mystics*, 216.

48   Gelpi, *Denise Levertov*, 4.

a self-destructive course in the exploitation of nature and their fellow human beings. Life's mystery has become a faded image for most people. *The Sorrow Dance* and next several volumes concentrate on themes such as the Vietnam War, the oppression of the Third World by capitalist imperialism, ecological disaster, racism and sexism. In these publications, she grapples with the problem of evil and postulates that collective and institutional violence disrupts a sense of harmony.[49]

The despair Levertov felt concerning unjust and oppressive regimes caused her to lose her poetic voice repeatedly. The sufferings she perceived in the world blotted out any sense of God's presence, and with it, her ability to find inspiration. It was for these reasons that she turned her attention to theodicy. It must have been with some difficulty, as she remembered her Jewish ancestors that she attempted to take an 'unbiased' look at Adolf Eichmann, the man tried in 1960 for his participation in the suffering of many in Nazi concentration camps.[50] In her poem 'During the Eichmann Trial',[51] Levertov specifically employs the metaphor of the eye.[52] This is the first of her poems where she seems to express her view of the social responsibility of a poet. This poem demonstrates her sense of a breakdown of social consciousness and disavowal of responsibility for the horrors of the Holocaust to which she wants to awaken people. The epitaph chosen by Levertov is a quote from Robert Duncan: 'When we look up each from his being'. Her suggestion is that all people must recognise through their shared humanity with Adolf Eichmann the latent potential for evil inside each and every one of us. Specifically, Eric Sterling argues, Levertov is suggesting here that people habitually adopt the blinkered stance that 'the fate of others does not affect their own lives;

---

49   Ibid.
50   Adolf Eichmann was a member of Hitler's regime who masterminded the 'Final Solution' to exterminate the Jews during the Second World War. He was eventually tracked down in South America and was consequently put on trial in Israel in 1960.
51   Levertov, *Poems 1960–1967*, 61–65.
52   Eric Sterling, 'The Eye as Mirror of Humanity: Social Responsibility and the Nature of Evil in Denise Levertov's "During the Eichmann Trial"', in Little & Paul, *Denise Levertov*, 139.

they refuse to see and to concern themselves with the suffering of others'.[53] Such a failure of empathy is by definition a failure of the imagination.

In the last section, 'The Peach Tree', Levertov imagines a scene in Eichmann's life prior to his Nazi crimes, a scene in which he murdered a Jewish boy for stealing a peach out of his orchard. Because of his inability to see the Jews as human he cannot imagine what it feels like to be this other person and does not hesitate to shoot him.[54] There is a further explanation of her stance on this in *The Poet in the World*:

> The imagination of what it is to be those other forms of life that want to live is the only way to recognition: and it is that imaginative recognition that brings compassion to birth. Man's capacity for evil, then, is less a positive capacity, for all its horrendous activity, that a failure to develop man's most human function, the imagination, to its fullness, and consequently a failure to develop compassion.[55]

Levertov shows through the Eichmann case how the failure to empathise or imagine the reality of others is in the first instance based on indifference, but led eventually to active barbarism or the murder of millions. In other words apathy might be the precursor to evil acts.

Levertov later engaged more specifically with the horrors of the Vietnam War. In 'Advent 1966',[56] Levertov reflects on the image of the 'Burning Babe' in Robert Southwell's (1561–1595)[57] well-known poem. Whereas Southwell imagines a 'pretty babe all burning bright' in whose heat the poet wishes to 'fry',[58] Levertov focuses on the plight of Vietnamese children who are burned alive by napalm, horrendous

---

53   Ibid., 141.
54   Ibid., 146. In a footnote to this poem, Levertov refers to the mention of this incident at the trial but stipulates that the details are not necessarily correct.
55   Levertov, 'Origins of a Poem', in *The Poet in the World*, 53.
56   Levertov, *Poems 1968–1972*, 124.
57   Robert Southwell was a Catholic martyr and poet. He was born in England and sent abroad for his education. He was an ordained priest of the Jesuit order who was tortured, imprisoned in the Tower of London and executed while on a mission to England. He was canonised by Pope Paul VI in 1970.
58   http://classiclit.about.com/library/bl-etexts/rsouthwell/bl-rsoutwell-burning_babe.htm

acts that are 'repeated, repeated, / infant after infant, their names forgotten, / their sex unknown in the ashes, / set alight, / flaming but not
vanishing, / not vanishing as his vision but lingering'. Here she criticises an ecstatic visionary for failing to recognise the sufferings of
others. Rodgers describes this poem as a 'death song' and an 'elegy
for the innocent', concluding that 'the distancing in the poem by juxta-
posing the sacred ritual with the infamy of Vietnam relieves the poem
of sentimentality and "personal" emotion'.[59] Through the ironical par-
alleling of the advent of Christ's birth with the 'cauldron of flame'
that is Vietnam in 1966, Levertov radically questions the political
stance of many Christians in the West.[60]

Nelson argues that Levertov ultimately fails to produce 'a poetic
world in which love is the goal; she would create a poetic world in
which love is the greater power, but she cannot'.[61] It is not possible to
redeem the harsh realities of war through poetic nostalgia. Indeed
Levertov continually grappled with the problem of how to discover
personal meaning against the backdrop of human indifference to suffering on the other side of the world. The most she could do was to
incite the reader to take action.

Dillard faces the same problem in *For the Time Being*. She dedi-
cates whole swathes of chapters to the topic of human evil. She recounts the horrendous act of cruelty by which the Emperor Hadrian
condemned Rabbi Akiva, and how the executioner Rufus proceeded to
separate the man's skin and muscles from his bones with curry-
combs.[62] Or what about the Chinese Emperor Qin who buried hun-
dreds of Confucian scholars up to their necks and allowed his soldiers
to behead them with axes.[63] It would appear that Dillard highlights the
deeds of tyrannical leaders who commit unspeakable acts against their
fellow humans in order to wake people up to the fact that God is not
going to step in and stop it happening, and make us, like Levertov,
aware of the human capacity for evil. Although there is a vast differ-

59   Rodgers, *Denise Levertov*, 96.
60   Ibid, 98.
61   Cary Nelson, 'Levertov's Political Poetry', in Gelpi, *Denise Levertov*, 164.
62   Dillard, *For the Time Being*, 28.
63   Ibid., 56.

ence between passivity in the face of evil and active participation in evil as regards to consequences, our writers certainly seem to be suggesting that the former may be implicated in the latter.

The Dark Night

The 'dark night of the soul' is a familiar phrase taken from St John of the Cross' book of the same name, a term that implies that doubt and despair are an inevitable stage in the *via mystica*. Contemporary psychoanalysis is more likely to refer to clinical depression or bereavement, but conceptually, these are the same things. Likewise, contemporary spirituality might refer to a spiritual crisis or fatigue. Either way, an encounter with the darker aspect of human quests is presented here as an unavoidable part of the search.

Doubt and Despair

What Levertov defined as 'the unknown' in her earlier poetry later became 'God revealed in the Incarnation',[64] but she acknowledges that she has never achieved the 'passionate knowledge' that her mother possessed in matters of faith.[65] In short, doubt for Levertov is never overcome completely. She understands that there is not a stage to be surpassed and followed by an absolute certainty in the matters of faith. However, she perceived that intellectualising could make matters worse. Too much thinking is detrimental to the life of faith, as she indicates in 'Flickering Mind:'[66] 'I elude your presence. / I stop / to think about you, and my mind / at once / like a minnow darts away.' It ends by asking 'How can I focus my flickering, perceive / at the fountain's heart / the sapphire I know is there?' Again she exemplifies

---

64   Levertov, 'A Poet's View', in *New & Selected Essays*, 241.
65   Levertov, 'Work that Enfaiths', in *New & Selected Essays*, 247.
66   Denise Levertov, *A Door in the Hive* (New York: New Directions, 1989), 64.

the need for balance — the 'sapphire' she knows is there refers to intuitive not factual knowledge. [67]

Levertov's conversion from an agnostic to believer was not an instant or dramatic one. She describes the writing of 'Mass' as a 'long swim through waters of unknown depth' as the final phase of her conversion.[68] She articulates her conclusions for overcoming the intellectual stumbling blocks concerning a God who continues to allow innocent suffering in her article 'Work that Enfaiths':

> God's nature, as Love, demands a freely given requital from that part of the creation which particularly embodies Consciousness: the Human. God therefore gives to human beings the power to utter yes or no – to perceive the whole range of dualities without which there could be no freedom. An *imposed* requital of love would be a contradiction in terms. Invisible wings are given to us too, by which, if we would dare to acknowledge and use them, we might transcend the dualities of time and matter – might be upheld to walk on water. Instead, we humans persistently say no, and persistently experience our wings only as a dragging weight on our backs. And so God remains nailed to the Cross – for the very nature of God as Love would be violated by taking back the gift of choice which is *our* very nature.[69]

Here she articulates the Judaeo-Christian understanding of freewill, where God gives human beings the choice to opt for good or evil. However, if there were no evil there would be no human choice. Levertov is also suggesting here that human choice means more than blindly obeying a set of rules. To reach beyond the dualities of time and space (which is basically a mystical concept) humans need 'to use their wings'. Resoundingly, faith for Murdoch, Levertov and Dillard is a matter of imagination rather that rational thought.

In her poem 'St. Thomas Didymus',[70] Levertov specifically explores the reality of doubt that faith inevitably encounters. 'Didymus' means twin, so here Levertov associates herself with 'Doubting Thomas'

---

67 An anthology that includes thirty-eight of Levertov's poems with religious themes took its title from this poem. See *The Stream and the Sapphire* (New York: New Directions, 1997).

68 Levertov, 'Work that Enfaiths', in *New & Selected Essays*, 250.

69 Ibid., 251.

70 Levertov, *A Door in the Hive*, 101.

in the Gospel narratives who doubts Christ's resurrection.[71] Despite having witnessed many miracles, Thomas is plagued with nagging doubt due to the continuation of suffering he sees all around him. It is only when he feels Christ's wound and his 'fingers [encounter] / rib-bone and pulsing heat' that he can testify to feeling 'not scalding pain, shame for my obstinate need, / but light, light streaming / into me, over me'. Following this experience, he can then move 'from tenuous be-lief to an illuminated conviction in which he can rest, like Lady Julian, from the nagging need for explanation'.[72] This emphasises Levertov's belief that mystical insight occurs through sensory and imaginative means as opposed to the probing of the intellect. As Dillard found out, rational thought is not much help in trying to understand the mysteries of suffering and pain.

In *Pilgrim at Tinker Creek* and *Holy the Firm*, the reader is fully aware of Dillard's anger at both the violence and waste in nature and the suffering of burn victims who experience no relief from their pain. Like Julian, Dillard wants intense experience of suffering in order to understand it, and it is clear that Dillard undergoes a 'dark night of the soul' on her forays into the wilderness. She endures a distinct stage wherein she suffers greatly due to her intense observations of nature that cause her to come to the pessimistic conclusion that 'evolution loves death more than it loves you or me'.[73] For Dillard, this is dia-metrically opposed to the human world, where '[we] value the indi-vidual supremely, and nature values him not a whit'.[74] This despair she endures comes about because of her sensory experiences of real suffering.

Her suffering intensifies in *Holy the Firm*. In her account of the young girl she names Julie Norwich, who receives horrific burns following a plane crash, her empathetic experience of the girl's suf-fering parallels Julian's desire for 'three wounds'. Dillard appears to conclude that the human situation is hopeless when she writes, '[k]knowledge is impossible. We are precisely nowhere, sinking on an

71   John 20:24–29
72   Levertov, 'Work that Enfaiths', in *New & Selected Essays*, 254.
73   Dillard, *Pilgrim at Tinker Creek*, 178.
74   Ibid., 178.

imaginary ice floe, into entirely imaginary seas themselves adrift.'[75] She sinks further into the realm of despair when she declares '[t]he universe is neither contingent upon nor participant in the holy [...] and we are not only its victims, falling always into or smashed by a planet slung by its sun – but also captives, bound by the mineral-made ropes of our senses.'[76] In a dramatic shift of perception, she then writes a few pages later, 'I know only enough of God to want to worship him, by any means at hand.'[77] The only response to the numerous brutalities that Dillard can think of is one of awe and worship, and so she sets off to the local parish church with a bottle of communion wine tucked under her arm.[78] An awareness and acceptance of suffering as part of the *via negativa* is the precursor to theological transformation and integration. Soelle grapples with this through suggesting that it is better to live with suffering than to exist in a state of numbness.[79] Soelle points to mystics such as Simone Weil who did not regard Christianity as a 'supernatural remedy for suffering', and believed that 'mystically experienced oneness of joy and suffering shines forth from the agony present in many experiences of suffering free of numbness'.[80] Twentieth century mystics such as Weil share this desire with Julian in the fourteenth century – to suffer in order to fully enter into Christ's passion. Weil took this to the extreme through living on the same rations as Jewish prisoners during the war, which resulted in her eventual death.

Soelle is careful to distinguish between two mystical trends concerning the nature of suffering: dolorousness (*dolorismus*) and compassion (*compassio*).[81] The former relates to what might be described as an obsessive preference to inflict pain on oneself, which bears all the hallmarks of sado-masochism. The latter, however, can be identified as vicarious suffering that truly allows one to enter into the suffer-

75   Dillard, *Holy the Firm*, 46.
76   Ibid., 48.
77   Ibid., 55.
78   Ibid., 63–64. It is on her journey to the church that she experiences the vision of Christ being baptised. See Chapter 2.
79   Soelle, *The Silent Cry*, 146.
80   Ibid., 151.
81   Ibid., 139.

ing of others. Julian experiences this in her vision of Christ's suffering when she bears his pain, as does Dillard mentally in the suffering of burns victim Julie Norwich. Although a fictional character, Julie Norwich was based on a neighbour's child who suffered similar burns. As noted previously, Dillard apparently kept a press cutting of a male burn victim who suffered the same fate twice to remind her of the pain in the world. Accordingly, suffering is

> not something bad to which one can surrender or stand up to in resistance. It becomes instead a reality that has something to do with the far-near God and that fits into God's incomprehensible love. The way of suffering that is not tolerated but freely accepted, the way of the passion, becomes therefore part of the disciple's way of life.[82]

It is possible however to 'stand up in resistance' to unnecessary suffering caused by human greed and the disregard of the suffering of others.

Befriending the Void

Antonaccio notices in Murdoch's *Metaphysics as a Guide to Morals* that there is a narrative flow that 'thematizes a pilgrimage from appearance to reality, from art to void, from the production of images to their dissolution or negation'.[83] The result is that, ultimately, we must move beyond familiar images and metaphors as they fail to capture the beyondness of the Good so that we must befriend nothingness or 'the Void'. Paradoxically, God's absence is where his presence is most keenly sensed.

Murdoch writes a small, penultimate chapter on what she terms 'The Void' in *Metaphysics as a Guide to Morals*, within which she puts forward her view that we need to 'befriend the void'. This is not

82   Soelle, *The Silent Cry*, 138.
83   Maria M. Antonaccio, 'Form and Contingency in Ethics', in Maria Antonaccio, & William Schweiker (eds), *Iris Murdoch and the Search for Human Goodness*, 136. This is most obvious in the first and last chapters entitled 'Conceptions of Unity', 'Art', and 'Void' respectively.

exactly unforeseen, as her life's work has centred on the need to get past sentimental or fantastical notions of existence as futile attempts to fill the void. Whilst not wishing to diminish the real agony and pain of people's lives, she suggests that in some ways we can learn from the void in that coming to grips with it is 'good for the soul'.[84] She refers to the classical dark night of the soul as the 'abyss of faith into which one falls',[85] and Murdoch believes a disavowal of this void or reluctance to face it leads to the filling it with fantasy that prevents progress. This is apparent in *The Bell*, where Murdoch communicates Michael's grief at finding the dead body of Nick this way: 'the landscape was blotted out'.[86] This is also a critical point in the narrative when he must absorb his pain and suffering in order to continue, to separate from his ego by realising he will never become an ordained priest.

The metaphor of the sea in biblical, mythical and philosophical texts invariably emerges as a representation of the Void, and indeed that image is one Murdoch repeatedly employs. In *The Sea, The Sea*, Charles Arrowby, the protagonist and narrator, imagines he will retire from his life as a famous stage actor to the sea to harmonise his life. However, he soon finds that the sea 'is not a place of rest, peace and knowledge [...] nor does it provide spirit over his parched life'.[87] Although he considers himself a strong swimmer, he finds himself constantly challenged by the sea, metaphorically representing the constant battering to his ego. Here Murdoch also powerfully evokes the metaphor of the sea to signify the realm of contingency within which human beings are subject to random instances of chance and to mortality.[88] A series of unforeseen and coincidental events forces Charles to come to terms with his own mortality and to ponder the emptiness of his past relationships with women. The sea mocks his desire to

---

84   Murdoch, *Metaphysics as a Guide to Morals*, 500.
85   Ibid., 501.
86   Murdoch, *The Bell*, 297.
87   Dipple, *Work for the Spirit*, 299.
88   Peter J. Conradi, 'Iris Murdoch and the Sea', in *Études Britanniques Contemporaines* 4 (Montpellier: Presses universitaires de Montpellier, 1994), http:// ebc.chez-alice.fr/ebc41.html

withdraw from the world to 'repent of egoism'.[89] Furthermore, the sudden death by drowning of his surrogate son Titus functions as a cautionary tale for the reader to remind them that life's tragedies should not be glossed over by a false sense of escapism. Inevitably, it is difficult to perceive a sacred presence at such times.

The belief that God is present in absence and that 'only in a vision of utter emptiness can the presence of God be perceived'[90] is a profound and unfathomable paradox; faith is only retained by the merest of tenuous threads due to belief in this unseen presence. In 'Suspended',[91] Levertov depicts this struggle in the fluctuations between belief and unbelief:

I had grasped God's garment in the void
but my hand slipped
on the rich silk of it.
The 'everlasting arms' my sister loved to remember
must have upheld my leaden weight
from falling, even so,
for though I claw at empty air and feel
nothing, no embrace,
I have not plummeted.

Despite her floundering faith, the poet is able to draw comfort from a sense of God's presence in his absence. George Steiner refers to this as the 'flickering of presence and absence' of God, which is of course characteristic of belief in postmodernity.[92]

Levertov addresses this issue in 'Mid-American Tragedy',[93] in which homophobia and unwillingness to face the void leads to the inability to love. A son, who is gay and has, presumably, contracted the AIDS virus, remains shut in a prison of silence and pain. More concerned with external appearances and unable to face up to the fact of their son's illness (probably due to the sexual nature of the disease);

89   Murdoch, *The Sea, The Sea*, 3.
90   James Gallant, 'Entering No-Man's Land: the Recent Religious Poetry of Denise Levertov', in *Renascence* (1997/1998) 50:1–2.
91   Levertov, *Evening Train*, 119.
92   Steiner, *Real Presences*, 123.
93   Levertov, *Evening Train*, 70.

the parents have built up a wall of denial. Instead, they cover their own emotional pain with fantasies of 'a trip to Disney World' and constant chatter while 'Jingle Bells pervades the air'. They do not know how to love and cannot therefore listen to their son or open their hearts to him. They cannot give 'the healing silence' that love requires due to their own biases concerning his sexual orientation and their denial of death. Again, Levertov manages here to rouse intense emotions in the reader in order to make them feel the injustices of social prejudices. By making us feel the terrible isolation of the dying son, we are stimulated to question our own biases and become aware of the walls we build around our own lives to keep death and the pain of others at bay.

It is in her one and only novel, *The Living*, that Dillard explores ways to come to grips with the fact of our mortality, or to accept the inevitability of death and therefore to 'befriend the void'. An example of this is an incident where the character Obenchain informs Clare Fishburn, who is one of the main protagonists, that he will kill him in the near future. Obenchain represents the rational philosopher who thinks that all life is in the mind and speculates that this threat will give him power over Clare by making his life impossible. On the contrary, Clare becomes exhilarated by the acceptance of the inevitability of his own death and is enabled to immerse himself more fully than ever before in the joy of living. Acceptance of the predictable and unavoidable brings freedom.

In *Teaching a Stone to Talk*, Dillard, despite her best efforts, concedes that nature does not reveal God, hence the title of the book. With a note of exasperation, she writes:

> You empty yourself and wait listening. After a time you hear it: there is nothing there. [...] You feel the world's word as a tension, a hum, a single chorused note everywhere the same. This is it: the hum is the silence. Nature does utter a peep – just this one. The birds, the insects, the meadows and swamps and rivers and stones and mountains and clouds: they all do it; they all don't do it. There is a vibrancy to the silence, a suppression, as if someone were gagging the world. But you wait, you give your life's length to listening, and nothing happens. [...] The silence is not actually suppression; instead it is all there is.[94]

94   Dillard, *Teaching a Stone to Talk*, 90.

She is not suggesting here that God is absent, but rather, that he is silent, so 'until Larry teaches his stone to talk, until God changes his mind, or until the pagan gods slip back to their hilltop groves, all we can do with the whole human array is watch it'.[95] The fact that life is a blessing, despite the fact of death and suffering, was an underlying theme of Julian's theological reflections, and likewise, Murdoch, Levertov and Dillard engage with the desperation that haunts human existence to suggest that we should accept with grace those things we cannot change and work diligently to correct those societal evils that we can.

The Apophatic Edge

In postmodernity, the meaning of both language and the self are under scrutiny, leading to a inconsistency between theories and experience of self: That is, humans have long depended on the functionality of language, and to one degree or another, on the dependable notion of selfhood, whether as a subjective statement or as an objectifiable body. Postmodernity has taken both of these away and neither language nor selfhood is definitive. In the discussion that follows, it will be suggested that the continuing quest to find language to express meaning is paradoxically a futile and yet necessary part of the *via negativa*, which is chiefly accomplished by embracing the concept of mystery as a theological category. Rather than denying subjectivity totally, there follows a suggestion that the temporary loss of self facilitates mystical and creative insights.

95   Ibid. Larry, Dillard tells us, is a man who lives on her island and is trying to get a stone to talk. She obviously finds it a useful analogy for her own mystical quest.

Where am 'I' in Mystical and Creative Pursuits?

Soelle utilises Eckhart's phrase 'Go where you are nothing' repeatedly to emphasise how important she feels it is that we free ourselves of our egos.[96] The way of nothingness is commonly used within the mystical apophatic tradition to indicate both the loss of self and the nothingness of God. In *Ascent to Mount Carmel*, for example, John of the Cross advocates 'the cleansing and the purging of a soul' as a necessary precursor to experiencing the presence of God.[97] In post-modernity, Thomas A. Carlson poses the question of whether 'the creative self-expression of God, which issues from and returns to Nothingness is imagined perfectly in the creative self-expression of the human'.[98] What Carlson suggests here is that God is only made visible through human creation but in such a way as it renders the individual invisible to him or herself.

In the same way, Earle Coleman suggests that 'greatness in art or religion requires a non-egoistic answer to the question: Who am I?'[99] That is to say, the true aesthetic experience requires the suspension of the egotistical self in order for the subject (the writer in this case) to merge with the object of attention. Coleman further comments that an artist's 'narcissistic preoccupation with finding his self' will eventually result in the loss of the creative self – in order to create the artist must become 'a vessel that is empty of ego'.[100] Coleman usefully clarifies this by asserting that there are existential and conceptual links between the creative artist and the religious contemplative as indi-

---

96 I have been unable to find out whether this is a direct quote, a paraphrase by Soelle, or something that has got lost in translation. It does however capture the general focus of Eckhart's thought paralleled in phrases such as 'where the creature stops, there God begins to be', and 'go out of yourselves'. Edmund Colledge, *Meister Eckhart* Vol. 2 (New York: Paulist Press), 184.

97 John of the Cross, *Ascent to Carmel* at http://www.ccel.org/ccel/john_cross/ascent.pdf, 68.

98 Thomas A. Carlson, 'Locating the Mystical Subject', in Kessler & Sheppard, *Mystics*, 228–29.

99 Earle J. Coleman, *Creativity and Spirituality: Bonds between Art and Religion* (Albany: State University of New York Press, 1998), 73.

100 Ibid., 73–74.

vidual selves. This also opens up a controversy over the extent that the author is justified in transposing 'the self' into the literary work of art. While Murdoch clearly avoids the confessional approach, she does admit that the author is never completely annihilated in the text. Many of Levertov's poems feature a grappling with the social and gender roles associated with being a woman and yet she was a firm believer in the non-confessional approach. Additionally, although Dillard on the surface appears to be writing spiritual autobiography, it is clear she writes from the perspective of a partially fictional author.

Leo Schneiderman depicts Murdoch's use of imagination as 'a non-chimerical process' that pays 'attention to the uniqueness of individuals, without subjective distortion dictated by the author's unconscious conflicts or ideological obsessions'.[101] Consequently, to produce an authentic work of art, the author's subjective and unconscious distortions' typically experienced in egotistical fantasies must be purged from the text. Always keen to maintain a sharp distinction between her philosophical works and her novels, Murdoch proposes that each requires a different mode of writing:

> Philosophical writing is not self-expression, it involves a disciplined removal of the personal voice. [...] But there is a kind of self-expression which remains in literature, together with all the playfulness and mystification of art.[102]

In Murdoch's opinion, the novelist needs to maintain a creative tension between objective depiction of the world around her and subjective experience and self-expression. The philosopher, by pretending to be wholly objective, is perhaps under the greater illusion or is hindered at the very least by a lack of imagination.

Murdoch provides the most vivid portrayal of these tensions in her novel *The Black Prince*. Here Murdoch explicitly examines the spiritual quest of a writer, but in such a way that the role and gender of the author are deliberately confused. In this novel, she splits her own conflicting desires and views on writing between two characters, the

---

101 Leo Schneiderman, 'Iris Murdoch: Fantasy vs. Imagination', in *Imagination, Cognition and Personality*, 16:4 (1996–97), 379.
102 Iris Murdoch, 'Literature and Philosophy', in Conradi (ed), *Existentialists and Mystics*, 5.

male narrator Bradley Pearson and his protégé Arnold Baffin. While Bradley experiences writer's block, waits for his Muse to inspire him, and is committed to the elusive 'spiritual and artistic goal of self-transcendence',[103] Baffin appears not to have much sense of ego and approaches writing in a pragmatic way.[104] Interestingly, but perhaps not surprisingly, Baffin is portrayed as the more successful of the two.

Baffin, like Murdoch, commands a very wide readership and similarly confronts the uncertainties of critical reception and inevitably mixed responses. Like Baffin, Murdoch writes out of evident enjoyment, as a writer who delights in the creation of separate, self-contained fictional worlds. But at the same time, she is able to project her more personal sense of connection between artistic, erotic and religious experience through the meditative narration of her *persona*.[105] It is through the portrayal of these two writers that Murdoch reveals some of the uncertainties and pretensions that accompany the literary life. As she says through the 'mask' of Baffin, 'every book is the wreck of a perfect idea' and 'it would be unthinkable to run along beside it whimpering "I know it's not good."' One keeps one's mouth shut for 'one must do it and keep on and on and on trying to do it better'.[106]

Levertov was deeply opposed to confessional poetry. In an interview with Sybil Estees, Levertov stated,

> I don't think that a lot of confessional poetry *is* good poetry. Sometimes poets writing in confessional modes are gifted poets, if their language instinct is good. But I think that this is the exception rather than the rule. As I understand it, the confessional poem has as its motivational force the desire to unburden the poet of something which he or she finds oppressive. But the danger here is reducing a work of art simply into a process of excretion. A poem is not vomit! It is not even tears. It is something very different from a bodily purge.[107]

103   Deborah J. Johnson, *Iris Murdoch* (Brighton, Sussex: The Harvester Press Ltd, 1987), 45.
104   Ibid.
105   Ibid.
106   Murdoch, *The Black Prince*, 172.
107   Sybil, Estess, 'Levertov Interviewed by Sybil Estess', originally appeared in Joe Bellamy (ed), *American Poetry Observed: Poets on Their Work*, University of Illinois 1984), http://www.english.uiuc.edu/Maps/poets/gl/levertov/estess .htm

What Levertov implies here is that confessional poetry is not creative. Paradoxically, according to Dillard, a 'fiction of aestheticism' is comparable to 'a kind of *via negativa* in which the writer [...] finds himself by losing himself'.[108] Dillard recounts her own joy during the writing of her first novel: 'to switch to fiction was really wonderful because you get rid of the daggone [sic] increasingly empty narrative eyeball. The "I" person whose voice I was getting truly sick of.'[109] Dillard's narrative voice is, as we have seen, partially fictional, but she shows an awareness of the dangers of lapsing into too egotistical a perspective. Using the creative voice to express individual anxieties or to expunge deep-seated psychological distress is not the purpose of writing for Murdoch, Dillard and Levertov. Indeed, the diminishment of ego proves to be a source of creative energy for all three of these popular writers.

Losing The Ego

All humans in Murdoch's view are 'by nature selfish and sunk in a reality deformed by their own fantasies'.[110] Close attention to reality enables a person to purge these 'fantasies' and illusions that prevent clear vision, which instigates 'a transformation of the self through the purification of the psychic eros'.[111] It is interesting to note that this subtly reinvigorates the classic Purgative Way as the first stage of the mystical search in a postmodern context. David Perrin defines *purgatio* as being essentially a move from 'self-centredness' to 'other-centredness', referring to the desire to lose the self in order to unite the soul with God, of whom Jesus Christ is the exemplar. For some religious ascetics this has historically led to a highly disciplined life or permanent withdrawal from the rest of the world. In traditional mysticism, success rests on the seeker's willingness to hand all aspects of his/her

108   Dillard, *Living by Fiction*, 156.
109   Mary Cantwell, 'A Pilgrims' Progress', http://www.nytimes.com
110   Maria Antonaccio, *Picturing the Human: The Moral Thought of Iris Murdoch* (New York: Oxford University Press, 2000), 15.
111   Ibid.

life over to God, so that his grace can enter and redeem the individual soul.[112] As a development to this, Murdoch argues that in postmodernity the moral agent is required, through an act of will, to orientate his/her life towards the Good and others, as opposed to an illusionary God figure that will make all things good. In effect, this means a move from retreating to the inner, passive self towards actively attending to the needs of others.

Murdoch highlights the dangers present in postmodernity – the focus on the self only provides illusions of happiness. This concept surfaces in the novel *Henry and Cato*, in which the two brothers operate as metaphors for the modern and postmodern understanding about God. Henry seeks the Good in the secular world, while Cato turns to religious orders. In the latter's case, the ego diminishes in the classical mystic way, but in the case of the former, individualism in the context of postmodern atheism and religious fundamentalism allows the ego to flourish. Henry is writing a book on the life of artist Max Beckmann, an artist who 'crammed his canvases with tortured images' characteristic of a troubled society. But it was the image of Beckmann himself which provided a role model that Henry wished to emulate:

> Henry envied that vast self-confidence, that happy and commanding egoism. How wonderful to be able to look at oneself in a mirror and become something so permanent and significant and monumental. [...] That great calm round face was a light in Henry's life. Two-wived Beckmann treading underground paths of masculine mysticism which linked Singorelli to Grünewald, Rembrandt to Cézanne.[113]

Ironically, Beckmann himself struggled constantly to assert his ego, especially in his fight to be accepted as an artist in his homeland.[114] Therefore, through Henry's affinity with Beckmann, Murdoch is able to illustrate 'both the inadequacies that fuel a lack of self-esteem and

112 David Perrin, 'The Purgative Way', in Philip Sheldrake, *The New SCM Dictionary of Christian Spirituality*, 517–18.
113 Iris Murdoch, *Henry and Cato* (London: Penguin, 1988), 13.
114 See Charles Kessler, *Max Beckmann's Triptychs* (Cambridge, Massachusetts: The Belknap Press of Harvard University Press, 1970), and Max Beckmann, *On My Painting* (New York: Buuchholz Gallery, Curt Valentin, 1941).

the egocentric delusions that help to transcend them'.[115] Murdoch here suggests that there is a delicate balance between self-defeating fatalism and healthy self-assertion. Interestingly, it is through a female character, Henry's girlfriend Colette, that Murdoch is able to illustrate this best, thereby replacing the illusionary 'masculine mysticism' that Henry holds dear with Colette's assertive claim on Henry. The following is addressed to his latest girlfriend, Stephanie: 'Miss Whitehouse, I just want to tell you this. I am going to marry Henry Marshalson. I have known him and loved him all my life and he belongs to me. That's all. I am going to marry Henry. He is mine. Good-bye.'[116] This pragmatic approach seems preferable to fantasy or illusions. While Colette is not an ideal 'good' person, Murdoch appears to be saying that selfish behaviour is sometimes warranted and is to be preferred to self-negation and a distorted vision of the self.

In many of Murdoch's novels, a passage through troubled waters is a metaphor for the self grappling with its own psychic energy and signifies illumination of one's self and an apprehension of others. This is also a common metaphor in mystical writing. Soelle tells us that it represents 'the depth into which the soul penetrates when it learns to deny itself'.[117] Anne Cavidge's experience of swimming in the sea is a good example of this in *Nuns and Soldiers*. Despite being a strong swimmer, she nearly succumbs to the sea but battles her way to shore. Her survival of this incident parallels her spiritual pilgrimage from the impersonal Christ of her religious order to a secular personalised Christ. Tim Reede, in the same novel, also has to face trial by water. At one point, he is swept downstream by a 'water demon' or fast running stream during his visit to France. This forces him into an awareness of 'the fragile mortality of his own body'[118] and resolves his earlier encounter with the 'large circular pool of clear water [where] he was aware of the absolute silence, the absolute solitude, the darkening

115 Anne Rowe, *The Visual Arts and the Novels of Iris Murdoch* (Lewiston; Queenston; Lampeter: The Edwin Meller Press, 2002), 98.
116 Murdoch, *Henry and Cato*, 243.
117 Soelle, *The Silent Cry*, 84.
118 Murdoch, *Nuns and Soldiers*, 156–58.

air' from which he fled in a panic.[119] Clear and calm waters represent a mind freed from the clutter of distortion and ego, a consciousness that has been purified. 'The absolute silence' of a mind freed from the ego, which disallows easy consolations, is what Tim initially runs from; but he returns to this same state eventually and accepts it. Rather than creating more fear, his attention to reality provides him with peace.

This is of course more complex for many women who may need to find themselves before they lose themselves. Whereas a patriarchal culture allows men certain clarity of self almost by default, women can struggle to find an identity within the larger social construct. For many women, writing is the medium through which this happens, and among the writers we are discussing, this is more apparent in Levertov's work. In 'Relearning the Alphabet'[120] for example, Levertov depicts woman as the hero of the myth. She is both the seeker and the one who is found – the one who eventually 'rediscovers her authentic self'.[121] 'In childhood dream-play I was always / the knight or squire, not / the lady.'

Although, as Dillard writes, 'a fiction of aestheticism' is comparable to 'a kind of *via negativa* in which the writer [...] finds himself by losing himself',[122] the use of detailed descriptions of landscape is a common narrative device to depict this dynamic. One landscape in particular that appears to captivate Dillard is the open spaces of the frozen Arctic, which contrasts sharply with the dizzying array of detail Dillard describes at Tinker Creek. In particular, she has a lasting fascination with the primitive lifestyle of indigenous people who live there. She explains in a 1981 interview that she uses them 'and the spare landscape in which they live as an emblem for the barren landscape of the soul: the soul's deliberate preparation for the incursions of the Divine'. Primitive peoples, in Dillard's expansive view, are more able to attune themselves to the sacred through an intimate connection

119   Ibid., 152.
120   Levertov, *Poems 1968–1972*, 90–100.
121   R. B. Duplessis, 'The Critique of Consciousness and Myth in Levertov, Rich, and Rukeyser', in Gelpi, *Denise Levertov*, 226.
122   Dillard, *Living by Fiction*, 156.

216

to their environment. The climatic and seasonal peculiarities of these northern climes are especially suited for mystical illumination.[123] The extremes of dark and light in this landscape also parallel the metaphorical 'dark night of the soul' and the contrasting light of illumination, and provide an uncluttered horizon upon which to contemplate.

In all her keen observations of nature, however, Dillard is acutely aware of the need to empty the individual ego for mystical insight to occur. It is only by losing her consciousness of herself that she can really 'see'. Dillard additionally reflects upon the ironic fact that our consciousness is what uniquely separates us from God and other creatures. 'It was a bitter birthday present from evolution, cutting us off at both ends', she writes.[124] This does not deter her, however. Recalling an episode watching muskrats, she writes, 'I was focused for depth. I had long since lost myself, lost the creek, the day, lost everything but still amber depth.'[125] Here Dillard displays the archetypal characteristics of passive contemplation that requires a relinquishment of individual ego. Despite the fact that Dillard perceives the power of the Sacred as mostly ambiguous, this does not prevent a peaceful surrender of self into all that is.

Celebrating Mystery

It is not surprising that there is a linguistic connection between the English words 'mysticism' and 'mystery' – both derive from the Greek word *musterion*. Not coincidentally, integral to the *via negativa* is the acceptance of the mystery and incomprehensibility of that which is called God. In contrast to the God who reveals himself through Holy Scriptures, the incarnation of Christ in Christianity, and specially chosen prophets as in Judaism and Islam, the Good as defined by Murdoch is both indefinable and always beyond our grasp.[126] This

---

123   Karla M. Hammond, 'Drawing the Curtains: An Interview with Annie Dillard', *Bennington Review* 10 (1981), 32.
124   Dillard, *Pilgrim at Tinker Creek*, 80.
125   Ibid., 192–93.
126   Murdoch, *The Sovereignty of Good*, 62.

means that the Good cannot be easily explained through empirical methods as it is not an 'object' in the world, and thus neither can morality be reduced to a set of rules and regulations. So while God is manifest in his Word and morality is more generally concerned with social rules as interpretations of that Word, the Good moves beyond and is greater than both by virtue of being the unattainable Idea of Perfection. This links conceptually to Soelle's understanding of the *via negativa*, specifically through the sense that the Good remains 'beyond' our understanding and indefinable.[127]

In 'A Poet's View', Levertov wrote '[a]cknowledgement, and celebration, of mystery probably constitutes the most consistent theme of my poetry'. In short, mystery is something that we must attend to diligently. In her poem 'Primary Wonder'[128] she explores this theme more fully:

> Days pass when I forget the mystery
> .....
> the mystery
> that there is anything, anything at all,
> let alone cosmos, joy, memory, everything,
> rather than void: and that, O Lord,
> Creator, Hallowed one, You still,
> hour by hour sustain it.

Water, whether in the form of a river, lake or sea is a favourite image for Levertov to depict the mystery that we call God. The depth of this mystery and unseen force is pictured in 'Of Rivers'[129] as 'a touch / shuddering them forth, a voice intoning them into / their ebbing and flood: fingertip, breath / of god or goddess in whom / their fealty rests'. She suggests that rivers have 'their way / to know, in unknowing flowing, the God of the gods, whom the gods themselves have not imagined'.

Mystery can also be frightening, however. Her poem 'Embracing the Centipede'[130] demonstrates the same wonder and horror to be found

127 Soelle, *The Silent Cry*, 67.
128 Levetov, *Sands of the Well*, 129.
129 Levertov, *Oblique Prayers*, 65.
130 Levertov, *Evening Train*, 107–10.

in nature that Dillard's work does. During the course of this poem, Levertov takes on a number of personas, which change from concern to disgust to anxious curiosity in response to a centipede. 'Cherish the mystery' (a voice responds) 'the mystery of this metamorphic apparition'. Denise Lynch suggests that '[t]hese multiple reactions to the creature represent the human response to divine mystery as frightening, fascinating, unfathomable, but ultimately inviting the heart's embrace.[131] Dillard reaches the same conclusions.

By now, it should be apparent that mystery is at the heart of Dillard's worldview. Her phrase 'We wake, if we ever wake at all, to mystery...'[132] captures this succinctly. Later in *Pilgrim at Tinker Creek*, she reflects that '[o]ur life is a faint tracing on the surface of mystery, like the idle, curved tunnels of leaf miners on the face of a leaf'.[133] Despite all the advances in scientific enquiry and centuries of religious belief and practice, we humans have to face the fact that we are inextricably entwined with mystery. Her response to the horror she witnesses in the life of insects is her amazement that '[t]hese are mysteries performed in broad daylight before our very eyes; we can see every detail and yet they are still mysteries'. She continues by making the provocative statement that 'we ought to be displaying praying mantises in our churches'.[134] In other words, rather than turn away in fear and loathing from the life of insects, we should not only acknowledge the mystery inherent in what appears to us as a horrific existence but celebrate it.[135]

---

131 Denise E. Lynch. 'Denise Levertov and the Poetry of Incarnation', in *Renascence* 50:1–2 (1997/1998), 49–64.

132 Dillard, *Pilgrim at Tinker Creek*, 4.

133 Ibid., 11.

134 Ibid., 65.

135 Here Dillard juxtaposes the inherent metaphor, praying, with the fact that these particular insects are first-rank predators, killers. The female of course eats the head of the male after coitus, Dillard wrote about this earlier in *Pilgrim at Tinker Creek*, 58.

In the Protestant West, where the Word has dominated Christianity (the Quakers being the exception to this), there has been a marked shift away from stillness and silence as a source of theological knowledge. Disavowing the power of words and avowing the power of silence is a radical modification in this age and in this place. However, mystical discourse recognises the inadequacy of language to describe the sacred. Ultimately, Murdoch appears to be telling us that, in the end, words fail. The central theory of her first novel, *Under the Net*, is based on Wittgenstein's treatise on the failings of theoretical rationalism, giving the impression of 'the incapacity of language and theory [to] fully represent contingent reality, just as a net cannot contain whatever it is cast over'.[136]

The character Brendon Craddock, an ordained priest in *Henry and Cato*, appears to have resolved the contradiction between belief and unbelief. Through his remarks to Cato, Murdoch suggests that the intellect will always fail and that human beings must give themselves up to whatever the divine may be:

> The point is, one will never get to the end of it, never get to the bottom of it, never, never, never. And that never, never, never, is what you must take for your hope and your shield and your most glorious promise. Everything that we concoct about God is an illusion.[137]

Brendan's despair then is itself a reason for hope and faith. It is also standard apophatic language of denial. As Turner notes, 'since we have no language in which to describe the deficit between our metaphors and the reality they reach out to, we are in a position only negatively to express the deficiency'.[138]

Murdoch writes one particularly memorable scene of a Quaker meeting in *The Philosopher's Pupil*, which successfully captures the mystical power of silence, or no words.

136   Bran Nicol, *Iris Murdoch: the Retrospective Fiction*, 2nd Edition (Basingstoke: Macmillan, 2004), 15.
137   Murdoch, *Henry and Cato*, 398.
138   Turner, *The Darkness of God*, 39.

The silence breathed with long soundless exhalations, with slower deeper rhythms, seeming ever more unbreakable and profound, as if everyone in the room would soon come to some absolute stop, perhaps quickly peacefully serenely die. Sometimes during the whole meeting no one spoke. Gabriel liked that best. Human speech sounded so petty, so unforgivably stupid, after that great void.[139]

A number of Murdoch's relatives and friends were Quakers, which gave her some added insight into this outlook. It also encapsulates her view that the Good is ultimately beyond all images and human thought. Silence is a similarly profound concept for Levertov.

The epigraph chosen by Levertov for 'The Antiphon'[140] is revealing and reflects, I think, a dominant theme in her religious outlook: 'L'Esprit souffle dans le silence la où les mots n'ont plus de voix.'[141] Silence – the place of no words – is where moments of revelation and spiritual rejuvenation occur. Predictably, the world of nature often provides the setting for this silence. More specifically, we find in several of Levertov's poems, that mountains become metaphors of absence and presence. This is apparent in 'Morning Mist',[142] where she uses the shrouding of a mountain in mist and its invisibility to lookers-on as a metaphor for God's perceived absence from his creation: 'The mountain absent, / a remote folk-memory'. Yet Levertov is able to transcend this thought by re-interpreting the silence to represent a 'presence in absence',[143] a God 'who is imaged as well or better in the white stillness' – an echo of the small still voice of the unnameable God that Moses experienced on Mt. Sinai.

Dillard offers a less dramatic suggestion in a rather curious poem in her small book of poems *Tickets for a Prayer Wheel* simply called 'God':

Numbers from one to ten, however, are called
'God'. In other words, counting to ten you would
say, 'God, God, God, God, God, God, God, God, God,

139   Iris Murdoch, *The Philosopher's Pupil* (London: Vintage, 1983), 200.
140   Levertov, *Oblique Prayers*, 77.
141   Ibid.
142   Levertov, *Evening Train*, 5.
143   Gallant, 'Entering No-Man's Land', 4.

God'. It is possible to distinguish between these
Numbers by the tone in which each is pronounced.
'God,' for example, corresponding to our 'five',
is pitched relatively high on the musical scale,
and accordingly sounds an inquisitive, even plaintive,
note. It is a sharp contrast to the number corresponding to our 'ten', which has a slightly accented,
basso finality, thus: 'God.'[144]

No doubt, to a linguistic mind this conveys some interesting facets of
the use of tone, pitch and stress in the use of language. However, from
a theological viewpoint Dillard appears to be suggesting that God is
beyond syntactical language but might be expressed in some small
measure through the cadences and rhythms of the human voice. That
is, the word itself is perhaps irrelevant, but the human voice gives the
concept relevance nevertheless. It could also refer to human attempts
to divide God as creation, into knowledge and therefore representative
of both the function of logic in the understanding of the same and the
human effort to dismantle by numbering and naming the parts.

Twenty years later, Dillard continues to grapple with the inadequacies of language to describe the sacred in a postmodern context.
In particular, she addresses the implications of language for understanding the nature of Christ in a poem entitled 'The Sign of the Father',[145]
which appears in a collection of what she describes as 'found poems'
entitled *Mornings Like This*. In this publication, she plays around with
texts to change their meaning, although as she tells us, she 'did not
write a word of it', to produce 'an urban, youthful, ironic, cruising
kind of poetry'.[146] The fragmentary nature of the reworked poem in
this instance represents 'the baffling quality of Christ's utterances and
the absurdly fragmentary nature of spiritual knowledge'.[147] In this
example, she takes an authentic sacred text, the New Testament Apoc-
rypha, so that 'Jesus and his sayings appear in tantalising snatches,

---

144   Annie Dillard, *Tickets for a Prayer Wheel* (New York: Harper, 1986), 99.
145   Annie Dillard, *Mornings Like This* (New York: Harper, 1996), 8–9.
146   Ibid., ix.
147   Ibid., x.

then disappear into an ellipse or half-gone word, in a teasing game of hide-and-seek'.[148]

> (His) disciples ask him (and s)ay:
> How should we fas(t and how
> Should we pr)ay and how (...
> ...) and what should we observe
> (Of the tradition?) Jesus says (.....
> .....) do not (.....
> .....) truth (.....
> .....) hidden (.....

> 'This saying has been handed down
> In a particularly sorry condition.'

Dillard expresses the limits of language more poetically thus:

> You walk, and one day you enter the spread heart of silence, where lands dissolve and seas become vapour and ices sublime under unknown stars. This is the end of the Via Negativa, the lightless edge where the slopes of knowledge dwindle, and love for its own sake, lacking an object, begins.[149]

De Certeau describes a similar stage where 'we have indeed arrived at that expanse that no longer speaks to us, lies mute, and where the wanderer [...] no longer has anything to "say" but the "lie" of an image'.[150] This is where opposites merge, metaphors arise and the journey continues. As De Certeau reminds us,

> he or she is the mystic who cannot stop walking and, with the certainty of what is lacking, knows of every place and object that it is not that; one cannot stay there nor be content with that. Desire creates an excess. Places are exceeded, passed, lost behind it. It makes one go further, elsewhere. It lives nowhere.[151]

148 Peggy Rosenthal, 'Joking with Jesus in the Poetry of Kathleen Norris and Annie Dillard', in *Cross Currents* 50:3 (2000), 390.
149 Dillard, *Living by Fiction*, 60.
150 De Certeau, *The Mystic Fable*, 293.
151 Ibid., 299.

Chapter One introduced Murdoch, Levertov and Dillard as exemplars of mystical longing in postmodernity. Their vocations as writers and sense of mystical perception operate as parallel themes in their lives. Chapters Two and Three developed this assertion through examining their approach to discerning the sacred through contemplation and creativity, but it is desire that keeps the mystic on his or her path.

Jantzen posits that desire has been 'a significant if under-acknowledged ingredient [in the philosophy of religion] all along, at least in the conceptualisation of the divine'.[152] Intellectual rational-isation more often than not fails to reach the object of desire (God or Good), and in fact, desire stands in opposition to rationality and the corpus of Western philosophical thought.[153] As Jantzen points out, the longing for the divine was a central and preoccupying motivation be-hind Julian's writings.[154] Julian wrote, 'all who are under heaven and will come there, their way is by longing and desiring'.[155] This is the same human longing expressed in Soelle's 'hermeneutic of hunger', but Soelle's assertion takes into account theological and political cav-eats implicit in contemporary secular settings. Soelle believes that a 'hermeneutic of suspicion' provides a much needed critical edge but often avoids the reality of oppression and the possibility of liber-ation'.[156] In contradistinction, a 'hermeneutic of hunger' gives a name to 'this bottomless emptiness into which consumerism plunges people [which] transports women and men into a kind of spiritual anorexia where any kind of nourishment is nauseating'. She argues that the continual search for individual 'nourishment' impoverishes communal values and only feeds the ego and does not 'render reality more trans-lucent'.[157]

152   Jantzen, *Becoming Divine*, 88.
153   Ibid., 87.
154   Ibid., 86.
155   Julian, *Showings*, 276.
156   Soelle, *The Silent Cry*, 47.
157   Ibid., 48–49.

A mystic's desire to lose the self in order to experience God has been criticised in feminist discourse, because it suggests the denial of the body in general and female materiality in particular. According to Soelle, however, the suspicion is unfounded in as much as the mystical experience of losing oneself 'does not dismiss the body as an ill-functioning machine; rather, it sets the body free for a different and new self-expression'. In order to go beyond what Soelle terms a critique of 'the political domination religious power used to consolidate its own power', we need to ask 'what men and women are looking for in their cry for a different spirituality'. This she defines as a 'hermeneutic of hunger'. Soelle is careful to point out that her definition of spiritual hunger has nothing to do with 'a greedy hankering after experience' or 'an anaesthetizing longing, [which] incorporates mystical elements and appropriates them for the individual'.[158]

Likewise, Levertov tries to invoke desire and longing for a more just world by providing an image of a world devoid of beauty. Levertov utilises biblical and apocryphal images of a wasteland as a critical device to awaken people from their apathy. A wasteland, as both metaphor and depiction of reality, is startlingly present in her poem 'Silent Spring'.[159] The title deliberately invokes Rachel Carson's pioneering work of the same name, which arguably provided 'the cornerstone of the new environmentalism'.[160] Carson, a scientist and writer, was at the forefront of the crusade against chemical pesticides and corporate greed that she observed to be dominating factors in the destruction of natural landscapes. Levertov speaks sadly of the 'absence' of wildlife and decay of plant life that spraying with chemicals creates:

> no crisp susurration of crickets
> One lone frog, One lone
> faraway whippoorwill. Absence.
> No hum, no whirr.
> And Look:

158   Soelle, *The Silent Cry*, 47–49.
159   Levertov, *Oblique Prayers*, 30.
160   Rachel Carson, *Silent Spring* (London: The Folio Society, 2000), 18. Originally published in 1962 by Houghton Mifflin.

the tigerish thistles, bold
yesterday,
curl in sick yellowing.

Drop the wild lettuce!
Try not to breathe!

Laboriously
the spraytruck
has ground its way
this way.
Hear your own steps
in violent silence.

There is a direct allusion here to the way everyone is responsible for
the depletion of the natural world, and again, she questions the assumption that nature is merely for human beings to exploit for their
own needs by speaking of direct and indirect violence to it. The poem
also offers an image of a dystopic future if we do not resist such
exploitation. She also echoes Soelle's notion that the absence of God
is more keenly felt due to the destruction of our source of 'original
amazement'.[161] The last stanza where she speaks of 'violent silence' is
an example of mystical language that utilises an oxymoron but with a
political twist. To make the reader aware of the situation, Levertov
invokes empathetic engagement in her readers. In this poem, Levertov
has skilfully combined both emotion and intellect. As Murdoch and
Levertov explicitly (and Dillard implicitly) show us, the lack of imaginative apprehension and feelings for other living beings is at the
root of all oppression.

The 'absence' and desolation Levertov imagines in her dystopic
vision is reminiscent of the mythological spiritual wasteland. The use
of desolated landscapes to portray the potential for evil in humans and
the result of turning away from God abound in the prophets in the
Hebrew Scriptures. See for example:

I looked on the earth, and lo it
was waste and void;

161   Soelle, *The Silent Cry*, 92.

and to the heavens, and they
had no light.
I looked on the mountains, and
lo, they were quaking
and all the hills moved to and fro
I looked, and lo, there was no
one at all,
and all the birds of the air had fled.
I looked, and lo, the fruitful land
was a desert.[162]

In the modern world, the prophetic image is doubly potent because of recent advances in science and technologies with their accompanying capacity to harm. At least intuitively perhaps, we all know that our impoverished sense of the spiritual world and lack of connectedness with the natural contains the real potential for such a wasteland.

Dillard captures this spiritual hunger in *Teaching a Stone to Talk:*

It is difficult to undo our own damage, and to recall to our presence that which we have asked to leave. It is hard to desecrate a grove and change your mind. The very holy mountains are keeping mum. We doused the burning bush and cannot rekindle it; we are lighting matches in vain under every green tree.[163]

Early on in her writing career, in the poem 'The Man who wishes to Feed on Mahogany',[164] Dillard takes up a challenge from Chesterton, who states that poetry can't express the obscure desire someone might have to feed on mahogany. Dillard's response to what she sees as an artistic challenge is remarkable. What she actually does is to imagine the desire a man might have to eat mahogany as analogous to the love Christ displayed for the world. Christ here loves his 'fellow creature' with such a force that it 'holds him here, / [...] nails him to the world'. And humans in return long for him with equal force so that we 'desire to drink and sup at mahogany's mass'. Here it is the erotic desire for the other that characterises the mystic in postmodernity and not just the empty longing for an anaesthetising effect.

162   Jeremiah 4: 23–26.
163   Dillard, *Teaching a Stone to Talk*, 88.
164   Dillard, *Tickets for a Prayer Wheel*, 39–40.

227

The *via negativa* represents then the point where language fails, where doubt, fear and despair are constant companions. The searcher along the *via negativa* must readily accept an inability to maintain conceptual control over religious language, which is perhaps most ironic for a writer. Simply put, God or the sacred is not something that can be contained within human constructs. It is impossible to concretise Mystery – language, dogma or doctrine cannot contain it. The *via negativa* in Western consumer culture is also about 'resisting' the *status quo* and egotistical desires. It has become clear that, in order to nurture a mystical consciousness, we all need to work on suspending the ego – if only temporarily. Furthermore, following the *via negativa* in postmodernity necessitates the need to 'befriend' the void, which includes 'negative' experiences such suffering, doubt and despair. Mystical theologians have always recognised that affirmative and negative language are oppositional terms for the human encounter with the sacred, that together these oppositions represent the limits of human reason and imagination. In the next chapter, we will explore the necessity of holding oppositional concepts in tension in order that theological reflection in postmodernity may integrate the *via positiva* and the *via negativa.*

Part Three

Chapter Six
The *Via Integrativa*: Re-orienting Consciousness

Following from the processes of the mystic way as outlined in the *via positiva* and the *via negativa*, part three explores the distinctive ways that creative writing with a mystical focus is able to provide insights for the renewal of theology. In Chapter One, two fundamental characteristics of theological configurations in postmodernity emerged that make it distinct from variations that have preceded it. First, that theology must reflect the plural nature of diverse realities, and second, theologians must accept that only partial or temporary 'truths' are attainable. Consequently, due to the multiplicity and transitory nature of such an approach, a systematic or in-depth evaluation of recognised theological categories is not possible. Instead, the focus of this discussion will be on the development of an integrated theology that draws on the whole of human experience, the central objective of which is to contribute towards a joyful, just and peaceable future for all.

The *via integrativa* is here offered as a more holistic and realistic alternative model for theological reflection in postmodernity. The aim of this chapter is to demonstrate how Murdoch, Levertov and Dillard's writing, acts as a vehicle of integration between existential and conceptual polarities. The notion of integration, or the *via integrativa*, is therefore offered, first, to differentiate between the goal of spiritual annihilation as the sole purpose of the *via mystica* and the integration of body, mind and soul in mystical pursuits. The second purpose is to provide a view of mysticism that challenges dualistic thinking as regards both abstract philosophical thought as well as socio-political realities.

In the classic mystical tradition, spiritual progression through the stages of the *via negativa* and the *via positiva* ultimately leads to the *via unitiva*, or to the experience of unity with God. This signifies the point 'where the self ceases actively to surrender itself and instead suffers the blindingly superabundant presence of God'.[1] Similarly, in Platonic mysticism the ultimate goal is to emerge from the cave into the full light of the sun or 'truth'. Interpretations of both scenarios imply that there is a hierarchical movement away from the body, from matter generally, towards the spiritual realm. Underlying this largely premodern worldview is the assumption that God or the Good exists above and beyond reality.

From the Protestant Reformation onwards, and more than ever following the establishment of Enlightenment ideals, the individual, as an autonomous, thinking being was central to any Western theology. Personal faith developed into a key focus of religious belief and practice. In such a world, especially following the rapid and relentless rise of scientific discovery and the changes wrought by the Industrial Revolution, the model of 'mechanistic progress' soon dominated the discussion. This model created an imaginary 'picture of an upward line, graphing the abundant life in terms of consumer goods for more and more of the world's people'.[2] However, both views, theological and worldly, represent a single vision that eclipses the realities of non-Westerners and of non-traditional religious conceptions as well as the material or embodied nature of existence.

Whilst earlier mysticisms, especially those articulated by male religious leaders, tended to deny the corporal element of reality, post-modern consumer culture overtly celebrates it, and therefore, spiritual experience tends to become a commodity like everything else. Jeremy Carrette and Richard King explain the difficulties inherent in this transformation:

> Our understanding of the self and its desires is lost [...] when [Eastern practices such as yoga and Buddhist meditation are] transformed in modern western societies into an individualised spirituality of the self, or as we are increasingly seeing, repackaged as a cultural commodity to be sold to the 'spiritual consumer'.[3]

---

1   McIntosh, *Mystical Theology*, 191.
2   McFague, *Life Abundant*, 43–45.
3   Jeremy Carrette and Richard King, *Selling Spirituality: The Silent Takeover of Religion* (London: Routledge, 2004), 16.

Moreover, in this scenario, the realities of marginalised peoples are ignored at the expense of attaining pleasure in the accumulation of consumer goods. Despite the focus on the self, pleasure in postmodernity largely represents a *dis*-integration, or fragmentation, of self-identity. Dualistic constructs that debase the natural world and our bodies have proved to be detrimental to the psychic health of numerous individuals as well as compromising the sustainability of the earth's ecosystems. The *via integrativa* represents an alternative and more holistic theological model to the Plotinian image of the 'flight of the Alone to the Alone'.[4] Moreover, it also resists forms of contemporary 'holistic' spirituality that would aspire to repudiate 'oppressive material worlds' but can 'paradoxically reinscribe the forces of isolation by focusing upon the individual'.[5] Carrette and King echo Jantzen's argument concerning the dangers of interiorised spirituality here.

To cite Jantzen, a postmodern anchoress (or mystic) 'will need comfort for her own griefs, but a comfort that allows her to turn towards rather than away from the needs of the world'.[6] So transcendence and unity of self occurs alongside and through an integrated vision of the world in all its complexities. Jantzen's proposal also stresses the ethical and political characteristics of the mystic in postmodernity. The underlying notion of the *via integrativa* is the assumption that human selves are ontological entities that seek wholeness through their relationship to the cosmos, other beings and within themselves. This chapter argues that the mystic way in postmodernity must seek *integritas*, or 'wholeness', because as Dillard concludes in *Holy the Firm*, 'everything, everything, is whole, and a parcel of something else'.[7] And theology in postmodernity should reflect this understanding.

To develop an integrated theology that draws on the insights of writer-mystics such as Murdoch, Levertov and Dillard, I will firstly posit Julian's reflections as an espousal of a theology of integration. In fact, her sense of the undivided 'double' nature of human beings in relation to God provides a useful spiritual blueprint for the mystic way

---

4   Plotinus, *Enneads* VI.9
5   Carrette and King, *Selling Spirituality*, 82.
6   Jantzen, *Julian of Norwich*, xxii.
7   Dillard, *Holy the Firm*, 66.

in postmodernity. Secondly, I will explore the three philosophical categories of being, knowing and acting – or ontology, epistemology and ethics – through the lens of integration. To finish, I will posit a model of relationship as capturing the central tenets of Jantzen, Soelle and McFague's theology.

The Example of Julian

Jantzen aptly describes Julian as 'an outstanding example of an integrated theologian, for whom daily life and religious experience and theological reflection are all aspects of the same whole'.[8] An overriding vocational aim that Julian expresses in *Shewings* is her desire to help people become whole by healing the fragmented nature of the human self. Her response to what she saw as a universal human longing is an image of humanity's relationship with the Creator:

> I saw that we have, naturally from our fullness, to desire wisely and truly to know our own soul, through which we are taught to seek it where it is, and that is in God. And so by leading through grace of the Holy Spirit we shall know them both in one; whether we are moved to know God or our soul, either motion is good and true.[9]

The increased attention to the humanity of Christ and awareness that human beings are made 'in the image and likeness' of God were seen in the late medieval period as proof that humans are 'inextricably joined with divinity'.[10] So Julian assures us that 'our substance is in God [...] and God is in our sensuality',[11] that it is as sensual bodily creatures that we perceive God. Our 'substance' or essential selves

---

8   Jantzen, *Julian of Norwich*, 91.
9   Julian, *Showings*, 288.
10   Caroline Walker Bynum, *Jesus as Mother: Studies in the Spirituality of the High Middle Ages* (Berkeley; Los Angeles; London: University of California Press, 1982), 129–30.
11   Julian, *Showings*, 288.

remain united with God, but it is our 'sensuality', or 'consciousness and behaviour', which loses touch with God.[12] Jantzen notes that the way that 'bodily reality is integrated into [her] spirituality' differentiates Julian and other female mystics from male expressions of mysticism.[13] That is, rather than a flight from the material realm to the spiritual, the spiritual is realised within the material.

Because of the conjoining of the human and divine soul and the belief that God is the ground of our being, to Julian's mind, it follows that to know ourselves at a deep level is to know God:

> And so I saw most surely that it is quicker for us and easier to come to the knowledge of God than it is to know our own soul. For our soul is so deeply grounded in God and so endlessly treasured that we cannot come to knowledge of it until we first have knowledge of God, who is the Creator to whom it is united.[14]

Julian appears to suggest that it is only by embracing the human condition and striving for a unified consciousness that humans can overcome the false separation between the body and soul, which is not to say that we are totally pure. As Julian recognised, the human potential for sin blocks the possibility of receiving God's grace. She thought that a life's spiritual task should be to 'know and see, truly and clearly, what our self is, then we shall truly and clearly see and know our Lord God in the fullness of joy'.[15]

Behind Julian's revelations, and her years of pondering them, are the reality of God and the unfathomable mystery of love. The only way to transcend sin is through the power of love. Love is what binds the creature to the Creator. Indeed, Julian concludes that the meaning of her revelations was precisely 'love':

> So I was taught that love is our Lord's meaning. And I saw very certainly in this and in everything that before God made us he loved us, which love was never abated and never will be [...]. In our creation we had beginning, but the

---

12   Jantzen, *Julian of Norwich*, 148–49.
13   Jantzen, *Power, Gender and Christian Mysticism*, 147.
14   Julian, *Showings*, 288.
15   Ibid., 258.

love in which he created us was in him from without beginning. In this love we have our beginning, and all this shall we see in God without end.[16]

Murdoch shared Julian's sense of the power of love as reflected in her interest in 'the ways that love makes for wholeness of perception, wholeness of being', but of course she was equally interested in love's failings.[17] It is chiefly though her belief that poetry is an incarnation that links Levertov to Julian's integrated vision of reality. She insists that '[t]he substance, the means, of an art, is an incarnation – not a reference but phenomenon; a poem is an indivisibility of spirit and matter'.[18] The human imagination or soul is where this fusion takes place. Dillard's engagement with Julian is perhaps the most challenging. She uses the experience of watching a moth burn to death in a candle flame as a metaphor for a nun in postmodernity.[19] Like Julian, she yearns for an experience of the sacred but knows this does not come without being willing to look suffering and death in the face. The fact that the body of the dead moth continues to burn and give light after its death is a symbol of sacrifice. For Dillard, surrendering oneself to the blinding presence of God is not about escape from this world, but a deeper encounter with reality.

The Human Longing for Wholeness

There is an etymological link between the word 'wholeness' and 'holiness' in the Old English words *hal* for health and *halig* for holy. For a human being to be whole, or in full health, the body, mind and spirit need to be in an integrated state. Like Julian, Soelle appreciates that the overriding religious concern for human beings is the desire 'to be whole and not fragmented'. This need extends to all creation wherein she suggests that 'the wish of growing love is to bind and join

16   Ibid., 342–43.
17   Conradi, *The Saint and the Artist*, 324. Conradi links this to Romantic humanism.
18   Levertov, 'Origins of a Poem', in *The Poet in the World*, 50.
19   Dillard, *Holy the Firm*, 16–17.

together even larger entities'.[20] In postmodernity, this premise has urgent ethical repercussions, as individuals, in the first world in particular, have become 'enemies of the earth, enemies of the sky above us, and enemies of ourselves'.[21] In other words, we have lost a sense of relationship to creation, to the transcendent, and between our spiritual and material selves.

McFague, in the same way, states that 'the category "human being" is a construction with fuzzy edges; it is a category that makes no sense apart from the history of life on our planet and the interlocking networks of support that keep all of us in existence'.[22] She is adamant that the Enlightenment ideal of the rational autonomous individual who has the potential to force matter to give up its secrets through scientific discovery rests on an ontological mistake. Yet, despite the damaging effect of mechanistic thinking in the past, a scientific paradigm in postmodernity, in McFague's view, is still able to provide crucial insights for theology. Specifically, she refers to the scientific discovery that there is a 'continuum between matter and energy (or more precisely, the unified matter/energy field), which overturns traditional hierarchical dualism'. Not least is the fact that we are minds as well as bodies and that the former emerges from the latter.[23] The categorical quality of the language is different, but the mystical essence is the same as Julian's sense of love that exists 'in him from without beginning', through the conjoining of human and divine matter.

In postmodernity, humans tend to experience themselves progressively in terms of isolation from those around them. Murdoch was acutely aware of this disunity between self and the external world, contending that, '[t]o do philosophy is to explore one's own temperament, and at the same time to attempt to discover the truth'.[24] Philosophy's aim is to discover what is inside us as well that which resides

20   Dorothee Soelle, *Suffering* (trans. E. R. Kalin) (Philadelphia: Fortress Press, 1984), 137.
21   Soelle, *The Silent Cry*, 192.
22   McFague, *Life Abundant*, 46.
23   Sallie McFague, *The Body of God* (London: SCM Press, 1993), 16.
24   Murdoch, *The Sovereignty of Good*, 46.

beyond the tangible world. At a basic level, philosophy (and much of theology, we should add) is the human attempt to resolve these feelings of separation and disunity. Conradi points out that one of Murdoch's perennial problems was 'how to marry the inner and the outer worlds, how to create fictions that honour both a strict causality and a strict sense of privacy and "freedom" that the moral agent may experience himself as endowed with'.[25] At a subjective level, an existential tension exists between the self as an autonomous unique being and the larger world that appears to operate through randomness and chance, which creates an unresolved tension within the human mind. In one sense, humans have a unique awareness of their freedom, but in another they cannot escape the knowledge that we are all subject to events over which the individual has little influence.

As a novelist and philosopher, Murdoch sought to mediate a path between absolute principles (whether philosophical or religious) and human consciousness. Murdoch does not resolve existential anxieties, but she offers, through her novels, a way to acknowledge that, while death and randomness is real, so is goodness. Like Julian, Murdoch intuited that a part of human consciousness was always orientated towards the Good but our lower desires could lead us into immoral behaviour. In other words, although we need to foster our higher eros, we still need to keep our feet on the ground. The temptation to escape into pseudo-mysticism is a constant temptation within a consumerist construction of spirituality, one that would be robustly criticised by Murdoch as pertaining to fantasy and escapism if she were still with us today.

Again, Murdoch believed that a fundamental orientation towards the Good was present in human nature. In *Metaphysics as a Guide to Morals*, she imagines the Platonic notion of the Good as something 'distant and apart' that operates as 'a source of energy'. Further, she describes it as 'an active principle of truthful cognition and moral understanding in the soul, the inspiration of the love-object of Eros'. It is not an object as such, or a person as in traditional beliefs about God, but rather, Murdoch depicts the Good as a 'reality principle whereby

---

25   Conradi, *The Saint and the Artist*, 325.

we find our way about the world'.[26] Fundamental to her task as a novelist was her desire to reorientate people towards the Good, which is how she understands conversion or, in relation to the discussion here, a reintegrated self, so that by definition, Murdoch's way is one of integration.

In 'Sojourns in the Parallel World',[27] Levertov gives us her personal interpretation of how the two worlds of the material and the supernatural intermingle and she dissuades us from a mysticism of escapism. In the same poem, she tells the reader of the transcendental realm where 'we lose track of our own obsessions, / our self-concerns' and our earthly existence, where 'our lives of human passions, / cruelties, dreams, concepts' occur. She concludes of course that, however joyous the experience of the mystical realm is, 'we must / return, indeed to evolve our destinies'. As Linda Kinnahan reminds us, Levertov never 'occupies a place of separation from the world nor embodies a self innocent of its systems of power'.[28] Furthermore, Levertov was acutely aware at all times of her own complicity in systems of oppression. The Jesuit priest and peace activist Daniel Berrigan argues that, through her writing, she helped to restore the balance in the seventies between American writing that was 'disproportionately passionate about the self, and correspondingly numb [...] toward the public weal and woe'.[29] Levertov's poetry represented a synthesis of subjective insight and ethical concern.

In Chapter Two, we discussed how Dillard imagines herself as a blend of artist, nun and thinker in *Holy the Firm*. Ostensibly, Dillard is attempting to fuse these three roles within herself. She further seeks to harmonise her being with creation. One seemingly mundane incident in *Pilgrim at Tinker Creek*, depicts her as wholly integrated as a human as well as with her surroundings. It happens whilst she stops at

26   Murdoch, *Metaphysics as a Guide to Morals*, 474.
27   Levertov, *Sands of the Well*, 49.
28   Linda A. Kinnahan, *Poetics of the Feminine: Authority and Literary Tradition in William Carlos Williams, Mina Loy, Denise Levertov, and Kathleen Fraser* (Cambridge: Cambridge University Press, 1992), 156.
29   Daniel Berrigan, 'Denise Levertov's Prose', in Gelpi, *Denise Levertov*, 175. Daniel Berrigan and Denise Levertov travelled to Hanoi during the Vietnam War.

a gas station during a long drive on a hot day. She takes a coffee outside, finds herself alone, and dazzled by the mountainous landscape before her eyes, and she notices that

> the bare forest folds and pleats itself like a living protoplasm before my eyes [...]. I am more alive than all the world. This is it, I think, this is it, right now, the present, this empty gas station, here, this western wind, this tang of coffee on the tongue, and I am patting a puppy, I am watching the mountain. And the second I verbalize this awareness in my brain, I cease to see the mountain or feel the puppy. I am opaque, so much black asphalt.[30]

Sharon Chirban, who positions herself on the border between culture and clinical practice in psychology, finds in Dillard's *Pilgrim at Tinker Creek* a sound example of the experience of what she calls 'oneness'. This state of wholeness is achieved through attention to an individual dog in parallel with the broader landscape. In particular, she points to Dillard's experience of patting a puppy as an example of 'oneness experience', noting that 'it is this area of experiencing in the space between that Dillard's sense of self and the many stimuli emitted from the mountain contribute to form the substance of an oneness experience'.[31] Ross-Bryant similarly states that 'Dillard experiences herself as part of a supportive matrix which is more than herself and yet includes herself'.[32] As such, 'human meaning, as Dillard presents it, depends on being open to and true to the experience of the other'.[33] Murdoch, Levertov and Dillard clearly maintain that it is only by engaging with others that we get a fuller sense of self. What is more, following the path of the *via integrativa* does not entail an attempt to separate from existential surroundings, however painful they may be.

30   Dillard, *Pilgrim at Tinker Creek*, 79–80.
31   Sharon A Chirban, 'Oneness Experience: Looking Through Multiple Lenses', in *The Journal of Applied Psychoanalytic Studies*, 2:3 (2000), 253.
32   Lynn Ross-Bryant, 'The Silence of Nature', in *Religion and Literature* 22:1 (1990), 88.
33   Ibid., 91.

Embracing the Whole of Human Experience

In Chapter Four, we saw how Christ's death, as opposed to his resurrection, is the important point of the Gospel narratives in Murdoch's reconfiguring. Further, in an interview with Haffenden (1983), Murdoch suggests that death is not some 'terribly special' event at the end of life, but rather, something that could happen at any moment. Death by natural or unnatural means is a perennial feature of Murdoch's novels. Titus, the youthful protégé that Charles takes on in *The Sea, The Sea*, dies pointlessly in a drowning accident. The protagonist of this novel had hoped to find redeeming love in this newfound relationship, but Murdoch appears to suggest that we cannot pin our hopes on individual relationships. Likewise, in *The Sacred and Profane Love Machine*, the sudden death of Harriet at the airport by a random gunman reflects Murdoch's notion that life is tenuous and that we are all victims of chance. Trying to be good or moral does not mean we will exert any control over our destinies.

Integral to this pragmatic viewpoint is her belief that a redeemed life is one that accepts the reality of death. Murdoch's novel *Bruno's Dream* is a reflection on this fact. As Bajaj states, it also reflects the Platonic notion of love, which decrees that perfection cannot be attained without 'dying to imperfect desires'.[34] The dying Bruno prepares for death but is plagued by his past. His has been rather a sad life that involves harsh treatment from his father, an unloving wife and the death of a daughter, and to make matters worse, he has become estranged from his son Miles in the present. As he struggles with many questions, the only sure thing he can say is 'there was no God. [...] I have lived for nearly ninety years and I know nothing.'[35] Referring to Murdoch's *Bruno's Dream*, Conradi surmises that 'Bruno's dying is a moral summons to [those around him] to full life and to a consciousness that at last admits the reality and claims of other people.'[36] Bruno's death helps others face up to reality. The paradox of

34 Bajaj, *A Critical Study of Iris Murdoch's Fiction*, 145.
35 Murdoch, *Bruno's Dream*, 283.
36 Conradi, *The Saint and the Artist*, 124.

the book is, as Conradi suggests, that the human race is not only death defying, but also life denying.[37] In other words, Murdoch suggests the same philosophical stance as Dillard in her novel *The Living* – it is only by accepting the reality of our own death that we can fully participate in life – they come as a package. Morality is mystical in the sense that it has no objective reason but relies instead on surrender to goodness and beauty, and Murdoch often illustrates this point in her fiction through the unifying vision of a classic piece of art.

In *Henry and Cato*, for example, she explicitly refers to Max Beckmann's large triptych entitled *Departure*, which represents 'a secular reproduction of the Christian holy family and a reflection of transcendent achievement'.[38] Beckmann's own interpretation of the picture is illuminating:

> Life is what you see right and left. Life is torture, pain of every kind – physical and mental – men and women are subjected to it equally. On the right wing you can see yourself trying to find your way in the darkness, lighting the hall and staircase with a miserable lamp, dragging along tied to you, as a part of yourself, the corpse of your memories, of your wrongs and failures, the murder everyone commits at some time of his life – you can never free yourself from your past, you have to carry that corpse while Life plays the drum.

> And at the center?

> The King and Queen, Man and Woman, are taken to another shore by a boatsman whom they do not know, he wears a mask, it is a mysterious figure taking us to a mysterious land. [...] The King and Queen have freed themselves of the tortures of life – they have overcome them. The Queen carries the greatest treasure – Freedom – as a child in her lap. Freedom is the one thing that matters – it is the departure, the new start.[39]

Clearly, Beckmann, like Murdoch, sees the beauty, mystery and tragedy that make up life. Henry's disavowal of pain and suffering by choosing to look only at the beauty of art means that art for him is a consolation and that his life will only ever become 'mediocre'. His

---

37   Ibid., 125.
38   Dipple, *Work for the Spirit*, 254. This work is housed in the Museum of Modern Art in New York.
39   Ibid., 254. Dipple cites Stephan Lackner, *Max Beckmann* (New York: Abrams, 1977), 116.

words are: 'as a spiritual being I'm done for'.[40] Cato, on the other hand, finds that his love for Christ is blotted out when he falls in love with the young boy Joe. Bajaj concludes that Cato, like Michael Meade in *The Bell*, finds himself caught in 'the conflict between messy personal desires and the unrewarding even impossible demands of a strangely alien transcendence'.[41] Cato eventually kills Joe when he is forced by circumstances to face the reality of who he is deep within himself. Bajaj notices that

> during the course of the novel the moral dialectic results in a complete reversal of expected roles. The 'bad' Henry comes to terms with life, and integrates himself into a family and community [while] the 'good' Cato cuts himself off from family, friends, church and God and commits murder.[42]

So Murdoch focuses on the individual struggle to be moral or religious in relation to the particularities we find ourselves within, whilst at the same time she is suggesting that humans can only hope for integration of self by recognising a mutual relationship with others.

Levertov felt this more intensely and oscillated for a large part of her writing career between her perception of beauty, her spiritual vision, and a political anger that surfaced in response to the many political issues that prevent peace and the flourishing of life in postmodernity. For Levertov, there is very little difference between personal suffering and the sufferings of others; and in fact, she felt personally affronted by the suffering, indignity or injustices experienced by others. Levertov's poem 'Life at War'[43] depicts her reaction to the pain of others in a similar manner to Julian's perception of Christ's bodily sufferings as something felt in her own physical being: 'The disasters numb within us / caught in the chest, rolling / in the brain like pebbles [...] our lungs are pocked with it'. The final stanza indicates how this suffering thwarts her ability to write: 'the mucous membrane of our dreams / coated with it, the imagination / filmed over with the gray filth of it'.

---

40   Murdoch, *Henry and Cato*, 382.
41   Bajaj, *A Critical Study of Iris Murdoch*, 208.
42   Ibid., 211.
43   Levertov, *Poems 1968–1972*, 121–22.

Yet, by the time she wrote the poems in *Evening Train*, she can depict a sense of her own experience of wholeness or integration in a poem entitled 'Dream Instruction'.[44] Here she juxtaposes her own constant rush of thought, imaged as the rushing waters of Niagara, with those of the archetypal wise crone who 'just purely be's'. The basic premise here is an injunction to live in the moment or to simply 'be'. Gallant believes this indicates a sense of stillness in Levertov at this moment of time; she has reached a point in her life where the paradoxes of life that so disturbed her in the past have been replaced by an inner peace.[45] Levertov captures the essence of the paradoxical nature of a human life in 'Of Being'.[46]

> I know this happiness
> is provisional:
>
>   the looming presences–
>   great suffering, great fear–
>
>   withdraw only
>   into peripheral vision:
>
> but ineluctable this shimmering
> of wind in blue leaves:
>
> this flood of stillness
> widening the lake of sky:
>
> this need to dance,
> this need to kneel:
>   this mystery:

There is an acknowledgement here of the coexistence of beauty and tragedy within a human life. Although the pain of losing loved ones, for example, never goes away, beauty remains a continual mystery that

44   Levertov, *Evening Train*, 60.
45   Gallant, 'Entering No-Man's Land', 5.
46   Levertov, *Oblique Prayers*, 87.

evokes praise and wonder in the beholder.[47] The same vision is evident in Dillard's account of her mystical journeys.

Previously, we discussed how Dillard's worldview in *Pilgrim at Tinker Creek* centres on the two contrasting images of 'the tree with lights in it' and the frog sucked dry by the water bug, how her experiences during her contemplation of nature range from the ecstatic to the repulsive. She holds these oppositional reactions to her observations of nature in tension throughout *Pilgrim at Tinker Creek*. It is the overwhelming gratuitousness of creation that appals her so. This is most apparent in her observations of insects. She writes:

> the faster death goes, the faster evolution goes. If an aphid lays a million eggs, several might survive. Now, my right hand, in all its human cunning, could not make one aphid in a thousand years. But these aphid eggs – which run less than a dime a dozen, which run absolutely free – can make aphids as effortlessly as the sea makes waves. Wonderful things, wasted.[48]

Clearly, she does not romanticise nature; she sees no point in getting emotional about tragedy because it is going to happen anyway. Towards the end of *Pilgrim at Tinker Creek*, she envisions herself as 'a sacrifice bound with cords to the horns of the world's rock altar, waiting for worms'.[49] She has been through both the glorious and the terrifying and 'been baptized both into the world – united with it – and separated from it'.[50] Ritual is her way of establishing a relationship with nature that does not try to resist the realities of death and decay.

Of the three authors whose work we are examining, it is maybe Dillard who makes the most unequivocal statement concerning the co-existence of life and death:

---

47 The notion of all of existence being provisional is of course intrinsic to Buddhist belief and practice. At some level, good and evil, suffering and transcendence are equally transient. It is not clear whether Levertov had this in mind here or not.

48 Dillard, *Pilgrim at Tinker Creek*, 177.

49 Ibid., 246.

50 Margaret Loewen Reimer, 'The Dialectical Vision of Annie Dillard's *Pilgrim at Tinker Creek*', in *Critique* 24 (1983) 197.

The world has signed a pact with the devil; it had to. It is a covenant to which every thing, even every hydrogen atom, is bound. The terms are clear: if you want to live, you have to die; you cannot have the mountains and creeks without space, and space is a beauty married to a blind man. The blind man is Freedom, or Time, and he does not go anywhere without his great dog Death. The world came into being with the signing of the contract.[51]

Later, explaining her motivations for writing the novel *The Living* to Mary Cantwell, Annie Dillard states,

I wanted to write about little-bitty people in a great big landscape, the way Turgenev does. I wanted to tell the story of the Northwest region, which I think is so wonderful. Most of all I wanted to give the sense – because it makes life so interesting – of knowing that you are alive in a generation that will die. Because these people who are so alive to themselves, so vivid to themselves, so on the cutting edge of the present – they're now underground...[52]

Life is about holding opposites such as life and death, joy and despair in tension. The offshoot of taking this ontological stance seriously is the route to liberation. It also allows us to resist the individualistic stance of many worldviews for the simple reason that our existence ceases to be more important than anyone else's.

Perceiving the Self in Relation to Others

In Chapter Two, it was noted that McFague's notion of looking derives in part from Murdoch's concept of attentive. She shares Murdoch's belief that good art can help us to pay attention to others:

Art frames fragments of our world: paintings, poetry, novels, sculpture, dance, music help us to look at colors, sounds, bodies, events, characters – whatever – with full attention. Something is lifted out of the world and put into a frame so that we can, perhaps for the first time, *see* it. Most of the time we do not see: we pass a tree, an early spring crocus, the face of another human being, and we do

51   Dillard, *Pilgrim at Tinker Creek*, 183.
52   Mary Cantwell, 'A Pilgrims' Progress' (1992). http://www.nytimes.com/books/ 99/03/28/specials/dillard-pilgrim.html. Ivan Turgenev (1820–1910) was a Russian author best known for his novel *Fathers and Sons*.

not marvel at these wonders, because we do not see their specialness, their individuality, their difference.[53]

It is only with the help of the artist who captures the duality of existence that we can begin to discern truth. In McFague's ecological model, the categories of knowing, being and acting must include the 'otherness of the other [as a] total way of being in the world'.[54] She further points out that the difficult task of attending to another fundamentally means paying attention to difference.[55] This section explores how Murdoch, Levertov and Dillard attempt to bridge the gap between self and others.

A central feature of Murdoch's moral philosophy is her notion of 'loving attention'. Her view on pornography demonstrates her reasoning behind this assertion. She opposed the sex industry generally because it 'displays [a] lack of honour and restraint', arguing that sexual promiscuity is to be discouraged because people do not really care for each other.[56] In *The Sovereignty of Good*, Murdoch expresses her opinion that art provides more appropriate clues for the apprehension of reality:

> The great artist sees his objects [...] in a light of justice and mercy. The direction of attention is, contrary to nature, outward away from the self which reduces all to a false unity, towards the great surprising variety of the world, and the ability to direct attention is love.[57]

Murdoch states that 'looking at other people is different from looking at trees or works of art'.[58] Looking at people has an extra layer of meaning or power dynamics whereby 'a loving just gaze cherishes

---

53   McFague, *Super, Natural Christians*, 29.
54   Ibid., 149.
55   Ibid., 28. McFague rightly points out here that this has been one of the prime contributions of feminism.
56   John Fletcher and Cheryl Bove, *Iris Murdoch: A Descriptive Primary and Annotated Secondary Bibliography* (New York & London: Garland Publishing, Inc, 1994), B0126, 209.
57   Murdoch, *The Sovereignty of Good*, 66.
58   Murdoch, *Metaphysics as a Guide to Morals*, 463.

and adds substance, a contemptuous gaze withers'.[59] Significantly, pornography falls into the latter category. In her view, the way we look at others actually takes effect in the world and has the potential to empower or disempower others.

As a case in point, Gabriele Griffen suggests that the portrayal of women in Murdoch's novels appears to represent them as 'externalisations of male needs, men who need women as mother figures, virgins, whores or goddesses.[60] Consequently, women's issues are only raised marginally and women characters are cast in conventional roles of femininity.[61] Most notably, women function as mirrors of men's needs where their individual being is not fully recognised.[62] Murdoch indicates in several novels that men are unable to 'see' women as separate individual beings. *The Sandcastle* illustrates a universal characterisation of the male ego, where Bledyard explains to Mor who is married but has a fixation on another woman, that

> there is no such thing as respect for reality. You are living on dreams now, dreams of happiness, dreams of freedom. But in all this you consider only yourself. You do not truly apprehend the distinct being of either your wife or Miss Carter.[63]

The ability to 'see' another person is primarily bound to the ability to love others, and undoubtedly, her assertion that the 'inner' life of others needs attending to was influenced by the writings of Simone Weil. When someone tries to assess another's situation, there may be no comprehension of the introspective life.[64] Much space is given over

59   Ibid.
60   Gabriele Griffen, *The Influence of the Writings of Simone Weil on the Fiction of Iris Murdoch* (San Francisco: Mellen Research University Press, 1993), 8.
61   Ibid., 7. In her later novels it should be pointed out that women do seem to become more real and less mythological figures – they do not mirror men's desires and fears to the same extent.
62   See also Mary Daly's 'The Looking Glass Society', in Ann Loades (ed), *Feminist Theology: A Reader* (London: SPCK, 1990).
63   Iris Murdoch, *The Sandcastle* (London: Penguin, 1957), 213.
64   Also see *The Sovereignty of Good*, 17–23 for Murdoch's example of a mother-in-law who feels hostility towards her daughter-in-law but learns to see her in a good light.

to such inner musings in her novels. The inclusion of such insight into moral reasoning, in Murdoch's language, means that the capacity for empathy has more to do with 'vision' than 'choice'. In other words, the ability to 'see' or empathetically enter into another's world enables more advanced moral insight than does reason alone. The mystical or imaginative approach to morality is equally present in Levertov's writing.

Levertov expresses an affiliation with Albert Schweitzer's under-valued doctrine of Reverence for Life, with the recognition of 'oneself as *life that wants to live* among other *forms of life that want to live*'.[65] Levertov further maintains that there can be 'no self-respect without respect for others, no love and reverence for others without love and reverence for oneself; and no recognition of others is possible without the imagination'.[66] It is uniquely through attention that this reverence or compassion for other life is achieved. In 'Watching, Dark Circle',[67] Levertov highlights our inability to feel the pain of others. Here she refers to an actual event through the graphic description of the use of pigs for testing the effects of a nuclear blast. She quite rightly points out that 'the Pentagon wants to know something a child could tell it: it hurts to burn', and she criticises the notion that the deliberate harm done to these animals can be called a 'simulation' because the agony is real for the pigs. Instead, she suggests that the so-called simulation is in fact 'the simulation of hell'.[68]

In order to imagine a more mutual understanding between sen-tient beings, McFague develops the metaphor of vision through the idea of 'locking eyes'. 'When we lock eyes something happens: we become two subjects, not subject and object [...] so that we relate to

65   Levertov does not reference Schweitzer here but she most probably refers to the sentence 'The most immediate and comprehensive fact of consciousness is that I am life which wills to live, in the midst of life that wills to live', in *The Philosophy of Civilisation*, trans. C. T. Campion (New York: Macmillan, 1950; reprint, New York: Prometheus Books, 1987), 310.
66   Levertov, 'Origins of a Poem', in *The Poet in the World*, 53.
67   Levertov, *Oblique Prayers*, 37
68   Ibid.

others more like a Thou than an It'.[69] In this subject–subject relationship, the 'other' may be human or non-human. An example of a 'locking of eyes' was experienced by Dillard while sitting by a pond, through a sudden encounter with a weasel:

> He had two black eyes I did not see, any more than you see a window. The weasel was stunned into stillness as he was emerging from beneath an enormous shaggy wildrose bush four feet away. I was stunned into stillness, twisted backward on the tree trunk. Our eyes locked, and someone threw away the key.
>
> Our look was as if two lovers, or deadly enemies, met unexpectedly on an overgrown path when each had been thinking of something else: a clearing blow to the gut. It was also a bright blow to the brain, or a sudden beating of brains, with all the charge and intimate grate of rubbed balloons. It emptied our lungs. It felled the forest, moved the fields, and drained the pond; the world dismantled and tumbled into that black hole of eyes. If you and I looked at each other that way, our skulls would split and drop to our shoulders. But we don't. We keep our skulls.[70]

This is illustrative of Buber's concept of an 'I–Thou' relationship as opposed to an 'I–It', one that relates to the meeting of two equals rather than an objective gaze that seeks to dominate. Dillard recounts a similar experience in contemplating her goldfish Ellery: 'Our eyes meet; a consciousness snaps back and forth'.[71]

On an epistemological level, Murdoch, Levertov and Dillard portray encounters with other beings in a manner that challenges harmful dualistic constructions. If others are seen as objects rather than subjects in their own right, it affords them no moral significance and allows the justification of abuse and exploitation. Paramountly, the *via integrativa* prioritises radical engagement with other beings. While there is no denying the fact that human existence consists of duality, shifting to one extreme is disastrous for the individual, society and the natural environment as the balance is tipped in favour of those with the most power.

---

69   McFague, *Super, Natural Christians*, 35. McFague uses Martin Buber's phrase here.
70   Dillard, *Living by Fiction*, 67.
71   Dillard, *Pilgrim at Tinker Creek*, 129.

250

Blurring the Boundaries of Knowledge

By definition, the *via integrativa* subverts dualistic thinking or ways of explaining human existence. The separation between love and knowledge, between reason and imagination, is not evident in Julian's theology, and that separation is also absent in Murdoch, Levertov and Dillard's work. In fact, in postmodernity, it is perhaps more important to acknowledge that we must interrogate and assimilate knowledge within a context that values both individual existential knowledge as well as considering global implications.

Matthews suggests that a mystical person in postmodernity becomes a 'liminal witness'.[72] As *limen* is Latin for 'threshold' this implies that this 'witness' is someone who operates as a mediator between various social, religious and disciplinary groups, particularly those on the margins. It is important to note, therefore, that Murdoch, Levertov and Dillard draw upon many academic disciplines and literary genres in order to incorporate an eclectic range of knowledge and thought into their work. Murdoch was of course a respected philosopher, but she was also well versed in theological and religious studies. Levertov, whilst heavily steeped in her literary heritage and Judeo-Christian context had a good knowledge of a range of spiritual traditions.[73] Dillard brings insights from natural history, philosophy, literature, biblical exegesis, theology and science into her mysticism. In fact, more of a generalist than a specialist, Dillard is the hardest to contain within any particular genre or discipline.

Subverting Dualistic Thinking

Any knowledge about God, due to the invisible nature of the subject matter, can never be purely a matter of rational discourse but must

---

72　Matthews, *Both Alike to Thee*, 139.
73　Levertov published a book with Edward C. Dimock, Jr. of translated Vaishnava poetry from the Indian religious traditions, *In Praise of Krishna: Songs from the Bengali* (Chicago: The University of Chicago Press, 1965).

draw equally on imaginative and emotive elements of an embodied life. Beginning with the late medieval period and extending through to the Enlightenment there was an increased separation of the creature from the Creator in metaphysical thought, and predominately in the Protestant tradition, God became a transcendent object, distant and outside of Creation in order to preserve God's sovereignty. McIntosh sums up this theological stance:

> God is a particularly powerful and invisible subject who acts over against human subjects, and must withdraw in order to permit their freedom to act autonomously. [...] Likewise the human person comes to be understood as human subject over against whom exists the range of objects for potential mastery and subordination.[74]

Hence, God and the human subject are mutually exclusive, each with power over others. The human mind by virtue of our radical capacity for self-consciousness became the sole source and centre of meaning, whilst God ceases to be perceptible in creation. This results in the dualistic separation of the object and subject as characterised in the modernist agenda and brings with it an elevated notion of the free and autonomous individual. In short, the over-emphasis on God as Other has resulted in both denying God and an exaggerated view of human power.

Jantzen reminds us that it was Christian theologians who utilised Plato's thought to set up binary dualisms. This led to the association of the mind with the divine, so that 'the Divine One, who has pure spirit, pure goodness, and thought of as male, was contrasted with the material world, which was dependent, chaotic, and thought of as female (as in "Mother Earth")'.[75] Jantzen also points out that the Protestant German theologian Karl Barth sought to retain the oppositional characteristics of dualism and that he maintained that any attempt to treat them as equal was a 'false realism'.[76]

If God as a moral absolute moves further and further out of the picture, correspondingly, moral thinking becomes more and more rela-

---

74   McIntosh, *Mystical Theology*, 211.
75   Jantzen, *Becoming Divine*, 267.
76   Ibid., 269.

tive. The claims that the autonomous individual has superseded absolutes and universal laws in postmodernity present the real possibility that ethics as a set of virtues and moral values common to all could disappear before a horizon of free choice in a consumer society. Murdoch, through her model of the spiritual journey towards the Good, intends to pre-empt such a decline; Levertov refuses to separate faith from political agency; while Dillard aspires to bring an unpredictable God devoid of human construction back into the picture.

Dialectical Ways of Knowing

Systematic theologians provide a thematic, or systemised, summary of the main doctrinal positions in Christian theology, and by so doing, they seek to provide a unified vision of biblical teachings relevant for contemporary contexts. Often, in order to achieve such a systematic description, there is inevitably some selective pruning in order to achieve a sense of coherence.[77] In this manner, theology tends to adopt a somewhat blinkered and unhelpful response to the human condition by bracketing off anything that sits outside its field of vision. In the main, this systematic approach requires the use of reason and logic to characterise and identify key terms and concepts. A mystic, or as we have seen, a creative writer, is more likely to use the senses, emotion, intuition or imagination to apprehend and describe the sacred. Within the former category, there are clear boundaries such as the difference between right and wrong and between the divine and human. In the latter category, the boundaries blur so that knowledge is dialectical and flexible and does not therefore provide rigid structures of thought. Likewise, mystical perception relies on paradoxical and ambiguous language, terms that suggest 'an encompassing, elemental, or ultimate unity through a juxtaposition of opposites that frustrate the analytic

---

77 Rosemary Radford Ruether would be a typical example of this theological method. She has pruned away everything that she sees as being unhelpful or inherently sexist or able to support systems of domination from the Judaeo-Christian tradition to provide a form of Christianity liberated from colonial or patriarchal biases.

intellect's conventional attempt to join them'.[78] While Murdoch, Lever-tov and Dillard build bridges between bipolar opposites using their imaginations, they do not offer easy answers or find permanent resolutions to life's conundrums.

According to Lorna Sage, Murdoch's writing occupies what she terms the 'middle-ground'.[79] As such, Murdoch creates and inhabits a mediating space between the symbolic narratives of orthodox philosophy and the popular genre of the novel. Her philosophy relates to a conceptual space, while her novels occupy a cultural space. Murdoch's focus on the concept of the Good, which, like God and Kant's Universal Law, is unrepresentable and transcendent and is based on an aspiration towards perfection in lived experience. She asserts that the 'intellect naturally seeks unity',[80] and it is only through the intellect and emotions together that progress towards the Good can be made. She does not seek to replace reason with emotion, but rather, to enter into a creative space of dialogue between the two.

There is, as Dipple aptly demonstrates, an important point of separation in Murdoch's philosophy, which departs from Plato's ideal of the absolute in favour of a realisation of our 'entrapment in a perpetual, flawed selfhood almost entirely incapable of moral advancement'.[81] In 'The Fire and the Sun' Murdoch comments that

> Plato spent some extremely valuable time (*Parmenides, Theaetetus, Sophist*) dismantling his earlier imagery, but then invented some more, marvellous, entirely new, mythological but still explanatory images in the *Timaeus*. [...] However, his failures do not lead him (as they might lead a later, Christian or liberal, thinker) to conclude humbly or tolerantly that the human mind is essentially limited and fallible. They lead rather to a firmer sense of Hierarchy. Wisdom is *there*, but belongs to gods and very few mortals *(Timaeus, Laws)*.[82]

78   Joseph Keller, 'The Function of Paradox in Mystical Discourse', in *Studia Mystica* 6:3 (1983), 5.

79   Lorna Sage, *Women in the House of Fiction* (Basingstoke: Macmillan, 1992), 72.

80   Murdoch, *Sovereignty of Good*, 57.

81   Dipple, *Work for the Spirit*, 78.

82   Murdoch, 'The Fire and the Sun', in Conradi (ed), *Existentialists and Mystics*, 445–46.

This highlights the major flaw in Plato's thought that is corrected by the humility of mystics such as Julian. A single-minded focus on wisdom outside of the world leads to the false belief in the potential of humans to escape their imperfect nature. Instead, as Murdoch demonstrates through her novels, overcoming our fallibility is a continual struggle.

Undoubtedly, philosophical reflection spills over into her novels, so that the difference between truth and fiction becomes blurred.[83] Yet her attention to detail and local particularities question the logic of dualistic or oppositional thinking, which radically separates the mind from experience. In other words, thought and emotion move together to create a scepticism towards the bipolar separation of good and evil, right and wrong, or truth and fiction.

Likewise, Levertov continually breaches the boundary between imagination and intellect. When properly utilised, she argues, imagination is the key to moving beyond what might be termed 'the feel good factor' or an artificial consolation:

> The action of imagination, if unsmothered, is to lift the crushed mind out from under the weight of affliction. The intellect by itself may point out the source of suffering; but the imagination illuminates it; by that light it becomes more comprehensible. [...] Though imagination's wings can lift the individual out of private pits of gloom, it is a *creative* function, producing new forms and transforming existing ones; and these come into being *in the world*, autonomous objects available to others, and capable of transforming *them*.[84]

In Levertov's reasoning, intellect, although invaluable to comprehend things, remains a passive and static force if not 'illuminated' by imagination. Poetry that accurately depicts the horrors of our time can only make readers really know by appealing to human imagination

---

83   Murdoch, 'Literature and Philosophy: A conversation with Bryan Magee', in Conradi (ed), *Existentialists and Mystics*, 4–5. As noted previously, Murdoch makes it clear that literature and philosophy are two distinct disciplines. Among other aspects, art is more widely accessible while philosophy tends to be more elitist. Philosophy requires exactness and logical thinking while art can be ambiguous and appeals aesthetically.

84   Levertov, 'Poetry, Prophecy, Survival', in *New & Selected Essays*, 145–46.

and emotion, by 'giving flesh to the abstract.'[85] As Levertov succinctly puts it, 'Just to tell the tale and walk away isn't enough.'[86] She sums up her own stance by denying that she is 'specifically an intellectual'. An artist, she suggests, has to '[draw] upon a wider range of intelligence – sensory, intuitive, emotional – than the term intellect connotes'.[87] In the final instance, Levertov's intellectual creed was undeniably an aesthetic that was 'bound up with artistic integrity'.[88]

Indeed, Levertov feels that it is her responsibility as a poet to inhabit the space between different realities, causing her to write in 'The Life of Art:'[89] 'the borderland – that's where, if one knew how, / one would establish residence. That watershed'. She acknowledges that as a creative poet she needs to be constantly aware of what is happening in the world and to offer interpretations, thereby becoming, from a position on this borderland, a 'locus of change'.[90] This balance is a rare and difficult thing to obtain though: 'there's an interface, / immeasurable, elusive – an equilibrium / just attainable, sometimes, when the attention's rightly poised'. So this 'equilibrium' that remains 'elusive' is something to be strived for in the creative working life. It is from this position on the borderland that the writer can transcend both themselves and the contingent in order to see 'what lies beyond the window, past the frame, beyond...' in order to offer new insights. The poet then operates in the tension between what is factual and what is ideal – moves to 'some place part fantasy, part truer-than-fact, where the life of the imagination supersedes commonplace activity'.[91] Yet it is only by holding firmly onto reality that the ideal can be aspired towards – to let go of reality opens the way for escapism into the world of fantasy.

Dillard describes the end of the *via negativa* as 'the lightless edge where the slopes of knowledge dwindle, and love for its own

85   Ibid., 147.
86   Ibid., 146.
87   Levertov, 'A Poet's View', in *New & Selected Essays*, 239.
88   Ibid., 240.
89   Levertov, *A Door in the Hive*, 85.
90   Victoria Harris, 'Denise Levertov and the Lyric of the Contingent Self', in Little & Paul, *Denise Levertov*, 22.
91   Wagner-Martin, *Critical Essays on Denise Levertov*, 1.

sake, lacking an object, begins'.[92] This is the recognition that the mystical journey must ultimately move past the intellect and reason and move towards love, that knowledge is only a means to an end – not the end in itself. Elsewhere, Dillard raises her fears that language may not be able to convey any real meaning beyond individual understanding when she asks,

> Is the search for meaning among the high heaps of the meaningless a fool's game? Is it art's game? What is (gasp) the relationship between the world and the mind? Is *knowledge* possible? Do we ever discover meaning, or do we make it up?[93]

The claim that 'true' knowledge is never possible is self-evident to mystics.

The same notion is present in *Holy the Firm*, where she states: 'Knowledge is impossible. We are precisely nowhere, sinking on an imaginary ice floe, into entirely imaginary seas themselves adrift'.[94] Language, although always imprecise, is the only means available to us. It follows that fluctuations of an imperfect world will necessitate a continual requirement to revision the notion of the sacred, for to treat anything in the finite world as beyond criticism is to render language idolatrous. This is what has tended to happen in religious discourse, where the dynamic functions of metaphors and symbols have become concretised and operate as idols rather than means to go beyond the more familiar interpretations of things they represent. Conversely, the potential for a symbol to 'act at the level where the scarcely understood fades into the unknown', Dillard suggestion allows it to act as 'an instrument of new knowledge'.[95] She elaborates:

> Symbol does not only refer; it acts. There is no such thing as a *mere* symbol. When you climb to the higher level of abstraction, symbols, those enormous, translucent planets, are all there is. They are at once your only tools of knowledge and that knowledge's only object. It is no leap to say that space-time is itself a symbol. If the material world is a symbol, it is the symbol of mind, or of

92   Dillard, *Living by Fiction*, 60.
93   Ibid., 14
94   Ibid., 46.
95   Ibid., 168–169.

God. Which is more or less meaningless – as you choose. But it is not *mere*. In the last analysis, symbols and art objects do not stand for things; they manifest them, in their fullness. You begin by using symbols, and end by contemplating them.[96]

Symbols and metaphors are the only means available to us by which we can articulate our sense of the sacred. Even philosophy, in the end, has to rely on metaphor to speak about its concepts. Symbols and metaphors step in 'at the rim of knowledge where language falters'.[97]

Although Dillard recognises that each progressive generation has the task of dedicating themselves 'to more comprehensive forms of beauty and understanding',[98] she tends to be sceptical about what she calls the 'human emotional stew' because it might provide a false ego-centric view of the world.[99] Additionally, Dillard is somewhat unusual in that she fuses a scientific approach with a mystical one in the contemplation of nature. Susan Felch observes that *Holy the Firm* contains a 'reflection thoroughly informed by modern physics'.[100] If science tells her one thing, it is that life is chaotic and random; '[n]othing temporal, spatial, perceptual, social or moral is fixed'.[101] In other words, she has confidence in the ability of science to broaden our mystical understanding of the world, and for example, suggests that Isaac Newton's discovery of gravity under the apple tree provides an interesting parallel to Buddha's enlightenment under the Bo tree and aligns herself with both.[102]

Time and space is a further continual fascination to Dillard.[103] Webb notices that, in Dillard's thought, 'the irregularities of time and place are hyperbolically condensed to produce a sudden illumination, sublime, mystical and yet troubling'. Thus, an epiphany is produced

96   Ibid., 169–70. I suggest that Dillard's statement here applies equally to the use of metaphor.
97   Ibid., 170.
98   Ibid.,
99   Dillard, *Pilgrim at Tinker Creek*, 181.
100   Susan, M. Felch, 'Annie Dillard: Modern Physics in a Contemporary Mystic', in *Mosaic* 22:2 (1989), 2.
101   Dillard, *Living by Fiction*, 24.
102   Dillard, *Pilgrim at Tinker Creek*, 186.
103   Dillard, *Living by Fiction*, 24.

through 'a disruptive suspension of ordinary time, a moment of eternity in the here and now'.[104] These moments appear to be unstable, yet as Humble-Johnson notes, it is 'the illuminated moment [that] has the potential to steady a wobbling universe'.[105] It is in fact her knowledge of Einstein's work that encourages her to seek this timeless moment that is an in between place. In was Dillard's belief that spiritual intuition and creative writing, as with Einstein's hypothesising, could lead to '*true* knowing'.[106] However, developing such knowledge and understanding only functions as a transformative power if it transposes onto practical or political matters.

Towards a Theology of Integration

Because the notion of dualism is so firmly ingrained in Western culture, one of the overriding problems that theologians face in postmodernity is that of merging conceptual opposites such as theory and practice, secularism and spirituality, intellect and emotion, and what approach to take to insights from other world religions. Here the model of relationship is evoked to imagine a theological integration of these polarities. This effectively enables personal spiritual experience to feed into the wider communal theological enterprise, thus avoiding the exclusive, ego-ridden, journey of individual faith.

Mysticism as Praxis

Since the 1960s, liberation theologians have endorsed the belief that theology cannot be divorced from political reality. The word *praxis* stems from the Greek verb *prassien*, which means 'to do'. By defin-

---

104   Stephen H. Webb, 'Nature's Spendthrift Economy: The Extravagance of God in *Pilgrim at Tinker Creek*', in *Soundings*, 77 (1994), 435–36.
105   Humble-Johnson, *The Space Between*, 20.
106   Ibid., 21.

ition, praxis involves the integration of ideas and actions, of theory and practice. I suggest that mystical praxis is about paying attention to the world around us, continuing the quest for spiritual insights, taking ethical responsibility for our actions, and having the courage to speak out – ultimately reaching out to others. The Greek term *phronesis*, which means to act truly and rightly, perhaps captures this best. This is a term developed by Aristotle as an alternative way of knowing, standing in contradistinction to *sophia*, which means to be more concerned with universal truths. *Phronesis* is usually translated as 'practical wisdom' and refers to the development of a habitual or virtuous way of living that will inevitably include a concern to further the well-being of all.

In Chapter Two the roles of Mary and Martha were discussed as the role models for the *via contemplativa* and the *via activa*. A crucial dimension of a mystic's life past and present is the ability to build a bridge between the outer or active life and the inner or contemplative life. Historically, Mary who sits at Christ's feet in quiet contemplation has been valued over Martha, who attends to his bodily needs. In theological terms, this relates symbolically to the elevation of theory over praxis. Eckhart, however, did not separate 'Martha's acting from Mary's contemplative devotion but rather, conceiving of Mary in Martha' as the more spiritually developed. The point that Soelle makes is that the aim of the mystic life should not be

> to practice an introverted mysticism nor to engage in an extroverted critique of the age alone, but to find one's *vita mixta* in this sense between contemplation and activity. [...] This combination of contemplating and acting is rooted in the mystical understanding of the relationship to God as a mutuality of receiving and giving.[107]

The fact that Julian wrote in the vernacular so that 'even Christians' could share her revelations as well as acting as a spiritual advisor exemplifies this dual achievement of the mystic.

Murdoch's approach, while not explicitly political or radical, inspires moral action at a public and private level. Her attempts to recover Plato's concept of the Good can contribute to ideological re-

---

107   Soelle, *The Silent Cry*, 200–1.

structuring at a communal level, while her concerns about illusion and self-deception encourage a reorientation of individual consciousness. Of our three literary writers, Levertov is the most overtly political. She felt obliged to work for peace and justice, and for her, prayer and politics play an equal role in Christian discipleship. Carley depicts Dillard as 'an axe for the frozen sea within us [...] breaking through the frozen separating the modern self from the world'.[108] The goal is not just to bring comfort to their readers, but rather, like Julian, these writers want their audiences to learn from and act upon their experiences.

For Murdoch, contrary to popular notions of mysticism, a mystical orientation directs humans away from the self and towards others. She believed that people are not one-dimensional, but varied and complex, and it is only by incorporating a spiritual element into their lives, which she defines as 'attention' towards others, that people can make sense of the world. Abstract theory does not account for real people's lives. In the real world, people have a tendency to use other people for their own ends. A focus on the self, whether it is selfish love or lust, guilt, anger or intellectual pursuits, distracts us from reality. In few words, Murdoch's moral philosophy can be summed up in the phrase 'loving attention'.

Levertov demonstrates a more proactive understanding of love that leads to action through her political activities during the seventies. For her, to transform the world through love means being vocal, being active and being prepared to break the law in the name of peace and justice. Cary Nelson observes that, within Levertov's poetic vision, there emerges a 'moral commitment to practical action *outside* poetry [which] enters the poetry itself'.[109] Levertov was involved in 'Ban the Bomb' demonstrations in the fifties, but her leftist political views did not appear in her poetry until the late sixties. Patricia Hampl describes Levertov as 'a reporter or witness at the political front [...] a *soul* at the front'.[110] As Hampl realises, Levertov feels acute guilt for being

---

108 Burton Carley 'Annie Dillard: Getting a Feel for the Place', in *The Journal of Liberal Religion*, 2:1 (2000), http://www. meadville.edu/gibbons_2_1.html
109 Cary Nelson, 'Levertov's Political Poetry', in Gelpi, *Denise Levertov*, 162.
110 Patricia Hampl, 'A Witness of Our Time', in Gelpi, *Denise Levertov*, 167.

alive at all; as long as someone on earth was suffering and dying, she felt guilt for having herself survived. Then, moreover, she feels complicitous in human-caused suffering. For example, she feels implicated in the American involvement in the war in Vietnam. At times, her anger spills over into her poetry, which she argued should not be the purpose of poetry, but it was as if she could not contain her rage at injustice. This is something she had to overcome to live and work at her full potential.

During the Vietnam War, Levertov adopted an anti-war stance that was, largely, contrary to popular opinion in America at the time. Although there were growing voices of dissent, especially from the younger generation, the average American was firmly committed to their country's involvement in the conflict. It was only through the concerted efforts of committed pacifists, in whose number Levertov can be counted, that the American public gradually became aware of atrocities inflicted on the Vietnamese people in the name of democracy. The fact that a poet engaged in what is essentially a political issue through poetry led to disagreement among literary critics and politicians alike, but Levertov believed passionately that she was morally obligated to respond to issues of inhumanity and injustice that she perceived to be all around her.[111] This is vital if we wish to eliminate disillusionment and despair in postmodernity.

Unlike Levertov, Dillard does not attempt political polemic or moral teaching. She said, 'I don't write at all about ethics. I try to do right and rarely do so. The kind of art I write is shockingly uncommitted – appallingly isolated from political, social, and economic affairs.'[112] To many, her policy of non-intervention is problematic. Pamela Smith speculates that this could partly be due to a feeling of 'estrangement […]' of an 'overwhelming sense of separateness'.[113] In addition, she offers no alternative visions of Western thought and practice. But she does urge her readers through her reflections on her own experience to become fully alive and awake through an evocation

111   Her good friend Duncan was firmly against her politicising poetry early on, and it caused a rift between them.
112   Philip Yancy, 'A Face Aflame', in *Christianity Today*, 22 (1978), 960.
113   Smith, 'The Ecotheology of Annie Dillard: A Study in Ambivalence.'

of consciousness.[114] Above all else, she wants to make her readers conscious of the supernatural, and surely to grow in consciousness means to become more aware. Although Dillard concentrates on her own personal growth (leaving her open to the criticism of egocentrism), the contemplative requirements of a mystic discussed previously pre-empt too much navel gazing.

The Model of Relationship

Julian's teachings are undoubtedly entrenched in the Augustinian tradition and the doctrines of the Church. More importantly, however, her theology is fundamentally Trinitarian, for the Trinity is the expression of integration *par excellence*. Philip Sheldrake, in his exposition of the divorce between spirituality and theology, suggests that the Trinity represents 'a creative tension within God that is inherently dynamic rather than static. [As such] it holds together unity and diversity, oneness and distinction, communion and individuality, fixed ground and fluid relations.'[115]

Although the Christian Trinity as a metaphysical reality is not of great significance for Murdoch, Levertov and Dillard, its metaphorical implications are evident. Indeed, it is interesting to note that ways of knowing and being tend to be represented by triadic structures in more holistic viewpoints rather than binary oppositions as found in mechanistic modes of understanding the world.[116] Trinities are therefore common metaphors in world religions to represent the idea of the one

114   Carley, 'Anne Dillard: Getting a Feel for the Place.'
115   Sheldrake, *Spirituality and Theology*, 49.
116   Trinities exist in most world mythologies as a natural metaphor of the concept
        of the tension or space between opposites. Trinities typically represent the idea
        of the one and the many, or the sense of unity at the heart of creation. In Maha-
        yana Buddhism, for example, the *dharmakaya* represents the cosmic body of
        Buddha, *nirmanakaya* the cosmic body incarnate in Gautama Buddha, and *sam-
        bogakaya* is the cosmic body present in the intersessionary bodhisattvas. In
        ancient Egyptian mythology, there was the Osirus-Isis-Horus trinity. Another
        example would be the Hindu *trimurti* of Brahma, Vishnu and Shiva as aspects
        of the universal Brahman.

and the many, or the sense of unity at the heart of creation. This represents a perceived unity present within the universe. It is also a model of relationship. It is a metaphor representing the mysterious and inexhaustible mystery of God. It is also a metaphor for the human being made in the image of God. An integrated view of the human person would include body, mind and soul, and in short, triadic structures resist dualistic modes of thinking by suggesting a more holistic or integrated vision of reality.

Mystical perception of a Transcendent Absolute, whether we call it the Good or God, or anything else, cannot materialise in the 'dress' of language without the combined efforts of both mind and heart. Moreover, without a corporeal body, humans would be unable to think or write. We can conclude, therefore, that our cognitive faculties (mind), our emotions (heart), and physical attributes (body) are three interlinked and necessary components to make the conveyance of a mystical consciousness possible. Language, particularly mystical language, has the potential to provide the bridge between these ontological realities. The poem, according to Levertov, is a 'communion [...] between the maker and the needer within the poet; the makers and needers outside him [sic] [...] and between the human and divine in both poet and reader'.[117]

McFague has made her most prominent mark on the theological enterprise through her reconfigured Trinitarian model of God as Lover, Mother and Friend as outlined in *Models of God* (1987) and *Body of God* (1993). This conceptualization of the Trinity reflects her view that relationship is an ontological reality. Humans are literally made from stardust and are part of the same 'primal explosion' as is the rest of the cosmos, for example, and thus emblematic of interrelationship in the extreme.[118] Salvation in McFague's theology is within this world and sin is categorised as 'turning away not from a transcendent power but from interdependence with other beings, including the matrix of

117   Levertov, 'Origins of a Poem', in *The Poet in the World*, 47. Note that Levertov speaks of the divine somewhat ambiguously here, as 'a vast, irreducible spirit', as this was before her conversion to Roman Catholicism.
118   McFague, *The Body of God*, 104.

being from whom all life comes'.[119] By the time McFague writes *Life Abundant*, she has changed her metaphors for the Trinity to 'Creator, Sustainer and Liberator'. The metaphors will no doubt continue to change, but the Trinity as a metaphor for relationship in the context of unity and diversity has much potential. Of course, the relationship that individual humans have with multiple others is but one dimension of this.

The Personal to the Communal

The totality of human existence consists of both the universal and the particular; every living thing has its own peculiarities whilst at *the same time* participating in the whole of all that is – and theology must relate to and express both. Murdoch persuades us that

> [o]ur pilgrimage (in the direction of reality, good) is not experienced only in high, broad or general ways (such as in increased understanding of mathematics or justice), it is experienced in all our most minute relations with our surrounding world, wherein apprehensions (perceptions) of the minutest things (stones, spoons, leaves, scraps of rubbish, tiny gestures etc., etc.) are also capable of being deeper, more benevolent, more just (etc., etc.) [*sic*][120]

So, like Julian, Murdoch recognises that both our 'substance and sensuality' are part of a larger unity. In an attempt to provide moral inspiration, however, Murdoch includes, through the personal fable, a means by which individual vision enters into a dialogue with public moral debate at a time when religious belief appeared to be in decline. Murdoch questions the logic of universal rules by suggesting that certain stories 'incarnate a moral truth that is paradoxical, infinitely suggestive and open to continual reinterpretation'.[121] In particular, the space given to ambiguity and paradox in her novels effectively

119   McFague, *Models of God*, 139.
120   Murdoch, *Metaphysics as a Guide to Morals*, 474. It is poignant that at the end of her life Murdoch took to collecting bits of rubbish like old envelopes and cigarette ends. Bayley, *Elegy for Iris*, 80.
121   Iris Murdoch, 'Vision and Choice in Morality', in Conradi (ed), *Existentialists and Mystics*, 91.

highlights the complexities of many moral choices. Moral reasoning is not a fixed absolute, but rather, is in continual flux.

Perhaps more accurately stated, she creates contexts that enable an objective reflection on moral and ethical concerns. Her oft-quoted metaphor of 'great hall of reflection where we can all meet and where everything under the sun can be examined and considered'[122] offers an interesting divergence from Plato's myth of the cave. In Plato's thought, the conception of ideas only takes place outside the cave away from illusion, whilst Murdoch, conversely, 'sees thinking as rooted in body-language'.[123] Murdoch here calls into question the idea of the disembodied intellect. Through attention to the 'stuff' of an ordinary life, she similarly denounces the notion of an abstract individual that dominates Western philosophy. It is only through our interaction with others as part of different communities that moral or mystical insight occurs.

It took Levertov many years and much wrestling with her conscience to harmonise the relationship between her personal life and the public world of politics. Lorrie Smith puts it succinctly when she concludes that,

> Not until she learns to live with paradox, relinquishing the desire to reconcile good and evil, can Levertov move beyond defeat toward new, though diminished, forms of affirmation. Her deep yearning for synthesis gradually moderates into a sort of détente which eases the polarized tension between the personal life and public contingency, lyric revelation and didactic statement. [...] Though 'inner' and 'outer' are often painfully separate in Levertov's fallen world, they are also paradoxically united because one person suffers and another records the dissonance. Her most successful political poems neither collapse the distinctions between these terms nor flatly oppose them, but sustain an equilibrium in which the integrity of each is preserved and enlarged by the other.[124]

---

122 Murdoch, 'The Fire and the Sun', in Conradi (ed), *Existentialists and Mystics*, 461.
123 Sage, *Women in the House of Fiction*, 83.
124 Lorrie Smith, 'Songs of Experience: Denise Levertov's Political Poetry', in Gelpi, *Denise Levertov*, 181.

In Levertov's affirmative vision, 'her knowledge of evil is mitigated by a deep reverence for earthly life'.[125] She does not attempt to offer specific solutions to problems, but as a socially engaged poet, she feels equally compelled to point out that which is worthy of praise and that which should be protested against. This is an exemplary example of the *via integrativa*. Hampl also makes the point that, unlike feminist poets such as Adrienne Rich and Marge Piercy, who hoist a large part of the blame for the Vietnam War onto men and patriarchy, Levertov recognises herself 'as a citizen of an oppressive nation, rather than as a victim of it [so] she could not separate herself physically from that paralyzing guilt that war brought with it'.[126] In other words, for Levertov, true liberation happens at both the personal and political levels and as a member of the community, not in separation. A succinct example of how the particular and the general are linked in Levertov's work surfaces in 'The Batterers'.[127] Levertov uses a man beating a woman and his 'astonished' realisation that he begins 'to cherish her' as an allegory for the way human beings have mistreated the earth. 'Earth can we not love you unless we believe the end is near?' Levertov uses domestic violence as a metaphor for the mindless destruction of the natural environment to suggest that we only love what we are in the midst of destroying.

The fact that Dillard moves from her solitary experience in *Pilgrim at Tinker Creek* to include the experiences of others in *Holy the Firm* and *Teaching a Stone to Talk* prompts Ronda to assert that 'a kind of tension is created between personal vision and collective insight'.[128] It is particularly in her essays 'Expedition to the Pole' and 'Total Eclipse' that this is evident. In the latter, Dillard, through dialogue with the Other, treads the *via media* between self-absorption and communal loyalties so that an engagement with others 'completes the incomplete self'.[129] An essential element of Dillard's writing that is

---

125 Ibid., 192.
126 Patricia Hampl, 'A Witness of Our Time', 170–71.
127 Levertov, *Evening Train*, 1.
128 Bruce A. Ronda, 'Annie Dillard's Fictions to Live By', in *Christian Century* 101:35 (1984), 1062.
129 Ibid., 1066.

often overlooked due to the solitary nature of her work is her sense of community. One of the most memorable of Dillard's accounts of her forays into nature is 'Total Eclipse', which appears in *Teaching a Stone to Talk*. She gathers with a crowd 'of rugged individualists' on a mountain in Washington State to watch the event[130] and describes how 'wrong' the world looked once the sun was covered up:

> The sky snapped over the sun like a lens cover. The hatch in the brain slammed. Abruptly it was dark night, on the land and in the sky. [...] There was no sound. The eyes dried, the arteries drained, the lungs hushed. There was no world. We were the world's dead people rotating and orbiting around and around, embedded in the planet's crust, while the earth rolled down. Our minds were light years distant, forgetful of almost everything.[131]

Time stood still on that mountainside, and Dillard, in the face of 'the power and indifference of nature', here 'claim[s] a place with others'. Ronda suggests that she imagines this as an apocalyptic scenario similar to a nuclear disaster, but what is clear is that Dillard wants to be with others, and in fact, in other writings, she has identified herself, 'however ambivalently, [with] the Christian community'.[132] Dana Wilde argues that, compared to Dillard's vision of 'the tree with the lights in it', this is not a 'real' mystical experience.[133] But the argument here maintains that all experience has the potential for mystical insight. For Dillard in this piece, her revelation is somewhat sinister and provides a prophetic insight into the outcome of thinking ourselves too powerful. However, I would argue that, by situating herself with others, Dillard emphasises the communal aspect of mysticism. After the eclipse she and her companion go back to a restaurant and eat among some of the other watchers, reinforcing the fact that she perceived herself as part of the human community. In fact, a young man suggests that the eclipse 'looked like a Life Saver up in the sky',[134] Dillard agrees with him and describes him as a 'walking alarm clock' who brings her back to the

130   Dillard, *Teaching a Stone to Talk*, 13.
131   Ibid., 18.
132   Bruce A. Ronda, 'Annie Dillard's Fictions to Live By', 1062.
133   Dana Wilde, 'Annie Dillard's "A Field of Silence": The Contemplative Tradition in the Modern Age', in *Mystics Quarterly* 26:1 (2000), 31–45.
134   Dillard, *Teaching a Stone to Talk*, 23.

world of reality, ready for 'the mind to begin its task'.[135] This helps her to realise that the 'vision' is useless unless she continues in her task of waking people up, through her creative ability to manipulate language, to the sacred.

Re-orientation of Private and Political Consciousness.

Murdoch, Levertov and Dillard provide clues that help us find our real selves by incorporating the whole array of human experience into their mystical reflections. Theological knowledge must include emotion and rational argument as a way of living in a dialectical tension between our private and public selves. At the microcosmic level, the writings of Murdoch, Levertov and Dillard contain a subjective view of the world through their individual mystical quests. At the macrocosmic level, however, their voices are prophetic by protesting against injustice and reading the signs of the time. The *via integrativa* is about the integration of our experiences, our ideas and ourselves, but more importantly, this stage in the mystic's path ensures that private contemplation does not exclude right actions – moral outrage and mystical vision must be parallel motivations for the mystic way in postmodernity. This will inevitably require a radical change of consciousness at both a personal and social level, which is a crucial step in order to maintain the *via transformativa*.

135   Ibid., 23–24.

Chapter Seven
The *Via Transformativa*: Likely Stories

In the preceding chapter I argued that Murdoch, Levertov and Dillard encourage their readers to strive for integration of body, mind and soul and to orientate perceptions and actions consciously towards others. I further argued, based on my reading of Soelle, Jantzen and McFague, that incorporating such insights into theological expression provides a middle path between postmodern consumer spiritualities and modernist discourses that seek a universal set of claims regarding the truth, whether those claims are religious or scientific. It should be clear by now that the writer as mystic (or vice versa) is someone who is ideally situated ideologically, spiritually, intellectually and imaginatively to facilitate the evocation of this middle-path and to show us 'new ways'. Therefore, this final chapter seeks to outline how the mystic way in postmodernity may contribute in a constructive way to theological reflection with a view to personal and communal transformation, or by way of the *via transformativa*.

In the end, to take literature seriously in a theological context is to talk about transformation, and it is a primary assertion of this study that stories and poetic imagery open up ways to imagine and then to create new futures. In postmodernity, there is an increasing awareness that, rather than there being just one definitive story that provides ultimate meaning in all times and places, as adherents of Christianity perceive the Bible, there are many stories that evolve and diversify over time. That is not to say that the historically revered scriptures cannot function as foundational narratives that may be woven into other new stories that 'testify through diversity and particularity to a God who is known through the stories we tell, as individuals or communities, about the experiences that have become revelatory for us'.[1]

---

1   Elaine Graham et al, *Theological Reflection: Methods* (London: SCM Press, 2005), 47.

I have been arguing throughout that the mystic way in postmodernity is not solely about those epiphanic moments that reveal the sacred. Soelle goes so far as to suggest that 'mysticism and transformation are indissolubly interconnected. [...] A genuine mystical journey has a much larger goal than to teach us positive thinking and to put to sleep our capacity to be critical and to suffer.'[2] It is inherently an ethical position that calls for active participation to create a community of justice. Soelle's understanding of mystical life is far removed from those practices that provide a soothing balm or quick release from the anxieties of modern living. We saw in Chapters Four and Five, for Murdoch, Levertov and Dillard, describing and interpreting the world is not about escaping from the unpleasant aspects of human life. Rather, the writing of writers with a mystical orientation has a prophetic role in human becoming. To return to my original aims, I wish to highlight the latent potential for transformation in the writings of Murdoch, Levertov and Dillard. Soelle, from her reading of Fox, suggests that the *via transformativa* represents 'healing that is at the same time resistance'.[3] I want to demonstrate how literary texts specifically can carry these motivations into theological expression. Accordingly, this final chapter seeks to establish how creative writers as mystics might contribute in a constructive way to a theological agenda that incorporates contemporary cultural, political and social concerns.

From its inception, the goal of the Christian Church has been personal and communal transformation, identified in the gospels as 'the good news'. Christ in Mark's Gospel instructs his disciples to 'Go into the world and proclaim the good news to the whole of creation.'[4] A postmodern world, with the hindsight of the Holocaust, Hiroshima and other twentieth century atrocities, not to mention ongoing patterns of warfare and genocide in the Middle East and the Sudan and elsewhere, must ensure that transformation maintains a critical dialogue with political and social affairs. Any theology that is orientated solely towards

---

2   Soelle, *The Silent Cry*, 89.
3   Ibid., 93.
4   Mark 16:15. The openings of the Synoptic Gospels all recount the beginning of a new era as prophesied in the Hebrew Scriptures.

some ethereal paradisiacal realm diverts attention away from injustices in this world. Furthermore, science and technology have advanced to a stage in which former beliefs have lost much of their credibility.

Murdoch, Levertov and Dillard do remain embedded within the Christian tradition, although as we have seen, in a somewhat eccentric and unorthodox manner. For Murdoch, Christianity must survive 'without literal dogma'.[5] Overwhelmingly, her view is that the religious life is synonymous with the moral life, so it is not surprising that she found inspiration in Buddhism. Despite having converted to the Roman Catholic tradition, Levertov continued to find inspiration from her Jewish ancestry, which included a special and lasting affinity with Hasidic writings. She increasingly persuaded herself that a life of religious faith should involve an obligation to work for peace. Out of the three writers, Dillard's path is the most turbulent in that she continually grapples with the problem of finding ourselves as 'moral creatures [...] in an amoral world'.[6] Nevertheless, she does not resort to nihilism, as the love between human beings and faith in a higher power that eludes understanding remain constants providing certainty. In short, situating Murdoch, Levertov and Dillard into a conventional theological position is impossible, but neither did they abandon completely the cultural context within which they were born as regards theology. Rather, they incorporated much more into that context, and indeed such diversity as is found in their writings naturally merges with theologies that acknowledge the peculiarities of postmodernity.

Today, there appear to be as many theologies as there are social, political and ethnic groups. Moreover, in postmodernity, theologies continue to fragment and diversify further. Paul Lakeland has usefully summarised the status of theology in postmodernity as exhibiting three main trajectories: the radical postmodern, the nostalgic postmodern, and the pragmatic theologians.[7] Don Cupitt would be an example

5   Gillian Dooley (ed), *From a Tiny Corner in the House of Fiction* (Columbia: University of Carolina Press, 2003), 215.
6   Kendyl Gibbons, 'Brushed with a Clean Wing: A Response to "Annie Dillard: Getting a Feel for the Place" by Burton Carley', in *The Journal of Liberal Religion*, 2: 1 (2000), http://www.meadville.edu/
7   Lakeland, *Postmodernity*, 41–44.

of a radical postmodern theologian who adamantly believes that religious happiness comes about solely through human effort, which includes a need to detach from 'old dead gods'.[8] The nostalgic postmoderns resist such theological liberalism by seeking to maintain a distinct Christian identity. They typically achieve this by returning to an exclusive premodern form of theology. Lakeland identifies two different strands in this group: 'postliberal theology', such as that espoused by George Lindbeck, and 'countermodernism', which he associates with the Anglican theologian John Milbank. Although there are many conceptual and methodological differences between them, each is convinced that secular influence 'adulterates the gospel'.[9] In between these two extremes, we find the pragmatic theologians – or what Lakeland terms 'the soft-core postmoderns'. More explicitly, Lakeland defines this group as those who are

> aware of the negative consequences of an uncritical adoption of the Enlightenment spirit [and] are also understandably wary of incorporating the death of God too literally into their religious vision. [Most] would draw the line at eliminating all notions of divine agency, and would want to preserve some sense of 'God' as not simply identical with the universe or nature, while not outside it. [...] Their preservation of hope in the postmodern world is a counter-factual commitment to transcendence; thus they are more vulnerable even than the radicals, who have put their trust in the play of text.[10]

Lakeland situates McFague in this group as a theologian who does not anthropomorphise God and espouses a panentheistic theology.[11] Although Murdoch reconfigures the personal God as the impersonal Good, there is a strong desire evident in all three of our writers to maintain a sense of the transcendent. The writers we are discussing, as well as Soelle, Jantzen and McFague, can be identified with Lakeland's definition of a 'soft-core postmodern'. As such, they fall between what we can be called 'hard' postmoderns, or the radical position that offers no hope, and the nostalgic position that offers (it could be argued) a false hope.

8   Cupitt, *Mysticism After Modernity*, 122.
9   Lakeland, *Postmodernity*, 43.
10   Ibid., 43–44.
11   Ibid., 56–57.

A corollary to theological positions concerning the place of God or the transcendent in postmodernity is the consideration of other religious traditions; the pragmatic theologians tend to be the most open to the perspectives of other faiths while the nostalgic postmoderns will only tolerate them on sufferance. For those in the more conservative or fundamental strands of the tradition, to acknowledge the value of other religious beliefs is to diminish the power of Christian teaching. Pragmatic theologians are more able to accept that other religious traditions can offer fresh or additional insight.

Contemporary theologians base their arguments concerning the dilemma that this poses around three categories: 'exclusivist' (I am right, you are wrong), 'inclusivist' (if you are a good person you can be an anonymous Christian), and pluralist (all religions are equal and relative).[12] Lakeland further suggests two hybrids: exclusivist-pluralist and pluralist-inclusivist. The former recognises other faiths as of value but doggedly maintains its own hegemonic position. The Roman Catholic Church under Pope Benedict is moving towards this point. The latter emphasises

> the value and richness of the pluralistic abundance of ways of wisdom while insisting on the hermeneutical necessity of maintaining a specific, particular, context – and history-bound way into the diversity of religions. Thus, while I do not privilege Christianity in an absolute sense, I encounter other traditions through the lens of my own.[13]

This is perhaps a more honest approach to Hick's inclusivist and pluralist categories and takes into account shifting perceptions as we move into the new millennium. The 'pluralist-inclusivist' position is helpful in situating both our writers and our theological discussion partners.

To ascertain the extent to which our three literary writers offer valuable contributions to the *via transformativa*, I will explore two

---

12   It seems most likely that these terms were first discussed by John Hick in *God Has Many Names* (Philadelphia: Westminster Press, 1982), Chapter 2. See Michael Barnes SJ and Daniel W. Hardy *Theology and Dialogue of Religions* (Cambridge: Cambridge University Press, 2002) 8–9 for a criticism of Hicks.

13   Lakeland, *Postmodernity*, 78.

broad dimensions. The first phase examines the central motivations of our theological partners in relation to aspects of Murdoch, Levertov and Dillard's outlook. The second outlines specific ways in which literary mysticism transcends normative theological boundaries. The scope of this discussion is somewhat limited in that space does not allow for a full examination of key theological themes. However, in keeping with the spirit of this study, the task is to identify a general orientation, change of consciousness, or way of being rather than to offer detailed or systematic theological enquiry.

Mysticism, Literature and Theology in Dialogue

A concurrent theme of transformation is evident in the later works of Soelle (2001), Janzten (1998) (2005) and McFague (1997) (2000). We recall that in *The Silent Cry* Soelle's main concern is to challenge postmodern consumerism and Western domination along with subsequent suffering and injustices. Convinced that mysticism holds the key for future transformation, she is concerned to advocate a form of mysticism that is both inwardly contemplative and outwardly active in the world. Jantzen (1994) discloses unease with the current turn to mystical texts, which encourages individuals to seek solace in inner forms of spirituality, in isolation, and therefore that tend to encourage a denial of social injustices. She is equally anxious to challenge theological metaphors such as salvation, which she believes contribute to a culture of violence. McFague (1982) is interesting in our current discussion because her theological outlook overtly provides a 'bridge' between poetic forms of writing and theology in her idea of metaphorical theology. Further, she argues passionately in *Life Abundant* that the Christian life in postmodernity faces specific challenges to preserve our planet and the well-being of all its inhabitants.

Soelle suggests that the motto of the postmodern world is 'I consume, therefore I am.' In effect, the Western world has been educated consistently through media advertising to respond to basic human needs by buying more and more goods.[14] Part of the active life of a postmodern mystic is to resist the 'consumer culture of plundering' and 'over-choice'.[15] Soelle states that 'ego-lessness, propertylessness, and non-violence' are the cornerstones of the change of life that comes from the spirituality of mysticism.[16] The connection between owning things and violence is perhaps hard to digest in Western culture, where success is gauged by material wealth. Equally, the idea of suppressing the ego strikes an odd chord in a society where assertiveness and personal success are cultivated and prized. Soelle argues that we need to resist these cultural imperatives and adopt instead the mystic's path that requires us to 'go where we are nothing'.[17] I offer an incident from the life of each of the writers we are discussing to suggest that they embody this ideal – at least some of the time.

John Fletcher recalls an event when Murdoch visited him prior to staying the night in university accommodations. Apparently, she had her old battered suitcase with her, which had broken in the taxi on the way from the station and spilled its contents. She asked her host for some string to tie it up. Fletcher responds to this event thus:

> I was of course perfectly happy to provide this [the string], assuming that it was needed only until she could get to the shops and replace the superannuated item. Not a bit of it: she intended to return to Oxford with her luggage fastened with an old piece of string, she who could easily have afforded to buy the most luxurious suitcase that our local department stores had to offer.[18]

14   Soelle, *The Silent Cry*, 212.
15   Ibid., 213.
16   Ibid., 209.
17   Ibid., 214–18. Soelle utilises a phrase by Meister Eckhart.
18   John Fletcher, 'Review of *Iris Murdoch as I Knew Her* by A. N. Wilson', in *The Iris Murdoch Society Newsletter* 17 (2004), 17.

Murdoch did in fact leave nearly two million pounds in her estate,[19] which sits oddly with the fact that she, along with her husband John Bailey, mostly lived in 'benign chaos' with scant regard for their deteriorating and neglected surroundings.[20] In his account of the broken suitcase, Fletcher refers explicitly to A. N. Wilson, who labels Murdoch in his biography as showing 'middle-class meanness'. While this may well have been the case, I find the image of Murdoch with an old battered suitcase tied up with string emblematic of the mystic in postmodernity who persists in their 'blundering on' and cares nothing about outward appearances.

In Levertov's experience, resistance often meant putting oneself at risk. Although Levertov believed in non-violence as an ideal, she reluctantly began to realise that action, in her case civil disobedience, was sometimes required in order to effect change. Her friend Murray Bodo recalls an incident he shared with her:

> In 1990, Denise, my father, and I were together, travelling to Las Vegas to commemorate the tenth anniversary of Archbishop Oscar Romero's martyrdom. We were there to pray and make a weekend retreat with many others at the U.S. Government's nuclear test site in Nevada. [...] We realized that we were in the presence of a woman [Levertov] who radiated an aura of peace in that place of non-peace. [...] Denise and I crossed onto United States Government property and were arrested along with others, while my father remained on the other side of the line, unwilling to cross, but standing at attention and saluting our decision to do so.[21]

This reminds us that certain individuals have a presence that can become contagious. Therefore mysticism in postmodernity, according to Levertov's example, requires a willingness to step across the line; it requires the courage to speak out against injustices and oppressions. Dillard remains, for the most part, reluctant to do this overtly. But she provides instead an insight into the sporadically ascetic lifestyle of a mystic in postmodernity.

19   Conradi, *Iris Murdoch*, 593.
20   Ibid., 580–81.
21   Bodo, *Poetry as Prayer*, 19–20. The incident with Bodo's father is particularly poignant considering that he was an ex-Marine.

Dillard's personal life remains largely a private affair, and as indicated in Chapter One, her persona is partly fictional. What we are privy to however is her living arrangements whilst in the process of writing a book. It seems that in order to get in touch with her mystical and creative side, she seeks to recreate the solitary and austere conditions of a medieval anchoress or hermit. She describes one such modest shelter:

> The cabin was a single small room near the water. Its walls were shrunken planks, not insulated; in January, February, and March, it was cold. There were two small metal beds in the room, two cupboards, some shelves over a little counter, a wood stove, and a table under a window, where I wrote.[22]

Presumably, she lives in a house with proper heating and more than one room the rest of the time, but what is interesting is that, in order to extend her imagination, which I argued in Chapter One is synonymous with a certain understanding of mysticism, she has to divest herself of material comforts in order to intensify her mystical sight.

From these brief examples, it is apparent that Murdoch, Levertov and Dillard consciously adopt a mystical and prophetic stance in postmodernity. Murdoch through non-conformity to current consumer trends, Levertov through her willingness to break the law, and Dillard through her physical isolation are all willing to tread the *via transformativa*. They challenge us to consider how our lifestyles prevent our own spiritual development and contribute towards the oppression of others.

Jantzen: The Horizon of Human Becoming.

In *Becoming Divine*, Jantzen argues for a new cultural symbolic of natality in an attempt to reverse the violent tendencies underpinning the focus on human mortality in orthodox Christian theology. Before her death, Jantzen published one volume, entitled *Foundations of Violence* (2004), of an intended trilogy that develops this concept more

---

22   Dillard, *The Writing Life*, 41.

fully. The book project is entitled *Death and the Displacement of Beauty* to capture her contention that

> [t]he habitus of Western society is a disposition toward the enactment of death and its concomitants, especially anxiety and a drive to control, to exert mastery over anything perceived as threatening. Natality, creativity and beauty have been displaced, despised or ignored; at best seen as unnecessary if pleasant extra to the real business of living. While there is an insatiable desire for novelty, there is little attention to the springs of creativity, the resources of newness that can redeem the present.[23]

Here the potential for creative writing to contribute towards the *via transformativa* is explicit. Furthermore, as discussed in Chapter Three, creativity links conceptually and experientially with natality. Murdoch certainly contributes to this notion by highlighting the will-to-love over the will-to-power, but I find one of Levertov's poems, 'A New Flower',[24] in which she imagines the new life that is not yet visible, to be an apt metaphor for this 'newness that can redeem the past'. As this is among the poems she wrote at a time when she was probably aware of her own impending death, this seems doubly poignant.

> Most of the sunflower's bright petals
> Had fallen, so I stripped the few
> poised to go, and found myself with the new flower: the centre
> [...]
> On this fall day, revealed within
> the autumn of its own brief bloom.

Within the seeds at the centre, she can perceive the new life lying dormant.

Furthermore, Levertov's invocations for peace remain optimistic about new beginnings. Levertov was passionate about the power of

23   Grace M. Jantzen, *Foundations of Violence* (London and New York: Routledge, 2004), 10. The 'habitus' Jantzen refers to is based on Pierre Bourdieu's term for the social, cultural and behavioural norms of society found in *The Logic of Practice*, trans. Richard Nice (Cambridge: Polity, 1990) and *Practical Reason: On the Theory of Action* (Cambridge: Polity, 1998). See also Grace M. Jantzen, *Violence to Eternity* (London and New York: Routledge, 2008).

24   Levertov, *This Great Unknowing*, 25.

poetry to instigate social change, and in common with Murdoch, she believed that the inner change of individuals was required in order for external manifestations to emerge. She argued that

> [w]e need life, and abundantly – we need poems of spirit, to inform us of the essential, to help us *live* the great social changes that are necessary. [...] All authentic art shows up the vagueness and slackness of ninety per cent of our lives – so that art is in its nature revolutionary, a factor instigating radical change, even while (giving 'the shock of recognition', and naming and praising *what is*) it is conservative in a real sense.[25]

Additionally, the ability to maintain an equilibrium between 'what human beings are capable of doing' and aesthetic beauty in a work of art is termed by Levertov as a 'paradoxical achievement'.[26] The poet needs to keep a balance between depicting 'the grime and gore, the torture, the banality of the computerized apocalypse' with 'the vision of the potential for good even in our species which has so messed up the rest of creation'.[27] Levertov too would appear to complement Jantzen's symbolic of natality.

One of the most enduring metaphors for life that aptly captures Jantzen's concept of 'natality, creativity and beauty' appears in Dillard's *The Writing Life*, where the aerial acrobatics of the stunt pilot Dave Raum were to make a lasting impression on her. Mesmerised by his performance, Dillard writes, 'he furled line in a thousand ways, as if he were inventing a script and writing it in one infinitely recurring utterance until I thought the bounds of beauty must break.'[28] Based on her own epiphanic experiences, she imagines him as wholly inside the moment, largely unaware of either his own discomfort or the 'picture' created by his fuel trail only visible to the outside observer. She quotes Pierre Teilhard de Chardin, who wrote '[p]urity does not lie in separation from but in deeper penetration of the universe'.[29] Dillard

25   Levertov, 'Great Possessions', in *New & Selected Essays*, 127.
26   Levertov, 'Paradox and Equilibrium', in *New & Selected Essays*, 141.
27   Levertov, 'Poetry, Prophecy, Survival', in *New & Selected Essays*, 144.
28   Dillard, *The Writing Life*, 109.
29   Ibid., 110. Dillard does not reference de Chardin's writing but I presume she refers to 'The Spiritual Power of Matter'. See Ursula King (ed), *Pierre Teilhard de Chardin* (New York: Orbis Books, *Modern Spiritual Masters* series, 1999), 142.

imagines Rahm to be both artist and priest who takes this to the outer limit of human experience. In her mind, she makes a link between de Chardin's declaration that the 'the world is filled, and filled with the Absolute' and that 'to see this is to be made free' and the passion and abandon Rahm the stunt pilot exhibits.[30] The stunt pilot reminds Dillard that humans have huge creative potential to bring forth new forms.

McFague: Mysticism as the Key to 'Planetary Theology'?

It is fundamental to McFague's theology that humans – Christians specifically – need to take responsibility for their actions to ensure our planet provides a safe and sustainable home for future generations. This section considers the extent to which Murdoch, Levertov and Dillard encourage what McFague terms 'planetary living' in *Life Abundant* (2000) – the title itself appears to have a double meaning: a biblical vision of what life should be like and a criticism of the consumerist Western lifestyle that relies on squandering natural resources.

McFague would hardly describe herself as a mystic, and neither does she give high priority to the term in her writings – perhaps her Protestant background makes her suspicious of the title. She does, however, demonstrate in *Life Abundant* that certain individuals (whom she calls saints) appear to have a special vocation to live and teach according to religious and political principles that have far reaching possibilities for social, religious and political transformation:

> The saints who work tirelessly for justice are spiritually alive. Persistent, life-long cruciform living appears possible only through immersing oneself in God's presence. Justice work and mysticism seem to be companions.[31]

It has taken her a lifetime of thinking, writing and teaching to reach this point. The book is partly an autobiographical plotting of her own spiritual development to the point where she recognises that we cannot have 'life abundant' unless we develop an alternative to individualistic

---

30   Dillard, *The Writing Life*, 111. Dillard refers here to Pierre Teilhard de Chardin's book *The World is Filled, and Filled with the Absolute* (Ives Street Press, 1992).
31   McFague, *Life Abundant*, 186.

consumerism. By her own admission, she wrote this book to correct the 'inadequacies 'of her previous books and to make sure her theology is 'functional'.[32]

It is perhaps pertinent to mention again at this point that Murdoch, Levertov and Dillard have all contributed in meaningful ways to McFague's ideas along her theological journey. For example, we saw in Chapter Two how Murdoch's notion of attention influenced McFague's construction of the 'Loving Eye' and the 'Arrogant Eye'. Levertov is mentioned in her early work *Speaking in Parables* as an example of an 'anonymous Christian' who produces 'secular literature in the parabolic *form*',[33] and by this she means that poets have a specialised 'way of locating the mystery of the universe within the ordinary and the mundane'.[34] Dillard is drawn on most extensively in *Super, Natural Christians* and is referred to briefly in *Life Abundant*. In the former, McFague refers to *Pilgrim at Tinker Creek* as enabling us 'to see things *differently* than we do most of the time – in more extreme, less balanced, less middle-of-the-road, but clearer, ways'.[35] Most of all Dillard's perspective forces us to have a more realistic view of what it means to be human in postmodernity.

The aim of *Life Abundant* is to challenge the current individualist market model, which 'is devastating the planet and making other people poor', by proposing an 'Ecological Model' for theology.[36] While theology is not wholly responsible for economic policies, she argues that theology should always remain in critical tension with public life. Intrinsic to this is the underlying premise that the individualist model based on Enlightenment ideals is outdated. What we need now is a theological model based on reality as it is in postmodernity. Science tells us that we are not the powerful individuals we once thought, but rather, 'we are *dependent* on nature and *responsible* for it'.[37] Accordingly, we need to live more economically and share with others. McFague

32   McFague, *Life Abundant*, xi–xii.
33   McFague, *Speaking In Parables*, 82.
34   Ibid., 103.
35   McFague, *Super, Natural, Christians*, 145.
36   McFague, *Life Abundant*, 205–7.
37   Ibid., 208.

suggests that the best way for Christians to imagine this model is 'to picture God's presence with us in the eschatological banquet to which all are invited, all people and all other creatures'.[38] A focus must be on ensuring that all peoples have the basic requirements of food, shelter and clothing as well as education and health care. Ultimately, it means sacrifice for many people living in the so-called West, especially in those stratas of society where an elite minority holds the majority of the wealth.[39]

A careful reading of McFague's theology suggests a number of points where it may be possible to see how Murdoch, Levertov and Dillard's writing has contributed towards her theology. The conclusion of *Life Abundant* captures this:

> We were created in God's image, in the image of love, and our goal is to grow more fully into that image by loving each other and the world in concrete, practical, daily ways; in other words, in just and sustainable ways. [...] Our task is to become aware of God's presence. As we do so we will both see the world differently and be empowered to act differently in and toward it. We are called to see differently – and then to live differently, as differently as we can, with God's help.[40]

Murdoch appears to have particularly influenced McFague's ability to articulate how apprehension of others is an ethical task. She also shares her awareness of the self-conscious thinking about the language we use that needs to be done.[41] However, Murdoch and McFague's overall philosophical and theological outlook is obviously very different.

Levertov shares with McFague a love of metaphor to speak about the things that matter most and a compassionate commitment to justice and concern to protect the environment. Although Levertov only

38   Ibid., 209.
39   I do not wish to make an over-generalisation here as I am aware that many people in Europe and America live below the poverty line and that there is an new underclass developing in many towns and cities across Europe and America. At the level of government, however, Western hegemony is still operative as recent events in Iraq portray.
40   Ibid., 202.
41   McFague, *Speaking in Parables*, 19.

appears briefly in McFague's work, I can speculate that she and other poets have contributed to her theological outlook. Dillard shares Mc-Fague's love of nature as well as an excellent grounding in scientific viewpoints. Overall, the way that Dillard contributes to this economic ecological model is the most subtle, however. In the end, her ontological position offers the most effective way of changing consciousness.

After reading Dillard's *For the Time Being*, the reader understands without doubt that he or she is no more than a 'dot' that exists among other 'dots' briefly and randomly, that life is both wonderful and terrible.[42] When readers try to imagine themselves amid such exuberance and seemingly mindless waste, they are forced to realise that it is futile to take themselves too seriously. Above all, Dillard makes clear that the individualistic model makes no sense whatsoever. This is a different approach to Murdoch's unselfing, but it achieves the same effect. Dillard's approach is not to encourage compassion for others, but rather, she forces her readers to see themselves as a somewhat insignificant part of a much larger whole.

This section has consolidated the dialogue between theological and literary insights and confirmed a common agenda and the possibility of a mutually enhancing enterprise, which is only possible if there are commonalities or similar aims to begin with. In order to achieve the aims stated at the outset of this study, it is now necessary to evaluate the various ways in which literary texts and our engagement with them enable theological transformation.

Transcending Theological Boundaries

As we discovered in Chapter Three, Soelle herself wrote poetry. She also described theology as more of an art than a science in that it attempts 'to cross the bounds of everyday language, [and is] orientated

---

42   Annie Dillard, 'Tsunami Commentary: Dots in Blue Water' (6 January 2005) http://www.npr.org/templates/story/story.php?storyId=4270641

towards art rather than to the abstract, rational and neutral'. She actually suggests a name for this literature – 'theopoetry'.[43] Sarah Pinnock discerns that what Soelle is actually saying is that literature and theology both suffer if they separate. The consequences are twofold: scientific discourses take over that are 'of no ultimate concern to much of humankind', and theology focuses on producing 'ordinances, pronouncements, how-to-manuals, etc.', thus preventing the more profound theological insights.[44] Poetry in Soelle's understanding is ultimately crucial for the well-being of all and is able to provide significance due to the freedom and diverse nature of the genre.

McFague argues that the best way of conceptualising theology in a postmodern context is through poetic language, particularly the choice of metaphors, understood to represent 'the halting attempts by specific individuals' to describe their perceptions of the sacred.[45] Again, McFague reminds us of the provisionality of religious language. Murdoch alone attempts to provide a root metaphor in 'the Good', which in the end I argue remains too abstract to permeate the religious imagination, however. By contrast, Levertov and Dillard utilise many metaphors in their attempt to find words that enable the gap between the mundane and sacred world to be crossed.

Writing, and the thought that it represents, therefore has the potential to impose new meaning. It is easy to forget that the language of philosophy and theology equally relies on metaphorical language. In many cases, individual specialists coin specific terms and phrases that the majority later assume to be absolute. Humans are, in fact, in a continual state of arrival and departure, always on the cusp of what they were and what they will become, and language is the medium that facilitates this. With each new discovery comes the recognition that more exists just over the horizon. Mystical language has always reflected this, but theological language outside of the mystical traditions

43   Dorothee Soelle, *Against the Wind: Memoir of a Radical Christian*, trans. B. & M. Rumscheidt (Minneapolis: Fortress Press, 1995), 152.
44   Sarah K. Pinnock (ed), *The Theology of Dorothy Soelle* (New York: Trinity Press International, 2003), 77.
45   Sallie McFague, *Metaphorical Theology: Models of God in Religious Language* (Philadlephia: Fortress Press), 3.

has tended to opt for preciseness and clarity at the expense of stifling further development.

We will discuss Murdoch, Levertov and Dillard's theological contribution within four broad areas. First, we will explore the wide-ranging ways in which Murdoch, Levertov and Dillard incorporate the Bible into their writing. They do not read the scriptures literally, yet neither have they diminished the Bible's importance to a mere cultural artefact. Second, there will be an assessment of selected theological categories in the writings of Murdoch, Levertov and Dillard. To conclude, I pick up Julian's well-known phrase 'all shall be well and all manner of things shall be well' to explore the place of hope in a time when redemption is conceived of as primarily centred within this world. Lastly, we will explore McFague's dynamic concept of 'parabolic theology' as the way towards an intermediary theology that incorporates mystical and literary insights.

Mystical Meaning in the Bible

One thing that Murdoch, Levertov and Dillard have in common, apart from their love of literature generally, is the influence of the *King James Bible* on their moral and spiritual education. Accordingly, this section identifies the continuing relevance of the Bible for our mystic-poets by exploring selected texts that contain either an overt reference to biblical material or, alternatively, one that is less obvious. The object here is not to identify a particular hermeneutical approach or to seek to capture a premodern understanding of the mystical meaning of the passage, whereby everything has a hidden or secret meaning centred on Christ.[46] Rather this discussion demonstrates how the Bible as a sacred text continues to operate as a mystical resource due to an on-going imaginative and lifelong engagement with its wisdom.

Biblical scholar Sandra Schneiders reminds us that the Hebrew Scriptures were integral to the vision embodied in the life and teaching of Jesus and his subsequent followers. Numerous references to the Hebrew Scriptures established the life and teachings of Christ to be

46   See Jantzen, *Power, Gender and Christian Mysticism*, 67–85.

the fulfilment of Messianic prophecies. Further, the developing Church continued its self-definition by using biblical imagery and symbolism in the writings of its founding members.[47] In subsequent centuries, Church fathers such as Origen, Tertullian, Augustine and Justin encouraged a creative approach to the interpretation of scripture. They believed that there were two senses in the texts, one historical or literal and the other allegorical. The latter, Schneiders informs us, included all forms of language and meaning other than the literal and so had a much broader definition than modern definitions of the term. Thus, a text could be read metaphorically and symbolically to ascertain moral, theological and eschatological meaning.[48] In the context of the contemporary reader, Schneiders calls for an interpretative project that engages with 'the transformative potential of the text [...] attention to the spirituality [that] attends to the life possibilities that the text opens out before the reader'.[49]

In postmodernity, many theologians, like Schneiders, are now recognising that the primary biblical texts require an imaginative approach.[50] As suggested above, this is not without its precedents. One particular example is found in the monastic tradition, which developed the practice of *lectio divina* that required the religious to absorb the texts into living memory.[51] Specifically, the Alexandrian school developed an allegorical exegesis, such as Origen's threefold sense of scripture, which related to the tripartite nature of human beings: body, soul and spirit. John Cassian developed this in the context of Western monasticism into the *lectio divina*, which had a fourfold approach to interpretation. The literal sense of the bible was just one of the four areas of interpretation, of course, and the other three related to the

<hr />

47   Sandra M. Schneiders, 'Scripture and Spirituality', in Bernard McGinn, et al (eds), *Christian Spirituality: Origins to the Twelfth Century* (New York: Crossroad, 1985), 2–4.

48   Schneiders, *Written That You May Believe* (New York: The Crossroad Publishing Company, 1999), 16–17.

49   Ibid., 22.

50   See for example David Brown, *Tradition & Imagination: Revelation & Change* (Oxford: Oxford University Press, 1999), and *Discipleship and Imagination* (Oxford: Oxford University Press, 2000).

51   Jantzen, *Power, Gender and Christian Mysticism*, 84–85.

spiritual or allegorical sense of scripture.[52] A Benedictine monk, Jantzen tells us, would be so immersed in Biblical language that all their life and thought flowed from scriptural texts.[53] This was not a purely personal matter, however, as the scriptures were 'received, shared and tested' in the community. Jantzen argues,

> It is no accident that the monasteries, devoted to learning the mystical meaning of Scripture, were often oases of social justice, and addressed themselves to the problems of poverty, illness, and ignorance and to political and ecclesiastical structures that reinforced these social ills. The measure of the encounter with the *caritas* of Christ in Scripture is the measure of the transformation of life, individually and communally into his likeness. [54]

From the Renaissance onward, there was an increasing turn to the literal sense of scripture, which was unable to 'transcend the world of the author'. While Jantzen recognises that we cannot ignore the legacy of the Reformation and the Enlightenment, or the gains of historical and literary insight into scripture, she does believe, like Schneiders, that we remain impoverished if we ignore the potential for spiritual or mystical insights.

There is also a long tradition of spiritual interpretations of sacred texts such as the Torah, the Talmud and the Mishnah in the Jewish tradition known as Midrash. The term *midrash* derives from the verb *darash*, which means 'to seek'. As with the medieval approach to the Christian scriptures, this tradition recognises there is a hidden meaning that the seeker can find. George Robinson, an American Jewish writer, describes *darash* as an interpretative technique that 'uses homily and parable to inquire into the text its latent meaning as opposed to its "plain" meaning'.[55] Rabbinic schools of interpretation developed the *aggadic midrash* to fill in unexplainable gaps present in

52   Schneiders, Sandra M., 'Scripture and Spirituality', 10–16.
53   Grace M. Jantzen, 'The Mystical Meaning of Scripture: Medieval and Modern Presuppositions', in *King's Theological Review*, 21 (1988), 42.
54   Ibid., 43.
55   George Robinson, *Essential Judaism: A Complete Guide to Beliefs, Customs, and Rituals* (New York: Pocket Books, 2000), 304.

sacred texts such as the Torah and the Tanakh.[56] The principles of classic *midrashic* interpretation (650–1200 C.E.) are not easily accessible to the modern non-Jewish reader, but it is an important principle that the interpretation of foundational sacred texts as an ongoing process is important if they are to continue to function within living memory. In fact, Julian's revelations, as well as Murdoch, Levertov and Dillard's interpretations of biblical texts, can be interpreted as creating new *midrashim*.[57] The key point about *midrash* is that the rabbinic scholars who wrote it recognised that the interpretation of sacred texts is an evolutionary process.

Considering the number of times the Bible is alluded to in Murdoch's novels, she obviously found it to be a continuing source of meaning. In an interview with Jonathan Miller, Murdoch revealed that, despite the fact that she had rejected any notion of a personal God or divine Christ, 'I still myself use the Christian mythology. I am moved by it and I see its religious significance and the way in which ordinary life is given a radiance.'[58] In short, the Bible formed part of her consciousness – as indeed it did for Dillard and Levertov. Although, of course, as Murdoch is quick to point out, this is an accident of life and that had she be born elsewhere Buddha or Krishna would have formed her consciousness.[59] Indeed, Dipple informs us that Murdoch would often pick a primary biblical text to underpin her novels.[60] *The Good Apprentice*, for example, is a retelling of the parable of the Prodigal Son in a contemporary setting. Similarly, *The Green Knight* revisions the story of Cain and Abel in postmodernity.

As well as these more obvious biblical themes, Murdoch would also periodically insert favourite biblical passages throughout her novels

---

56 Ibid., 357. There are three categories of *midrash*: exegetical, homiletical and narrative.

57 Ibid., 359. For an introduction to *midrash*, see Jacob Neusner's *The Midrash: An Introduction* (Oxford: Rowman & Littlefield Publishers, Inc, 2004).

58 'My God: Iris Murdoch interviewed by Jonathan Miller', in Dooley, *From a Tiny Corner in the House of Fiction*, 214. Murdoch's choice of the word 'radiance' is significant and correlates to Plato's 'light of the sun' in his cave myth referred to in Chapter Two.

59 Ibid., 215.

60 Dipple, *Work for the Spirit*, 27.

to convey her belief in a timeless wisdom or mystery at the heart of the world. One such example comes towards the end of *The Bell*, where she quotes Isaiah 55:9: 'For as the heavens are higher than the earth, so are my ways higher than your ways, and my thoughts than your thoughts.'[61] In this context, the quotation relays an acceptance on the part of Michael Meade, the failed priest, who despite an increasing conviction that belief in God is irrational, manages to maintain a sense of mystery and hope. The use of a biblical text that underpins our religious and cultural heritage also suggests a universal meaning that moves beyond the confines of the literary character. This is also reflective of Lakeland's inclusivist-pluralist position outlined at the beginning of this chapter.

One particular feature of Levertov's engagement with biblical texts is important for reading the Bible in the context of Christianity in postmodernity. She has a heightened ability to enter mystically into the spiritual life of characters found in the Gospel narratives. This derives largely from her interest in the meditative practices of St Ignatius of Loyola's *Spiritual Exercises*, which she experienced first hand. She also sought to offer further insights into biblical passages for which she believed that allegorical interpretations had missed the deeper meaning.[62] The poem 'Annunciation',[63] for example, represents Levertov's imaginative interpretation of the Gospel narrative of the Annunciation. She recalls the angel Gabriel's announcement to Mary, which '[s]he was free / to accept or to refuse', the offer to 'bear in her womb / [...] nine months of Eternity'. Levertov then relates the narrative to everyone's life by asking, '[a]ren't there annunciations / of / one sort or another / in most lives?' What she is saying in effect is that it takes courage to choose to follow those 'roads of light and storm' most of which 'are turned away from'. As she says, '[o]rdinary lives continue, / God does not smite them. But the gates close, the pathway vanishes'. This is a direct challenge by Levertov to take up the mystic path.

61 Murdoch, *The Bell*, 308.
62 Levertov, 'Some Affinities of Content' in *New & Selected Essays*, 14.
63 Levertov, *A Door in the Hive*, 86–88.

Like Murdoch and Levertov, Dillard displays a deep knowledge of the biblical texts. In fact, in *An American Childhood*, Dillard confesses that by her adolescence she

> had miles of Bible in memory: some perforce, but most by hap, like the words to songs. There was no corner of my brain where you could find, among the files of clothing labels and heaps of rocks, among the swarms of protozoans and shelves of novels, whole tapes and snarls and reels of Bible.[64]

No doubt, this was largely due to summers spent at Bible camp in her childhood. Her later apprehension of what she terms a 'scandalous document' was to prove far removed from the intention of her Presbyterian Sunday school teachers.[65] She summons the memory of her youthful encounter with elders, who would quote the Bible at length, in the character of Ada Fishburn in *The Living*, who represents 'a particularly gloomy brand of Protestantism'.[66] Yet Dillard cannot jettison these 'reels of Bible' from her being.

Many of Dillard's descriptions of her visionary encounters with nature reveal the extent to which biblical language has embedded itself within her consciousness. Take the following example that creatively recounts a numinous experience during a summer evening spent at Tinker Creek:

> Then I noticed white specks, some sort of pale petals, small, floating from under my feet on the creek's surface, very slow and steady. So I blurred my eyes and gazed towards the brim of my hat and saw a new world. I saw the pale white circles roll up, roll up, like the world's turning, mute and perfect, and I saw the linear flashes, gleaming silver, like stars being born at random down a rolling scroll of time. Something broke and something opened. I filled up like a new wineskin.[67]

Lorrainne Schaub suggests that Dillard is here describing a mystical experience of an apocalyptical vision reminiscent of John's in the Book of Revelation that speaks of the sky vanishing 'like a scroll

64   Dillard, *An American Childhood*, 133.
65   Ibid., 134.
66   Smith, 'The Ecotheology of Annie Dillard: A Study in Ambivalence'.
67   Dillard, *Pilgrim at Tinker Creek*, 34.

rolling itself up'.[68] Instead of reading the text, she is reading the landscape, but the biblical text has provided some of the language.

McFague argues that 'the Bible as model can never *be* the word of God, can never capture the ways of God [but] underscores the relative, groping character of this very human work'. For McFague, the Bible is a classical piece of *literature* that provides a central model for all Christians.[69] Therefore, reading the scriptures theologically is not about 'extricating an abstract concept but precisely the opposite, delving into the details of the story itself, letting the metaphor do its job of revealing the new setting for ordinary life'.[70] Inevitably, this means that theological concepts can never be stable categories and should be understood to represent 'the groping character' of what is a very human undertaking. Biblical language, the stories collected there, both as narratives and as allegories, permeates these writers' work. Murdoch, Levertov and Dillard consciously connect with their cultural and religious heritage and breathe new life into the words, the images, the metaphors. There is an intrinsic connection between the imaginative approach to biblical texts and the ways in which our writers approach theological categories such as God, Christ and evil.

Mystical Theology in the Literary Imagination

The consequences and possibilities for religion and society without God were favourite themes in Murdoch's novels. Indeed, all of her novels contain some discussion on the subject. The idea of God as articulated in the Christian theological tradition is for Murdoch a substitute for reality. As such, she feels it is a distraction; for believing in a personal God and the promise of eternal salvation for the human soul stops people from aspiring towards the Reality of the Good or

68 Lorraine Schaub, 'Tricks of Eye and Spirit: Invisibility and Illusion in Annie Dillard's *Pilgrim at Tinker Creek*'. http://www.hoardeordinaries.com/lori/research/tricks.html
69 McFague, *Metaphorical Theology*, 62. My italics.
70 McFague, *Speaking in Parables*, 8.

Perfection that lies beyond the human concept of God.[71] Not surprisingly, Christ is subsequently removed from any connection to a divine God in Murdoch's hands.

Christ as characterised in Murdoch's fiction becomes a human figure who is fallible like the person of Tallis in *A Fairly Honourable Defeat*. At the end of the novel, the crucifixion image is of 'a very battered Christ wearily opening his arms',[72] who shares in the suffering of humanity. Cato in *Henry and Cato* comes to the stark realisation that Christ is 'A marvellous religious symbol. But not God. Not the Redeemer. Not the kingpin of history. There is no kingpin, there is no redemption.'[73] Murdoch, through exploring the spiritual crises of fictional characters, avoids the polarisation of theism and atheism. Instead, she recognises the human longing for the transcendent but curtails it with pragmatic discussions.

Rejecting Christ as the Son of God is also to reject the historical event of the resurrection and, by implication, that there is a continuance of life after death. Through the character of Stuart Cuno in *The Good Apprentice*, Murdoch suggests that Christ was 'mistaken' and 'disappointed', and that he represents 'pure affliction, utter loss, innocent suffering, pointless suffering, the deep and awful and irremediable things that happen to people'.[74] In this light, the message of Christ's life is not that he provides escape from the finality of death, but rather, it affirms the 'human truth of pain, suffering and annihilation'.[75] Therefore, for Murdoch, Christ is of importance above all because of his death not his resurrection. However, the loss of belief in eternal salvation leaves a dangerous void.

The increasingly permissive society that Murdoch saw around her in the sixties contained the very real possibility in her view that the distinction between good and evil would be indiscernible in the

---

71   See Murdoch, 'On 'God' and 'Good', in Conradi (ed), *Existentialists and Mystics*.

72   Iris Murdoch, *A Fairly Honourable Defeat* (London: Penguin, 1970), 392.

73   Murdoch, *Henry and Cato*, 170.

74   Iris Murdoch, *The Good Apprentice* (London: Vintage, 1985), 147.

75   Caroline Guerin, 'Iris Murdoch – A Revisionist Theology? A Comparative Study of Iris Murdoch's *Nuns and Soldiers* and Sara Maitland's *Virgin Territory*', in *The Journal of Literature and Theology*, 6: 2 (1992), 162.

future.[76] For Good to exist, its opposite, evil must necessarily exist too. Murdoch denies the existence of evil as personified in the figure of Satan, but instead she directs attention towards the inability of humans to act in a selfless and loving manner in their relationships with each other. Through the characters in her novels, she suggests that people are foolish or confused and experience life as an incessant muddle. In *The Nice and the Good*, Theo, who had taken Buddhist vows in the past, thinks to himself '[t]he point is that nothing matters except loving what is good. Not to look at evil but to look at good.'[77] And furthermore, no supernatural being is going to intervene to save humanity from itself. It is only from this perspective that we can effectively build structures of value and begin to summon up 'possibilities [...] which go beyond what could be said to be strictly factual'[78] whilst avoiding the pitfalls of sentimentality and fantasy.

Not least, her idea of being 'good for nothing' and disavowal of a Saviour who rose from the dead destroys the certainty of the eternal existence of the individual soul. Any notion of redemption in Murdoch's thought is more aligned with the Buddhist notion of selfless perception and compassion towards others. In effect, Murdoch firmly believed that Buddhism could transform Christianity into a form of religion more appropriate for our times.[79] In fact, she wanted to make Christ more Buddha-like, 'an avatar of a transcendent Good that he cannot exhaust or even adequately represent'.[80] Murdoch attempted to depict this through characters such as James Arrowby in *The Sea, The*

76 Fletcher and Bove, *Iris Murdoch*, B0126, 209.
77 Murdoch, *The Nice and the Good*, 355.
78 Ibid., 151 cites Murdoch, 'Darkness of Practical Reason', *Encounter* 27 (July 1966), 49.
79 A number of spiritual and academic individuals and communities now actively pursues mutual dialogue. See for example, D. W. Mitchell, & J. Wiseman (eds), *The Gethsemani Encounter* (New York: Continuum, 1999). This is the outcome of a historic five day meeting in July 1996 between Buddhist and Christian monks and nuns. The Dalai Lama suggested the Abbey of Gethsemani in Kentucky, USA as the setting because it was the home of the mystic Thomas Merton, whom His Holiness had met and greatly admired. This is, however, a marked difference to the syncreticism that Murdoch proposes.
80 Alan Jacobs, 'Go(o)d in Iris Murdoch.' http://www.firstthings.com/ftissues/ft 9502/jacobs.html

Sea, Peter Mir in *The Green Knight*, and Jackson in *Jackson's Dilemma*. These figures represent more than a moral example to those they encounter. Rather, they embody 'a mystical vision of the Good that shines through [them]'.[81]

An overview of Murdoch's understanding of religion in postmodernity is most aptly captured in *The Philosopher's Pupil*, in which Father Bernard, who suddenly abandoned his priesthood and his parish in Ennistone to live in Greece, writes a letter to the mysterious N, the narrator of the novel:

> Nothing but true religion can save mankind from lightless and irredeemable materialism, from technocratic nightmare where determinism becomes true for all except an unimaginably depraved few, who are themselves the mystified slaves of a conspiracy of machines. [...] What is necessary is the absolute denial of God. Even the word, the name, must go. What then remains? Everything, and Christ too, but entirely changed and broken down into the most final and absolutely naked simplicity, into atoms, into electrons, into protons. The inner is the outer, the outer is the inner: an old story, but who really understands it?[82]

The phrase 'the inner is the outer, the outer is the inner' correlates to mystical metaphors of interiority and exteriority. It is interesting to speculate whether Murdoch was familiar with the apocryphal *Gospel of Philip* where this phrase appears.[83] Most importantly, Murdoch's view (presuming that she is N) here recalls the standard cry of mystics to 'Deny God for God's sake.' As soon as we try to pin the concept of God down, it loses its mystery and significance.

---

81   Ibid, The lack of female Christ or Buddha figures is noticeable in Murdoch's fiction.
82   Iris Murdoch, *The Philosopher's Pupil*, (London: Vintage, 1983), 552. It is significant that Murdoch's characters, even in her later novels, still communicate by letter and only rarely by phone. There is not an e-mail in sight. Neither do they watch TV or films let alone go anywhere near a computer. Resistant to postmodern technology to the end, Murdoch herself continued to write by hand.
83   *Gospel of Philip*, 55. Codex II 51, 29–86, 19. Translated by Wesley W. Isenberg. James M. Robinson (ed), *The Nag Hammadi Library* (San Francisco: Harper & Row, 1977), 131–151. http://www.Goodnewsinc.org. uk/OTHBOOKS/philip.html

It seems both ironic and significant that Murdoch chose to end *Metaphysics as a Guide to Morals*, following Tillich, with reassuring quote from Psalm 139 – from the *King James Version*, naturally:

> Whither shall I go from thy spirit, whither shall I flee from thy presence? If I ascend into heaven thou art there, if I make my bed in hell, behold thou art there. If I take the wings of the morning and dwell in the uttermost parts of the sea, even there shall thy hand lead me, and thy right hand shall hold me.[84]

Mystical perception is the only way left to apprehend the Ultimate; it always eludes rational explanation. The reflective element in Murdoch's novels enabled her to avoid making the truth claims that philosophy demands. Instead, within the structure of a novel she could provide free characters and moral dilemmas, in turn provoking the reader to reflect on their own life through the employment of imaginative perception.

Like Murdoch who finds resonances in Psalm 139, Levertov speaks of a 'beloved nugget' in 'Mass for the Day of St Thomas Didymus' within the human heart that we cannot expunge.

> O deep unknown, guttering candle,
> beloved nugget lodged
> in the obscure heart's
> last recess.
> Have mercy on us.[85]

She portrays how belief and unbelief coexist in her mind and soul. Yet this does not address the greatest paradox that has continued to plague Christian thinking – the image of a just, merciful and benevolent God who allows suffering, evil and pain to continue. Levertov does not shy away from this question and tackles it by imagining God as a 'lonely craftsman'[86] in her poem entitled 'The Task'.[87] She does not imagine him to be like 'an old man always, upstairs, sitting about in sleeveless undershirt, asleep, arms folded, stomach rumbling', but

---

84   Psalm 139:7–10, cited in Murdoch, *Metaphysics as a Guide to Morals*, 512.
85   Levertov, *Poems 1972–1982*, 266–72.
86   Lynch, 'Denise Levertov and the Poetry of Incarnation', 3.
87   Levertov, *Oblique Prayers*, 72.

rather, as a God who 'is absorbed in work, and hears the spacious hum of bees, not the din, and hears far-off our screams. Perhaps listens for prayers in the wild solitude.' Elsewhere, Levertov reveals that there were two main inspirations behind this poem. One was a friend's description of 'the awesome quiet near Mount Denali'[88] and the other was the writings of Julian who spoke of there being a divine plan, which will make sense of all the miseries of the world.

Elsewhere, she reimagines Christ to accommodate this perception and awareness of a near-far God. Levertov's image of Christ in the final section of 'Mass for the Day of St Thomas Didymus',[89] subverts traditional metaphors such as 'king' and 'lord' that imply power and dominion by depicting the *Agnus Dei* embodied in a newborn lamb.

> God then,
> encompassing all things, is
> defenceless? Omnipotence
> has been tossed away, reduced
> to a wisp of damp wool?
> ....a shivering God?

Christ in Levertov's intuitive understanding is 'born in bloody snowdrifts' and stands as a parable for 'a shivering God', who is both immanent and transcendent.

By way of contrast, God in Dillard's hands is highly unstable and infinitely more ominous. The possibility that God can and might do anything is fundamental to Dillard's religious outlook and springs from her understanding of the Incarnation. Rosenthal points to two poems about Christmas in her first publication, *Tickets for a Prayer Wheel*, that reveal her incarnational theology. In the first she writes, 'God empties himself, / into the earth like a cloud, / God takes on the substance, contours / of a man, and keeps them.'[90] And later in 'Christmas': 'This is the hour / God loosens and empties. / Rushing

88   Levertov, 'Work That Enfaiths', in *New & Selected Essays*, 252.
89   Levertov, *Poems 1972–1982*, 266–72.
90   Dillard, *Tickets for a Prayer Wheel*, 33.

consciousness comes / unbidden, gasping.'[91] Summing up Dillard's viewpoint here, Rosenthal suggests that it is 'because God does the wonderful crazy thing of "emptying" himself into human form [...] that all wildly improbably comings-to-life can happen'.[92] Indeed, throughout her writing career, Dillard maintains the tension between theology and reality that McFague argues for in *Life Abundant*. Cheney notices, for example, that

> there is a tension in *Pilgrim at Tinker Creek* between, on the one hand, a thoroughly naturalized and contextualized inquiry into the sacred and, on the other hand, a Western theological tradition of a transcendental creator-god which provides much of the explicitly theological vocabulary at work in the text.[93]

Dillard does not seek to resolve this tension. God appears to be stubbornly absent in her observations of nature, and neither does she see a logical God *behind* creation. Rather, she imagines a God who defies all human understanding, only observable as an overflowing of creation where waste and abundance co-exist. Webb observes that for Dillard nature is a 'flagrant profusion that can be terrifying as well as comforting, paralyzing as well as energising'.[94] In other words, nature conceals as much about God as it reveals. She arrived at a position in *Holy the Firm* where she realises that 'immanence needs a handle'. Gradually, she becomes aware of the necessity of a link between the world of matter where 'the world is flattened on a horizontal plane, singular, all here crammed with heaven, and alone', and the world of the mind where 'Christ touches only the top, skims off only the top, as it were, the souls of men.'[95] Christ and the incarnation are that link. Her task as a writer is perhaps to fill in the gaps and maintain that link – to remind readers of the sacred.

91   Ibid., 103.
92   Peggy Rosenthal, 'Joking with Jesus in the Poetry of Kathleen Norris and Annie Dillard', in *Cross Currents* 50:3 (2000), 149.
93   Jim Cheney, 'The Water of Separation: Myth and Ritual in Annie Dillard's *Pilgrim at Tinker Creek*', in *The Journal of Feminist Studies in Religion* 6 (1990), 48.
94   Webb, 'Nature's Spendthrift Economy', 433–44.
95   Dillard, *Holy the Firm*, 70.

The overall theme of her latest book, *For the Time Being*, concerns the place of God in a world of unspeakable horror and cruelty and shows that Dillard has come no closer to achieving any answers. Like her earlier works, she has one eye fixed on the contingent and one on the sacred throughout. She has arranged the work in seven chapters, which may or may not reflect the seven days of God's creation in Genesis. Each chapter contains a meditation of recurring themes of 'Birth', 'Sand', 'China', 'Clouds', 'Numbers', 'Israel', 'Encounters', 'Thinker', 'Evil', and 'Now'. The pressing theological question Dillard poses all the way through is: What sort of God does our world reflect?

Based on years of searching for and reflecting on the nature of God, Dillard speculates that

> God is not a member of the loop like the rest of us, passing the water bucket to splash the fire, kicking the bucket, passing the buck. After all, the semipotent God has one hand tied behind his back. (I cannot prove that with the other hand he wipes and stirs our souls from time to time, or that he spins like a fireball through our skulls, and knocks open our eyes so we see flaming skies and fall to the ground and say, 'Abba! Father!').[96]

In other words, we have to be God's hands. The use of metaphors relating to fire and light are used copiously throughout Dillard's work to describe her encounters with the sacred, but in this portion of text, there also appears to be a contradiction in this regard. Her perception of God ranges from the *deus absconditus* – where God is 'out of the loop' – to the ecstatic experience of a God who 'spins like a fireball through our skulls'. But as we have seen in Chapters Four and Five, these dialectical modes of describing encounters with the sacred in terms of presence and absence are common to those with a mystical outlook. Ultimately, despite the darker side of existence, like Julian who believed that 'all shall be well' Murdoch, Levertov and Dillard demonstrate a realistic optimism concerning the future.

---

96   Dillard, *For the Time Being*, 140–41.

Murdoch could be accused of a lacking social and political awareness as her novels do not address the injustices and oppressions of her time, unlike the way that Charles Dickens exposed the social ills of his day for example. Instead of providing social and political critique, however, Murdoch was committed to creating a more just and peaceful future through a transformation of individual conscience. Her existential and fictional world may have been parochial, but her vision was global. She also advocated spiritual beings that could inspire others. The 'Christ' figure in *The Green Knight*, whom she named Peter Mir, suggests that she sees such people as reaching out to others. '*Mir*' in Russian means both 'world' and 'peace'. Her 'good' characters do effect positive change in the lives of others, while the more scholarly characters in Murdoch's novels fail to extend their theoretical morality into praxis.[97]

One of the key visions Levertov presents in her work is that of a future peaceable world. The final lines of Levertov's poem 'Life at War'[98] look *towards* living in peace. Rodgers notices that there is also an interesting treatment of humanity's experience of duality, that the poet 'dictates the tone that vibrates between despair and hope'.[99] The title itself juxtaposes life and death, and there is clear evidence of the double vision of the poet that enables the reader to see the harsh reality of war as well as to realise the full potential human beings have to flourish.[100] She can find a remnant of hope in the fact that we 'go on knowing of joy, of love' and that 'nothing we do has the quickness, the sureness, / the deep intelligence living at peace would have'. Rodgers sums up the poem as ending

---

97 A few examples: Henry in *Henry and Cato*, Max in *The Unicorn*, Gaffe in *The Green Knight*, Benet in *Jackson's Dilemma* are all trying to write definitive texts of key philosophers – or artist in Henry's case.

98 Levertov, *Poems 1968–1972*, 127. Peggy Rosenthal has edited a new anthology of Levertov's poems entitled *Making Peace* (New York: New Directions, 2006), which has, not surprisingly, many resonances with contemporary global conflicts.

99 Rodgers, *Denise Levertov*, 85.

100 Ibid., 85–86.

with the need, in the face of desecration of war, to remember the joy and love intrinsic to the human condition. This is the faint hope for a dark moment in human history, but the final lines look *toward* living in peace.[101]

Some years later, in response to the debate on a panel at Stanford wherein the lack of poems of peace was lamented, she felt moved to write a poem that tries to imagine what peace would be like. The result was the poem entitled 'Making Peace'.[102] Levertov acknowledges that peace is something more than 'an interim between wars' and adds that it is something 'so unknown that it casts no images on the mind's screen'.[103] This peace in Levertov's mind is neither utopian nor a complacent belief that God will make all things new. Peace has to be both an internal conversion and *made*. That is, peace is both particular and universal and intrinsically connected to notions of justice, so that a poetry of peace is of necessity also a poetry of struggle.[104]

The reader could be forgiven for not picking up on Dillard's sense of hope and her motivations to work for a better world, as they appear briefly and randomly throughout her *oeuvre*. No doubt, this fact reflects her belief that there is a sacred power behind creation that remains eternally elusive. My reading of Dillard indicates that the Hebrew phrase *Tikkun Olam* (which she just calls *Tikkun*) provides Dillard with the best clue to understanding the mysteries she has scrutinised over the years. She refers to it in *For the Time Being* in relation to the creation of the world in the beginning, and the creation of a future world. She includes an account by Rabbi Isaac Luria that tells of how God withdrew from the world to leave room for creation with the intention that divine light was to filter through ten holy vessels to humans. However, something went cataclysmically wrong:

The holy light burst the vessels. The vessels splintered and scattered. Sparks of holiness fell to the depths, and the opaque shards of the broken vessels (*quelippot*) imprisoned them. This is our bleak world. We see only the demonic shells of things. It is literally sensible to deny that God exists. In fact God is hidden, exiled, in the sparks of divine light the shells entrap. So evil can exist,

101   Ibid., 86.
102   Levertov, *Breathing the Water*, 41.
103   Levertov, 'Poetry and Peace', in *New & Selected Essays*, 155.
104   Ibid., 169.

302

continue to live: The spark of goodness within things, the Gnostic-like spark that even the most evil tendency encloses, lends evil its being.[105]

Although to the sceptical reader this is purely an aetiological myth that accounts for moral evil and natural disasters, it equally offers a mystical understanding of creation that parallels Julian's. As such, it provides, through metaphorical language, a means to understand mystery. Certainly, the notion of the divine trapped in matter or 'exiled' fits into Dillard's understanding of the Creator. Embedded in the notion of *Tikkun Olam* is the belief that the world is broken and needs to be repaired, and moreover, there are theological links to the Jewish notion of social justice. Each small act contributes towards this reparation. It is the human task to release the divine sparks

> and return them to God. This is the human task: to direct and channel the sparks' return. This task is *tikkun*, restoration.
>
> Yours is a holy work on earth right now, they say whatever that work is, if you tie your love and desire to God. You do not deny or flee the world, but redeem it, all of it – just as it is.[106]

Not surprisingly, the recent tsunami on 26 December 2005 in Asia recalled Dillard's work in *For the Time Being*, and she was asked by an American News Agency to write an essay. The title she chose was 'Dots in Blue Water', which recollects her daughter's image of those drowned in Bangladesh in 1991 as the only way to imagine them. From the time of this catastrophe, Dillard cites a newspaper headline that pronounced, 'Head-Spinning Numbers Cause Minds To Go Slack'. A hopeful Dillard proclaims that

> we agree that our minds must not go slack, neither must our hands. We the living now enter the surf to form a human boom like a log boom. We try to encircle and enclose and bring in and burn or save the dots, all the dots, those Indian and Indonesian dots, those dots dropping everywhere in Iraq right now, the starving dots. We do not go slack. We secure the boom. We hold tight to

---

105 Dillard, *For the Time Being*, 50–51.
106 Ibid., 141. *Tikkun Olam* is a central concept in the Zohar, the most important book in Kabbalah.

other hands in the water. We save and rescue as many dots as we can whether we can see the people flail in front of us or not.[107]

Despite the fact that there is little point in trying to reconcile God's goodness to the reality of human suffering, there is still reason to remain optimistic. Even though there is no evidence of a personal God who is present in the multiplicity of human existence, human optimism refuses to not care. Instead of wrestling over pointless questions, we need to be working towards a better world by using our energies on those things where we can make an impact.

To conclude this discussion, I shall focus on metaphorical language and the parabolic form to demonstrate how it allows the Bible, mysticism and creative imagination to function within the context of 'parabolic theology'.[108] The very open-ended nature of metaphorical language is the meeting point between mystics and theologians.

Parabolic Theology

Throughout this discussion I have referred to metaphor as the basis of religious language, and McFague reminds us by way of an example that '[t]he Hebrew poet piled up and threw away metaphors of God, in the hope of both overwhelming the imagination with the divine richness and undercutting any idolatrous inclination to absolutise images.'[109] McFague actually argues that metaphor in a theological context does not take us 'out of ourselves', as in mystical vision, but rather 'returns us to ourselves with new insights'.[110] Therefore, it is possible to assess mystical writings as resources for metaphorical or parabolic theology.

McFague identifies three characteristics that metaphor and parable share: indirection, extravagance, and mundanity.[111] Irrespective of whether the writing is biblical or non-biblical, such writing involves an element of the unknown, a willingness to expend oneself

107   Dillard, 'Tsunami Commentary: Dots in Blue Water'.
108   McFague, *Speaking in Parables*, 70.
109   McFague, *Metaphorical Theology*, 42.
110   McFague, *Speaking in Parables*, 38.
111   McFague, *Metaphorical Theology*, 44.

with abandoned passion, and an overwhelming attendance to the things of this world. The result is that parables generally either helps the reader/listener to gain understanding of the sacred or prompt ethical action, and in order to achieve either result, parables need to retain a tension between two ways of being or living in the world: the ordinary and the extraordinary, the conventional and the radical. McFague clarifies this assertion this way:

> A parable begins in the ordinary world with its conventional standards and expectations, but in the course of its story a radically different perspective is introduced that disorientates the listener, and finally, through the interaction of the two competing viewpoints, tension is created that results in a redescription of life in the world.[112]

In other words, the world of the parable includes both the secular and religious dimensions of our world,[113] which enables the reader or listener to enter into the narrative subjectively, because they can relate to events, feelings and knowledge from their own experience, but at the same time to get a glimpse of future possibilities.[114] So the world a parable creates is paradoxical. McFague suggests that the parables of the Kingdom of God are an extended metaphor designed to make the listener or reader aware of the possibilities for the extraordinary within the ordinary realm of existence. Parable is thus an invaluable tool for the mystic treading the *via transformativa*.

The most important point about the parable that theologians must consider is that the parable 'is not translatable into concepts. [...] It is shot through with open-endedness, with pregnant silences, with cracks opening into mystery. But it remains profoundly inpenetrable.'[115] The parable is therefore impossible to systemise into theological concepts. Neither is it possible to interpret individual parables on any deeper level – they stand as they are. Murdoch would agree with McFague as she herself sought to emulate the parabolic form of story, stating that

---

112 Ibid., 46–47 McFague cites Paul Ricoeur, 'Biblical Hermeneutics', *Semeia* 4 (1975), 122–28.
113 McFague, *Speaking in Parables*, xvii.
114 Ibid., 46.
115 Ibid., 55.

Certain parables or stories undoubtedly owe their power to the fact that they incarnate a moral truth which is paradoxical, infinitely suggestive and open to continual reinterpretation. (For instance, the story in the New Testament about the woman who broke the alabaster box of very precious ointment). [...] Such stories provide, precisely through their concreteness and consequent ambiguity, sources of moral inspiration.[116]

A particularly keen sense of seeing the extraordinary within the ordinary is evident in Levertov's poem 'Meeting the Ferret',[117] in which she recalls an encounter with a boy's pet ferret in a park. This animal she noticed, appeared to have lost its 'natural' tendency for violence and was friendly and affectionate. In Levertov's words, it was 'a creature willing to try out the Peaceable Kingdom: to just begin it without waiting'.

This is perhaps an example of how theologians must be open to seeing reality in surprising and strange ways, and rather than striving to interpret the parable, we must allow the parable to interpret us.[118] Levertov demonstrates this through her interpretation of the parable of the fig tree in her poem, 'What the Fig Tree Said'. Here she imagines the fig tree that withers not as a symbolic foretelling of the fall of Jerusalem but as a 'metaphor for [the disciples'] failure to bring forth / what was within them.' Levertov suggests that the fig tree served 'Christ the Poet, / who spoke in images'. In opposition to the standard apocalyptic interpretation, Levertov imagines that Christ cursed '(ears that hear not, eyes that see not) / their dullness, that withholds / gifts *unimagined*'. Yet again, this is a call to the mystic path, to use those 'human fruits – compassion, comprehension'. In both cases, Levertov is espousing the value of imagination in religious perception as well as challenging conventional interpretations of the text. Theologically speaking, she challenges us to be responsible and proactive in the work of redemption. McFague sums up the power of parable as being concerned

116   Murdoch, 'Vision, Choice and Morality', in Conradi (ed), *Existentialists and Mystics*, 91.
117   Levertov, *Sands of the Well*, 47.
118   McFague, *Speaking in Parables*, 59.

not with what we believe, know, or are, but what we are in the process of believing, knowing, and becoming *in our lives*. [...] They are not primarily concerned with knowing but with doing (understood as deciding on a way of life based on new insight).[119]

McFague openly recognises that such a theology is risky, but points out that there are others (such as Paul, Pierre Teilhard de Chardin and Dietrich Bonhoeffer) who have adopted this model of theological reflection. She further offers three distinguishing features of such theologians. First, their choice of vocabulary is neither 'literalistically biblical nor highly abstract', sharing the poet's ability to utilise 'common language to evoke the uncommon'.[120] Second, coming to belief is a life process for these theologians rather than an adherence to a set of doctrines. Metaphor, the stories we tell, the poems we write are ways that 'human beings get from here to there'. Theology in this respect is not about 'formulations and systems', but has more in common with a story along with its 'stops and starts'.[121] The third characteristic is that the life of a theologian – or mystic we can now add – is metaphorical. This radically questions the neutral or objective position through recognising that there is no such thing as 'disembodied abstract theology'. As McFague posits, 'where does one start to theologize if not with oneself?'[122] I will offer three examples from the work of Murdoch, Levertov and Dillard that demonstrate the metaphorical aspect of the mystic-poet's life and work.

The final sentences of what was to be Murdoch's final novel are both poignant and illuminating in that they link the mystical moment with her own reality:

> Unobserved [Jackson] sat down in the grass and watched the boy [Bran] and the horse [Spencer], both his friends. He was also, he observed, now the companion of a very large spider who was busy completing a web between the tall grasses. [...] He breathed deeply. Sometimes he had a sudden loss of breath, together with a momentary loss, or shift, of memory. So he was to wait, once more forgetfulness, his and theirs. He thought, my power has left me, will it ever

119   Ibid., 66.
120   Ibid., 70–71.
121   Ibid., 71.
122   Ibid., 72.

return, will the *indications* return? [...] Madness of course always now at hand. He had forgotten where he had to go, and what he had to do [...] I have come to a place where there is no road. As, casting off all this, he began to rise, he felt something strange. The spider had discovered his hand and was now walking upon it. Gently he assisted the creature back into its web.[123]

This passage offers a unique glimpse into Murdoch's emotions at a time when her intellect was dimming. Her projection of an image of a Buddha-Christ, or modern incarnation of a *Bodhisattva* who sits in quiet contemplation in harmony with his surroundings, seems a fitting legacy. Spiders appeared in *Bruno's Dream* and *The Green Knight* too and may well be based on the *Upanishads*, in which the spider 'emphasises the sole reality of *Brahman*'.[124] The spider web is a symbol of unity in many cultures, as is the saint or mystic who is at one with nature. The whole scene can be interpreted as a metaphorical image of wholeness or oneness of which Soelle speaks. As ever, the reverence towards small insects is a recurring motif in Murdoch's fiction that is symbolic of someone who has achieved a high level of egolessness and goodness. As Jackson has completed his tasks and been instrumental in helping others find themselves, he ends by walking 'down towards the river and cross[ing] the bridge', and then as he gets nearer, he 'began to smile'.[125] Here in these last scenes, Murdoch provides a metaphor that envisions human redemption.

In a poem in her last collection, with the title 'A Clearing',[126] Levertov conveys her reflections on 'paradise as a paradigm for how to live on earth'. The image of paradise operates as a universal metaphor that points back to a time of harmony and looks to the future as an image of how life should be. Like many other metaphorical images in Levertov's poetry, it also represents the individual mystical and poetic quest. The paradisiacal garden has a long history stretching far back to pre-Islamic and pre-Judeo-Christian eras. The idea of an area that is isolated and protected from the outside world comes from the

123   Iris Murdoch, *Jackson's Dilemma* (London: Penguin, 1995), 248–49.
124   Nirmal Datta, *Iris Murdoch: Freedom and Form* (Delhi: Macmillan India, 2000), 137.
125   Murdoch, *Jackson's Dilemma*, 249.
126   Levertov, *This Great Unknowing*, 53.

ancient Persian word *parideqza* – 'pairi' means 'around' and 'daeza' means 'wall'.[127] This idea of a hidden or secret world corresponds to the inner or unconscious world, and in Levertov's vision of the sacred garden, human beings are harmonised with their surroundings, skilfully symbolising the private and public aspects of the human journey or the necessity of being both 'private' and 'open'.

Poetry, Levertov suggests here, provides 'inspiration', starts 'with the given', discovers 'unexpected harmonies', and is a source of 'revelations'. So poetry inspires the reader, attends to the world of things, continues traditions, seeks to harmonise and reveals. The metaphor of paradise in Islamic thought allows 'the visitor to draw closer to God'.[128] In Levertov's poem, the visitor is initially redirected to a vision of paradise on earth, and hence, the writer of this poem inspires the reader to hope for a better world by suggesting possible routes based on 'given' circumstances. McFague suggests that poetic metaphor or parable works due to the poet's ability 'to connect this with that, to make jumps, to see the part as a whole through imaginative association'.[129] Levertov connects herself through her metaphor to others.

> The big trees enclose an expanse of sky, trees and sky
> together protect the clearing.
> One is sheltered here
> from the assaultive world
> as if escaped from it, and yet
> once arrived, is given (oneself
> and others being part of that world)
> a generous welcome.
> It's paradise

She harmonises her own inner and outer worlds through the actualisation of a dreamlike vision into the poetic form of words and language. Lastly, through employing the metaphor of paradise, she 'reveals' the sacred in the natural world, presents the theological notion

127 Emma Clark, 'Water and Shade', in *Parabola* 26:1 Spring (2001), 37.
128 Ibid., 42.
129 Mc Fague, *Speaking in Parables*, 91.

of humans as co-creators, and suggests that artistic creation in the form of a poem contributes to the task of recreating the world.

Dillard presents us with a similar if slightly bleaker view. She starts with and returns to her fascination and horror of birth defects in *For the Time Being*. In the numbers sections, she lists those who died in earthquakes and floods, and millions of others who died through acts of genocide. Notably, she inserts her own journeys to Israel and China with other journeys of note so that her text is also a parable of the self. Throughout, she juxtaposes the beauty and tragedy that the history of human existence encompasses. Dillard's ability to maintain a tension between these two extremes and the fact that she ends up inverting the reader's expectations at the end characterises her work as parabolic theology.[130]

She offers an account of a Hasid girl, Suri Feldman, who had been missing but was found alive and well.[131] The girl is welcomed with joyous rapture by her Hasidic community. Wendy Lesser suggests that 'this concern about the relationship of the one to the many – the individual death, for which we feel grief, set against the incomprehensibility of numerous deaths – pervades Dillard's book'.[132] So like Levertov, she understands how this individual narrative relates to the whole human story. Additionally, this story invokes feelings concerning the loss and return of a loved one that everyone can understand. On the face of it, it appears to be an isolated tale, but in the context of Dillard's previous accounts of suffering and genocide it functions as a parable of hope. It also echoes parables such as 'The Lost Sheep' and 'Prodigal Son' that speak of God's extravagance. So the parabolic form allows us to imagine the extraordinary in the ordinary and is suggestive of the fact that the sacred can rupture the façade of the ordinary when we least expect it. Most of all it is a site of creative tension between the individual and the cosmos; between settling for mundanity and aiming at spiritual and moral excellence.

---

130 This reflects McFague's definition. See McFague, *Metaphorical Theology*, 46–60.
131 Dillard, *For the Time Being*, 199.
132 Wendy Lesser, 'Deliver Us From Evil', *The New York Times* (1999), http://www.nytimes.com/books/99/03/28/reviews/990328.28lessert.html

Likely Stories

I began this chapter by suggesting that creative writing is crucial to transformation in a theological sense. In his dialogue with Timaeus, Plato maintained that, whenever we are talking about human or divine matters (or when we are theologising), the best we can do is tell 'likely stories', or *eikôs muthos*.[133] The universe and our place in it is shifting and changing in character, so any account we give (whether it is mythological, scientific or theological) might be the best we can do, but it is never the full or complete story. In postmodernity, the need to acknowledge this incompleteness is crucial for transformation, and the mystic path is an effective model to embed this in the materiality of our lives.

Throughout I have been concerned to maintain a dialogue with theologians who offer their particular 'likely stories' and whose main objectives include the transformation of human beings, peace between peoples and the preservation of the world's depleted natural resources. Moreover, by putting carefully selected literary writers and theologians in dialogue with each other, a common picture emerges of the possibility of a less violent, less dogmatic and less personalised role for Christianity. The biblical narratives, lives of the saints and mystics all provide the narrative inspiration, vocabulary and wisdom to continue the story. Although there are points of divergence between our literary writers on issues such as the nature of God, Christ and evil, the crucial factor in determining their value for theological discourse is the evolutionary and participatory nature of their insights.

Any theological formulation (and I use this term in a loose sense here) emerges out of a life dedicated to observing and interpreting the world. In the main, Murdoch, Levertov and Dillard reflect on a mysterious force at the heart of the universe by bringing the metaphorical language found in the Christian tradition back to life. Rather than being a didactic mode of transferring knowledge, parabolic theology invites involvement through describing how reality is while at the

133   Plato, *Timaeus*, 29b 3–5, http://plato.stanford.edu/entries/plato-timaeus/

same time suggesting how it could be. The creative use of metaphor and parable are the vehicles that allow the reader to perceive the extraordinary that lies latent within the ordinary.

Conclusion

This book has countered the notion of mysticism as being solely about extraordinary religious experience by demonstrating that mysticism is more appropriately defined as an orientation of consciousness and way of being or process. In particular, in the first chapter, entitled the *via mystica*, it argued that the ability to extend the imagination is a common, but overlooked link between mystics and creative writers through the ages. Further it has taken up Soelle's challenge that the life of the person treading the *via contemplativa* must be complemented by the *via activa*. Throughout I have maintained that this should materialise in political action and compassion for others but that it is also indicated by the act of writing itself. The metaphor of 'seeing' has proved to be especially relevant for the life of the mystic-writer, as a way of fusing imagination and intellect.

In the discussion of the *via creativa* I gave an overview of the implications for taking human creativity seriously, as a means through which revelation is a continual and dynamic process rather than being limited to a specific historical event. Inherent in my choice of writers and theologians is an indication that women, in particular, have a heightened ability to access the world of the unconscious and imagine human becoming – an issue that fell largely outside of the scope of this study. Most of all, this portion of the discussion highlighted the role of human creativity and responsibility in the work of redemption by virtue of the fact that humans are made in the image of God. Jantzen's concept of natality links naturally to creative forms of mysticism.

Following on from this, the book redefines the traditional processes of mysticism – the *via positiva* and the *via negative*, with consideration to the peculiarities of postmodernity. The *via positiva* represents all we can say about God and results in a riot of metaphorical language in poetic and mystical texts, but in postmodernity I provide suggestions as to how selected literary writers and theologians can challenge us to awaken our sense of awe or wonder in the sacredness of life. Equally, there has been a strong emphasis on the fact that this cannot mean we can ignore the more unpleasant aspects of life. Hence, the materiality of our lives must be the starting place of mystical and metaphorical reflection about the sacred. To my way of thinking it is obvious that it is only by immersing oneself in the menial and muddled fabric of life that wisdom arises.

Along the same lines, I have argued that the *via negativa* in postmodernity is still about losing the self in spiritual contemplation but that it must further consciously adopt a position of resistance to systems of domination. Moreover, the process has proved that the practice of losing the self that is associated with mystical perception is paralleled in the creative writer's ability to suspend the ego in the interests of allowing insights to enter the imagination, or experience epiphanic moments. This book reinforces the fact that the *via negativa* represents the belief that that there is no effortless means to apprehend the nature of suffering and evil, although the mystic in postmodernity does not suggest that we merely accept it. We must struggle to right what we can, especially those evils born of human choice. The mystic accepts that God or the sacred is a mysterious and unpredictable force and that human linguistic constructs fail miserably to contain it – or as De Certeau puts it, we are in a continual state of departure.

The third part of the book synthesised literary insights into theological expression. In doing so, the *via integrativa* demonstrated that the mystic way in postmodernity is principally about an integration between ontological realities, mystical perception and theological understanding. The discussion centred on arguing that love and knowledge, subjective experience and communal vision constitute dialectical modes that represent the relationship between people as well as the visible and invisible (spiritual) world. Finally, I want to assert my contention that mystic vision in postmodernity is only of value if it aims to transform individuals both spiritually and morally.

My argument in the *via transformativa* reinforced the theological perspectives of Jantzen, Soelle and McFague who have been our theological conversation partners throughout this discussion. The conclusion that stands out from this conversation between mysticism, literature and theology is that global and planetary concerns must be an integral element of theological configuration as opposed to the passage of the human soul into an eternal life hereafter. If theology is to critique and inform contemporary concerns, I have demonstrated that theological reflection needs to be, like mysticism, in a continual state of departure. Any theological enterprise that takes mystical insight seriously is never content to settle on fixed terms that describe the sacred. From a Christian perspective, this is not to suggest that we should throw out old conceptions and create new ones to replace them, but rather, that we should continue to re-envision our most deeply held conceptions in our present context, moving outward and onward from the sacred texts and premises that have held sway for centuries.

At the outset of this book, I set out to redefine mysticism in relation to the specific context of postmodernity. I define the context of our present moment as designated by the term postmodernity as a period in history characterised by a deep sense of spiritual emptiness and an awareness of communal sin against others – the remedy for which is to replace old 'truths' that relied heavily on the power of reason and divine revelation with new everyday 'truths' that represent a shift in attention to the 'Other', the value of ordinary experience, and the celebration of diversity and difference.

Based on the preceding discussion I conclude that an inclusive definition of mysticism in postmodernity that addresses the above dilemmas might be as follows: an orientation of consciousness that facilitates an experiential perception of a mysterious force behind creation and a means to determine moral worth and purpose through the disciplined use of the imagination, attention to others and the ability to 'see' with three 'eyes': the physical, the spiritual and the cognitive. So postmodernity is a time that requires a theological renewal and shift in consciousness. I have explored how the life and writings of Murdoch, Levertov and Dillard reconceptualise the practice of contemplation and creativity that facilitates the conveyance of spiritual meaning to their readers.

More specifically this book has sought to demonstrate how such literature acts as a linking principle between ordinary life and theological perception. The suggestion that mystical insights found in creative writing can inform theological expression raises some key conceptual and methodological issues, not least because mystical

315

language avoids both. By citing ordinary experience as a primary category, I attempt to decentre, but not totally dismiss, abstract or invisible categories of rational thought. Lastly, the outline of the mystic way proposed in this book takes on a radical edge that opposes many contemporary understandings of spirituality by moving deeper into the world rather than trying to escape from it. Most importantly, the *via mystica* as outlined here demonstrates the ability to transcend the modernist view of individualism and scientific progress while at the same time resisting relativistic nihilism. Overall, I proffer the suggestion that the blurring of epistemological boundaries in our writers provides a useful methodological approach for theological development that is tenable in postmodernity. As such, the mystic way recaptures elements of premodern mysticism, such as that espoused by Julian, and transfigures them according to the context of postmodernity and its particular dilemmas.

Finally, I have placed Murdoch, Levertov and Dillard on a mystical continuum with other Christian mystics such as Julian whose theology is based on the principle of integration. The discussion has provided three examples of women who aptly fit into Jantzen's definition of a 'postmodern anchoress', as those who observe the world, are prepared to critique the status quo and have a special ability to write texts that convey their mystical or theological insights. In postmodernity, the writers discussed here have been paralleled with Julian's theology in three key ways. First, they share a common ability to see with the 'eye of reason' and the 'eye of imagination' that demarcates the mystic way in postmodernity. Second, I have identified their ability to integrate visionary experiences into theological reflection. Lastly, I have suggested that they display a common ability to convey these insights using parable, metaphor, and analogy in popular or vernacular forms of writing. While Julian's theology adheres strictly to Church doctrine and teaching, the postmodern mystic has greater freedom to experiment with language about the sacred and the overriding drive to reveal the sacred in the ordinary through the work of love.

There are three possible ways that these insights can enhance theological discourse. First, they can build upon the perspectives of writers such as Jantzen, Turner and McGinn who argue that mysticism

316

is not solely about extraordinary experience, in the context of post-modernity. Explicitly I have shown, through the texts and lives of Murdoch, Levertov and Dillard that mysticism is largely a way of being, an orientation of consciousness and a life's process as opposed to an ineffable or passively received experience. By referring to the examples of Murdoch, Levertov and Dillard in the present and Julian in the past it has been demonstrated that mystics are visionaries who help us deal with historical periods of religious flux such as the late fourteenth century and the period following modernity, which is still in the making.

Second, this book identifies how the idiosyncrasies of individual writers such as Murdoch, Levertov and Dillard can be taken seriously within a larger theological arena without imposing prefixed conceptual and methodological categories onto their work. One area that I have scarcely touched upon, and one that certainly warrants further discussion, would be a closer analysis of the nuanced ways Murdoch, Dillard and Levertov utilise mystical perspectives from worldviews such as Buddhism, indigenous religions and Judaism and the potential they have to contribute to Christian continuation and development,

Third, I have provided a model for incorporating literary texts, the Bible and theological reflection into a process that remains open-ended or in a continual state of departure. Theological expression that incorporates the mystical way of being into its paradigms posits a theological model that concurs with McFague who maintains that all statements about God, the world and human beings are 'hypothetical, partial, risky and limited'.[1] By moving through a reconfigured mystic way in postmodernity I have demonstrated how mysticism is the connecting principle that allows a democratic participation in this ongoing human effort to discern, describe and reflect on the sacred. This discussion appears to suggest a linear or sequential route to an ultimate goal of transformation, but in reality, the stages of *via mystica* represent different layers of human existence that incorporate conceptual understanding, contemplative methods, creativity and mystical longing that shift according to circumstances.

1   McFague, *Life Abundant*, 28.

Postmodernity accepts the imprecise and temporary nature of all our language. The fact that humans have the ability to create and understand metaphor underpins all human efforts to make meaning. Indeed, it is fundamental to all language; metaphor is the axis around which all human thought and creativity revolve. On an individual level, with the right attitude, a reader is able to develop his or her own mystical consciousnesses through accessing mystical texts. On a communal level, literary writers contribute to the horizon of human becoming within a long line of visionaries, like Julian, through wide dissemination. It is clear that Murdoch, Levertov and Dillard write from a sense of vocation rather than pandering to market trends or dominant ideologies, but unlike 'hard' postmoderns such as Cupitt, they maintain a sense of the mystery that perpetually eludes human language, aligning them with Lakeland's definition of 'soft-core post-moderns'.

To conclude, I maintain that literary texts by Murdoch, Levertov and Dillard demonstrate the appropriate parabolic and metaphorical qualities needed to jolt us out of our apathy and call us back to sacred living. Indeed McFague herself seems to suggest a link to a mystical sensibility when she states that metaphor is 'the intimation of our original unity with all that is [by] making novel connections within [...] familiar worlds in order to move beyond where they are'.[2] Therefore, it is with some surprise that I must agree with Cupitt that the 'Word' can save us in that 'it draws us out into reconciled, unified expression'.[3] That is, in the final instance, we are all potential mystics because of our ability to use metaphorical language.

2   Ibid., 46.
3   Cupitt, *Mysticism After Modernity*, 138.

Bibliography

Anderson, Pamela Sue, 'Myth, Mimesis and Multiple Identities: Feminist Tools for Transforming Theology', in *Literature and Theology* 10:2 (1996), 112–30.

Antonaccio, Maria, *Picturing the Human: The Moral Thought of Iris Murdoch* (New York: Oxford University Press, 2000).

Antonaccio, Maria & Schweiker, William (eds), *Iris Murdoch and the Search for Human Goodness* (Chicago: Chicago University Press, 1996).

Arendt, Hannah, *The Life of the Mind* (San Diego, New York & London: Harcourt, 1978).

Arnold, David Scott, 'Hermeneutic of Otherness: A Feeling of Deflection from a Viable Centre', in 'Reading A Severed Head', in *Liminal Readings: Forms of Otherness in Melville, Joyce and Murdoch* (London: Macmillan Press Ltd, 1998), 87–153.

Bajaj, Kum Kum, *A Critical Study of Iris Murdoch's Fiction* (New Delhi: Atlantic Publishing, 2001).

Bauerschmidt, Frederick, 'Order, Freedom and "Kindness": Julian of Norwich on the Edge of Modernity', in *Theology Today* 60 (2003), 63–81.

Bauman, Zygmunt, 'Postmodern Religion', in Paul Heelas, *Religion, Modernity and Postmodernity* (Oxford: Blackwell, 1998), 55–78.

Bayley, John, *Elegy for Iris* (New York: Picador, 2000).

—— *Iris: A Memoir of Iris Murdoch* (UK: Clipper Audio, 2002).

Beattie, Tina, Review of *Becoming Divine: Towards a Feminist Philosophy of Religion*, 1998 by Grace M. Jantzen, in *Reviews in Religion and Theology* 7:3 (2000), 308–10.

Block, Ed, 'Interview with Denise Levertov', in *Renascence* 50 (1997), http://www.questia.com/PM.qst?a=o&d=500124879.

—— 'Poet, Word, and World: Reality and Transcendence in the Work of Denise Levertov', in *Logus* 4:3 (2001), 159–84.

Bodo, Murray, *Poetry as Prayer* (Boston: Pauline Books & Media, 2001).

Bonaventure, *Bonaventure: Classics of Western Spirituality* (Mahwah, New Jersey: Paulist Press, 1978).

Brooker, Jewel Spears, *Conversations with Denise Levertov* (Jackson: University Press of Mississippi, 1998).

Brown, David, *Discipleship and Imagination* (Oxford: Oxford University Press, 2000).

—— *Tradition & Imagination: Revelation & Change* (Oxford: Oxford University Press, 1999).

Bynum, Caroline Walker, *Jesus as Mother: Studies in the Spirituality of the High Middle Ages* (Berkeley; Los Angeles; London: University of California Press, 1982).

Cantwell, Mary, 'A Pilgrims' Progress', http://www.nytimes.com/books/99/03/28/specials/dillard-pilgrim.html

Carley, Burton, 'Annie Dillard: Getting a Feel for the Place', in *The Journal of Liberal Religion*, 2:1 (2000), http://www.meadville.edu/gibbons_2_1.html

Carrette, Jeremy & King, Richard, *Selling Spirituality: The Silent Takeover of Religion* (London: Routledge, 2004).

Carson, Rachel, *Silent Spring* (London: The Folio Society, 2000).

Cheney, Jim, 'The Water of Separation: Myth and Ritual in Annie Dillard's *Pilgrim at Tinker Creek*', in *The Journal of Feminist Studies in Religion* 6 (1990), 48.

Chirban, Sharon A., 'Oneness Experience: Looking Through Multiple Lenses', in *The Journal of Applied Psychoanalytic Studies* 2:3 (2000), 253.

Clark, Emma, 'Water and Shade', in *Parabola* 26:1 (2001), 37–42.

Coleman, Earle J., *Creativity and Spirituality: Bonds between Art and Religion* (Albany: State University of New York Press, 1998).

Conradi, Peter J., *Going Buddhist: Panic and Emptiness, the Buddha and Me* (London: Short Books, 2004).

—— 'Iris and the death of God', *The Guardian*, http://www.guardian.co.uk/comment/story/0,3604,672531,00.html

—— *Iris Murdoch: A Life* (London: HarperCollins, 2001).

—— 'Iris Murdoch and the Sea', in *Études Britanniques Contemporaines 4* (Montpellier: Presses universitaires de Montpellier, 1994), http://ebc.chez-alice.fr/ebc41.html

—— (ed), *Iris Murdoch: Existentialists and Mystics* (London: Penguin, 1997).

—— Iris Murdoch: *The Saint and the Artist* (London: HarperCollins, 2001).

Cupitt, Don, *Mysticism after Modernity* (Oxford: Blackwell, 1998).

—— 'Iris and the Death of God'. Cupitt records a conversation with an unnamed person, http://www.guardian.co.uk/comment/story/0,3604,672531,00.html

Datta, Nirmal, *Iris Murdoch: Freedom and Form* (Delhi: Macmillan, 2000).

De Beauvoir, Simone, *The Second Sex* (London: Vintage, 1997).

De Certeau, Michel, *The Mystic Fable*, trans. Michael B. Smith (Chicago & London: The University of Chicago Press, 1992).

Dillard, Annie, *An American Childhood* (New York: Harper, 1988).

—— *For the Time Being* (New York: Vintage, 1999).

—— *Holy the Firm* (New York: Harper, 1988).

—— *Living by Fiction* (New York: Harper, 1988).

—— *Mornings Like This* (New York: Harper, 1996).

—— *Pilgrim at Tinker Creek* (New York: Harper, 1998).

—— 'Singing with the Fundamentalists', in *Yale Review* 74 (1985), 312–20.

—— *Teaching a Stone to Talk* (New York: Harper, 1992).

—— *The Living* (New York: Harper, 1993).

—— *The Writing Life* (New York: Harper, 1990).

—— *Tickets for a Prayer Wheel* (New York: Harper, 1986).

—— 'Tsunami Commentary: Dots in Blue Water' (2005), http://www.npr.org/templates/story/story.php?storyId=4270641

—— 'Winter Melons', *Harpers* 248 (1974), 87–90.

—— 'Write Till You Drop' (1989), http://www.nytimes.com.books/99/28/specials/dillard-drop.html

Dionysius the Areopagite, *Mystical Theology and The Celestial Hierarchies*, trans. The Editors of the Shrine of Wisdom (Godalming, Surrey: The Shrine of Wisdom, 1949).

Dipple, Elizabeth, *Iris Murdoch: Work for the Spirit* (London: Methuen, 1982).

Donovan, Josephine, 'Ecofeminist literary criticism: reading the orange', in *Hypatia*, 11:2 (1996) 161–184.

Dooley, Gillian (ed), *From a Tiny Corner in the House of Fiction: Conversations with Iris Murdoch* (Columbia: University of Carolina Press, 2003).

Dunn, Robert Paul, 'The Artist as Nun: Theme, Tone and Vision in the Writings of Annie Dillard', in *Studia Mystica* 1:4 (1978), 26.

Estess, Sybil, 'Levertov Interviewed by Sybil Estess', originally appeared in Joe Bellamy (ed), *American Poetry Observed: Poets on Their Work* (University of Illinois, 1984), http://www.english.uiuc.edu/Maps/poets/g_l/levertov/estess.htm

Felch, Susan, M. 'Annie Dillard: Modern Physics in a Contemporary Mystic', in *Mosaic* 22:2 (1989), 1–14.

Fletcher, John, 'Review of *Iris Murdoch as I Knew Her* by A. N. Wilson', in *The Iris Murdoch Society Newsletter* 17 (2004).

Fletcher, John & Bove, Cheryl, *Iris Murdoch: A Descriptive Primary and Annotated Secondary Bibliography* (New York & London: Garland, 1994).

Fox, Matthew, *Original Blessing* (New York: Tarcher, 2000).

—— *Creativity: Where the Divine and Human Meet* (New York: J P. Tarcher, 2002).

Frankenberry, Nancy, Review of *Becoming Divine: Towards a Feminist Philosophy of Religion, 1998* by Grace M. Jantzen, in *Hypatia*, 16:1 (2001), 98–100.

Gallant, James, 'Entering no-man's land: the recent religious poetry of Denise Levertov', in *Renascence* 50:1–2 (1997/1998), 122–234.

Gatens-Robinson, Eugene, 'Finding our feminist ways in natural philosophy and religious thought', in *Hypatia* 9:4 (1994), 207–22.

Gelpi, Albert (ed), *Denise Levertov: Selected Criticism* (Ann Arbor: The University of Michigan Press, 1993).

Gerstenberger, Donna, *Iris Murdoch* (Cranbury, New Jersey: Associated University Press, 1975).

Gill, Jerry H., *Mediated Transcendence: A Postmodern Reflection* (Macon, Georgia: Mercer University Press, 1989).

Gordon, David J., *Iris Murdoch's Fables of Unselfing* (Columbia & London: University of Missouri Press), 1995.

Gordon, Rosemary, *Bridges: Psychic Structures, Functions and Processes* (London: Karmac Books, 1993)

Graham, Elaine, Walton, Heather & Ward, Frankie, *Theological Reflection: Methods* (London: SCM Press, 2005).

Grey, Alex, *The Mission of Art* (Boston & London: Shambala, 2001).

Grey, Mary, 'The Praxis of Resurrection: Literature and the Feminist Quest', in *British Journal of Education* 21:2 (1999), 112–20.

—— *The Wisdom of Fools?* (London: SPCK, 1993).

Griffen, Gabriele, *The Influence of the Writings of Simone Weil on the Fiction of Iris Murdoch* (San Francisco: Mellen Research University Press, 1993).

Guerin, Caroline, 'Iris Murdoch – A Revisionist Theology? A Comparative Study of Iris Murdoch's *Nuns and Soldiers* and Sara Maitland's *Virgin Territory*', in *Journal of Literature and Theology* 6:2 (1992), 153–70.

Hammond, Karla M., 'Drawing the Curtains: An Interview with Annie Dillard', in *Bennington Review* 10 (1981), 30–38.

Hazleton, Roger, 'Believing is Seeing: Vision as Metaphor', in *Theology Today* 35:4 (1979), 405–12

Hederman, Mark P., 'Philosophy and the Feminine: The Novels of Iris Murdoch', in *The Haunted Inkwell* (Blackrock, Co. Dublin: The Columbia Press, 2001), 70–95.

Heelas, Paul & Woodhead, Linda, *The Spiritual Revolution: Why Religion is Giving Way to Spirituality* (Oxford: Blackwell, 2005).

Heschel, Abraham Joshua, *Man is Not Alone: A Philosophy of Religion* (New York: Farrar, Straus and Giroux, 1951).

—— *Man's Quest for God* (Santa Fe: Aurora Press, 1998).

Huffaker, Lucinda, *Creative Dwelling: Empathy and Clarity in God and Self* (Atlanta, Georgia: Scholars Press, 1998).

Humble Johnson, Sandra, *The Space Between: Literary Epiphany in the Work of Annie Dillard* (Kent, Ohio, & London: The Kent State University Press, 1992).

Jacobs, Alan, 'Go(o)d in Iris Murdoch', http://www.firstthings.com/ftissues/ft9502/jacobs.html

James, William, *The Varieties of Religious Experience* (New York: Modern Library, 1999).

Jantzen, Grace M., *Becoming Divine: Towards a Feminist Philosophy of Religion* (Manchester: Manchester University Press, 1998).

—— 'Eros and the Abyss: Reading Mystics in Postmodernity', *Literature and Theology* 17:3 (2003), 238–64.

—— 'Ethics and mysticism: Friends or foes?', in *Nederlands Theologisch Tijdschrift* 39 (1985), 314–26.

—— 'Feminism and Flourishing: Gender and Metaphor', in *Feminist Theology* 18 (1995), 81–101.

—— 'Feminists, philosophers, and mystics', Special Issue: Feminist Philosophy of Religion, in *Hypatia*, 9:4 (1994), 186–206.

—— 'Flourishing: Towards an Ethic of Natality', in *Feminist Theory* 2:2 (2001), 219–32.

—— *Foundations of Violence* (London & New York: Routledge, 2004).

—— *Julian of Norwich* (London: SPCK, 2000).

—— 'Necrophilia and Natality: what does it mean to be religious?', in *Scottish Journal of Religious Studies* 19:1 (1998b), 101–21.

—— *Power, Gender and Christian Mysticism* (Cambridge: Cambridge University Press, 1995).

—— 'The Mystical Meaning of Scripture: Medieval and Modern Presuppositions', in *King's Theological Review* 21 (1988), 39–43.

—— 'What's the Difference? Knowledge and Gender in (Post) Modern Philosophy of Religion', in *Religious Studies* 32 (1996), 431–48.

Jasper, David, *The Study of Literature and Religion: An Introduction*, 2nd edition (London: Macmillan, 1992).

Jenkins, David, 'Literature and the Theologian', in John Coulson (ed), *Theology and the University: An Ecumenical Investigation* (Baltimore: Helicon Press, 1964).

Jennings, Elizabeth, *Every Changing Shape: Mystical Experience and the Making of Poems* (Manchester: Carcanet, 1996).

Johnson, Deborah, *Iris Murdoch* (Brighton, Sussex: The Harvester Press, 1987).

Julian of Norwich, *Showings*, trans. Edmund College, O.S.A. and James Walsh, S.J. (Mahwah, New Jersey: Paulist Press, 1978).

Kaufman, Gordon D., *The Face of Mystery: A Constructive Theology* (Cambridge, Massachusetts: Harvard University Press, 1993).

Keller, Carl, *Mysticism and Language* (Oxford: Oxford University Press, 1992).

Keller, Joseph, 'The Function of Paradox in Mystical Discourse', in *Studia Mystica* 6:3 (1983), 3–19.

Kessler, Michael & Sheppard, Christian, *Mystics: Presence and Aporia* (Chicago & London: University of Chicago Press, 2003).

King, Ursula, *Christian Mystics: Their Lives and Legacies throughout the Ages* (London & New York: Routledge, 2001).

Kinnahan, Linda, A., *Poetics of the Feminine: Authority and Literary Tradition in William Carlos Williams, Mina Loy, Denise Levertov, and Kathleen Fraser* (Cambridge: Cambridge University Press, 1992).

Lacey, Paul A., 'Denise Levertov: Testimonies of a Lived Life', in *Renascence* 53 (2001), http://www.questia.com/PM.qst?a=o&d=5001050780

—— '"To Mediate a Saving Strategy": Denise Levertov's Religious Poetry', in *Renascence* 50 (1997), http://www.questia.com/PM.qst?a=o&d=5001524883

Lakeland, Paul, *Postmodernity: Christian Identity in a Fragmented Age* (Minneapolis: Fortress Press, 1997).

Lash, Nicolas, *Holiness, Speech and Silence: Reflection on the Question of God* (Aldershot: Ashgate, 2004).

Leonard, Philip (ed), *Trajectories of Mysticism in Theory and Literature* (Basingstoke: Macmillan, 2000).

Lesser, Wendy, 'Deliver Us From Evil', *The New York Times* (1999), http://www.nytimes.com/books/99/03/28/reviews/990328.28lessert.html

Levertov, Denise, *A Door in the Hive* (New York: New Directions, 1989).

—— *Breathing the Water* (New York: New Directions, 1987).

—— *Collected Earlier Poems 1940–1960* (New York: New Directions, 1979).

—— *Evening Train* (New York: New Directions, 1992).

—— *Light Up the Cave* (New York: New Directions, 1981).

—— *New & Selected Essays* (New York: New Directions, 1992).

—— *O Taste and See* (New York: New Directions, 1964).

—— *Oblique Prayers* (Newcastle upon Tyne: Bloodaxe Books, 1986).

—— *Poems 1960–1967* (New York: New Directions, 1983).

—— *Poems 1968–1972* (New York: New Directions, 1987).

—— *Poems 1972–1982* (New York: New Directions, 2001).

—— *Sands of the Well* (Newcastle upon Tyne: Bloodaxe Books, 1998).

—— *Tesserae* (Newcastle upon Tyne: Bloodaxe Books, 1997).

—— *The Poet in the World* (New York: New Directions, 1973).

—— *This Great Unknowing* (Tarset, Northumberland: Bloodaxe Books 2001).

Little, Anne Colclough, 'Old Impulses, New Expressions: Duality and Unity in the Poetry of Denise Levertov', in *Renascence* 50:1–2 (1997/1998), 33–48.

Little, Anne Colclough & Paul, Susie, *Denise Levertov: New Perspectives* (West Cornwall, CT: Locust Hill Press, 2000).

Little, Margaret Olivia, 'Seeing and caring: the role and affect in feminist moral epistemology', in *Hypatia* 10:3 (1995), 117–38.

Lloyd, Genevieve, *The Man of Reason: 'Male' & 'Female' in Western Philosophy* (London: Methuen, 1995).

Loades, Ann, *Feminist Theology: A Reader* (London: SPCK, 1990).

—— 'Iris Murdoch: the vision of the good and the *via negativa*', in *Culture, Education & Society* 40:2 (1986), 147–55.

Louth, Andrew, *The Origins of the Christian Mystical Tradition* (Oxford: Clarendon Press, 1981).

Lynch, Denise E., 'Denise Levertov and the Poetry of Incarnation', in *Renascence* 50:1–2 (1997/1998), 49–64.

Magee, Bryan, 'Iris Murdoch on natural novelists and unnatural philosophy', in *The Listener* 27 April 1978.

Matthews, Melvyn, *Both Alike to Thee: The Retrieval of the Mystic Way* (London: SPCK, 2000).

McClintock, James I., 'Annie Dillard: Ritualist', in *Nature's Kindred Spirits* (Wisconsin, USA: The University of Wisconsin Press, 1994) 88–108.

McDonnell, T. P. (ed), *A Thomas Merton Reader* (New York: Bantam Doubleday, 1996).

McFague, Sallie, *Life Abundant* (Minneapolis: Fortress Press, 2001).

—— *Metaphorical Theology: Models of God in Religious Language* (Philadlephia: Fortress Press, 1982).

—— *Models of God* (Philadelphia: Fortress Press, 1987).

—— *Super, Natural Christians* (Minneapolis: Fortress Press, 1997).

—— *Speaking in Parables* (London: SCM Press, 2002).

—— *The Body of God* (London: SCM Press, 1993).

McGinn, Bernard, *The Foundations of Mysticism* (London: SCM Press, 1992).

McGrath, Alister E., *Christian Spirituality: An Approach* (Oxford: Blackwell, 1998).

McIntosh, Mark A., *Mystical Theology* (Oxford: Blackwell, 1998).

Milburn, D., 'Iris Murdoch: Fragments of a re-cognition', http://www.texaschapbook press.com/magellanslog35/murdochfecundity.htm

Murdoch, Iris, *A Fairly Honourable Defeat* (London: Penguin, 1970).

—— *A Severed Head* (London: Penguin, 1961).

—— *A Word Child* (London: Chatto & Windus, 1975).

—— *An Accidental Man* (London: Penguin, 1971).

—— *An Unofficial Rose* (London: Vintage, 1962).

—— *Acastos* (London: Penguin, 1986).

—— *Bruno's Dream* (London: Vintage, 2001).

—— *Henry and Cato* (London: Penguin, 1988).

—— *Jackson's Dilemma* (London: Penguin, 1995).

—— *Metaphysics as a Guide to Morals* (London: Penguin, 1992).

—— *Nuns and Soldiers* (London: Chatto & Windus, 1980).

—— *New Revised Standard Version Bible* (London: Collins, 1989).

—— *The Bell* (London: Vintage, 1973).

—— *The Black Prince* (London: Penguin, 1973).

—— *The Book and the Brotherhood* (London: Penguin, 1987).

—— *The Flight from the Enchanter* (London: Vintage, 1956).

—— *The Good Apprentice* (London: Vintage, 1985).

—— *The Green Knight* (London: Penguin, 1993).

—— *The Italian Girl* (London: Penguin, 1964).

—— *The Message to the Planet* (London: Vintage, 1989).

—— *The Nice and the Good* (London: Penguin, 1968).

—— *The Philosopher's Pupil* (London: Vintage, 1983).

—— *The Red and the Green* (London: Penguin, 1965).

—— *The Sacred and Profane Love Machine* (London: Penguin, 1976).

—— *The Sandcastle* (London: Penguin, 1957).

—— *The Sea, The Sea* (London: Vintage, 1999).

—— *The Sovereignty of Good* (New York & London: Routledge, 1970).

—— *The Time of the Angels* (London: Chatto & Windus, 1966).

—— *The Unicorn* (London: Penguin, 1966).

—— *Under the Net* (Harmondsworth, Middlesex: Penguin, 1977).

Nicol, Bran, *Iris Murdoch: the Retrospective Fiction*, 2nd edition (London & New York: Macmillan, 2004).

Nussbaum, Martha C., '"Faint with Secret Knowledge": Love and Vision in Murdoch's The Black Prince', in *Poetics Today* 25:4 (2004), 689–710.

—— The Fragility of Goodness: Luck and Ethics in Greek Tragedy and Philosophy, revised edition (Cambridge: Cambridge University Press, 2001).

Nuth, Joan M., Wisdom's Daughter: The Theology of Julian of Norwich (New York: The Crossroad Publishing Company, 1991).

O'Connell, Nicholas, 'Levertov's Final Interview: A Poet's Validation', in Nicholas O'Connell, At the Field's End: Interviews with 22 Pacific Northwest Writers (University of Washington Press, 1998), http://www. english.unic.edu/maps/poets/g_l/levertov/oconnell.htm

O'Connor, Patricia, To Love the Good: The Moral Philosophy of Iris Murdoch (New York: Peter Lang, 1996).

O'Donoghue, Noel D., 'Mystical Imagination', in James P. Mackey, Religious Imagination (Edinburgh: Edinburgh University Press, 1986).

O'Flaherty, Wendy Doniger, The Implied Spider: Politics & Theology in Myth (New York: Columbia University Press, 1998).

Ostriker, Alicia Suskin, Stealing the Language: The Emergence of Women's Poetry in America (London: The Women's Press, 1986).

Pacernick, Gary, 'Denise Levertov', in Meaning and Memory: Interviews with Fourteen Jewish Poets (Columbus: The Ohio State University Press, 2001), 65–75.

Parrish, Nancy C., Lee Smith, Annie Dillard and the Hollins Group (Baton Rouge, LA: Louisiana State University Press, 1998).

Peterson, Eugene, 'Annie Dillard: Praying With Her Eyes Open', in Theological Students Fellowship Bulletin (1985), 7–11.

Pinnock, Sarah K. (ed), The Theology of Dorothy Soelle (New York: Trinity Press International, 2003).

Radaker, Kevin, 'Caribou, Electrons, and the Angel: Stalking the Sacred in 'Annie Dillard's Pilgrim at Tinker Creek', in Christianity and Literature 46:2 (1997), 123–43.

Rainwater, Catherine & Scheick, William J. (eds), Contemporary American Women Writers: Narrative Strategies (Lexington: University of Kentucky Press, 1985).

Ramanathan, Siguna, Iris Murdoch: Figures of Good (Basingstoke: Macmillan, 1990).

Reimer, Margaret Loewen, 'The Dialectical Vision of Annie Dillard's Pilgrim at Tinker Creek', in Critique 24 (1983), 182–91.

Robinson, George, Essential Judaism: A Complete Guide to Beliefs, Customs, and Rituals (New York: Pocket Books, 2000).

Robinson, John A. T., Honest to God (London: Westminster John Knox Press, 1963).

Rodgers, Audrey T., Denise Levertov (Rutherford; Madison; Teaneck: Farleigh Dickson University Press, 1993).

Rogers, Bobby Caudle, 'Denise Levertov's Poetics of Process', in D. J. N. Middleton, God, Literature and Process Thought (Aldershot: Ashgate, 2002), 207–25.

Ronda, Bruce A., 'Annie Dillard and the Fire of God', in Christian Century 100:16 (1983), 483–86.

Rosenthal, Peggy 'Joking with Jesus in the Poetry of Kathleen Norris and Annie Dillard', in Cross Currents 50:3 (2000), 383–92.

Ross-Bryant, Lynn, 'The Silence of Nature', in *Religion and Literature* 22:1 (1990), 74–94.

Rowe, Anne, *The Visual Arts and the Novels of Iris Murdoch* (Lewiston; Queenston; Lampeter: The Edwin Meller Press, 2002).

Ruddick, Sara, *Maternal Thinking: Towards a Politics of Peace* (London: The Women's Press, 1989).

Ruffing, Janet K., R.S.M. (ed), *Mysticism and Social Transformation* (New York: Syracuse Press, 2001).

Sage, Lorna, *Women in the House of Fiction* (Basingstoke: Macmillan, 1992).

Sayers, Dorothy L., *The Mind of the Maker* (London: Mowbray, 2002).

Schaub, Lorraine, 'Tricks of Eye and Spirit: Invisibility and Illusion in Annie Dillard's *Pilgrim at Tinker Creek*', http://www.hoardeordinaries.com/lori/research/tricks.html

Schneiders, Sandra M., 'Scripture and Spirituality', in Bernard McGinn et al. (eds), *Christian Spirituality: Origins to the Twelfth Century* (New York: Crossroad, 1985).

—— *Written That You May Believe* (New York: The Crossroad Publishing Company, 1999).

Schreick, William J., 'Annie Dillard, Narrative Fringe', in Catherine Rainwater, and William J, Schreick (eds), *Contemporary American Women Writers: Narrative Strategies* (Lexington: University of Kentucky Press, 1985).

Sells, Michael A., *Mystical Languages of Unsaying* (Chicago & London: The University of Chicago Press, 1994).

Sheldrake, Philip, 'Christian Spirituality as a Way of Living Publicly: A Dialectic of the Mystical and Prophetic', in *Spiritus* 3 (2003), 19–37.

—— *Spirituality and Theology: Christian Living and the Doctrine of God* (London: Darton, Longman & Todd, 1998).

—— *The New SCM Dictionary of Christian Spirituality* (London: SCM Press, 2005).

Smith, Pamela A., 'The Ecotheology of Annie Dillard: A Study in Ambivalence', *Cross Currents* 45:3 (1995), 341–59.

Soelle, Dorothee, *Against the Wind: Memoir of a Radical Christian*, trans. B. & M. Rumscheidt (Minneapolis: Fortress Press, 1995).

—— *Death By Bread Alone: Texts and Reflections on Religious Experiences* (Philadelphia: Fortress Press, 1978).

—— *Suffering* (trans. E.R. Kalin) (Philadelphia: Fortress Press, 1984).

—— *The Silent Cry: Mysticism and Resistance* (Minneapolis: Fortress Press, 2001).

—— *The Strength of the Weak: Towards a Christian Feminist Identity*, trans. R. & R. Kimber (Philadelphia: The Westminster Press, 1984).

—— *Thinking about God: An Introduction to Theology*, trans. J. Bowden (London: SCM Press, 1990).

Soskice, Janet Martin, 'Love and Attention', in Michael McGhee, *Philosophy, Religion and the Spiritual Life* (Cambridge: Cambridge University Press, 1992), 59–72.

Spear, Hilda D., *Iris Murdoch* (Basingstoke: Macmillan, 1995).

Steiner, George, *Real Presences* (Chicago: Chicago University Press, 1991).

Tacey, David, *The Spirituality Revolution: The Emergence of Contemporary Spirituality* (New York: Brunner-Routledge, 2004).

Taylor, Mark C., *Erring: A Postmodern Theology* (Chicago & London: The University of Chicago Press, 1984).

The Oxford English Dictionary, 2nd edition, Vol. X (Oxford: Clarendon Press, 1989).

Tracy, David, 'Theology and the Many Faces of Postmodernity', in *Theology Today* 51:1 (1994), 104–14.

Tucker, Lindsey, *Critical Essays on Iris Murdoch* (New York: G. K. Hall, 1992).

Turner, Denys, *The Darkness of God* (Cambridge: Cambridge University Press, 1995).

Von Hildebrand, Dietrich, *Transformation in Christ: On the Christian Attitude* (Fort Collins, CO: Ignatius Press, 2001).

Wagner, Linda Welshimer, *Denise Levertov* (New Haven, Connecticut: College and University Press, 1967).

Wagner-Martin, Linda, *Critical Essays on Denise Levertov* (Boston, Massachusetts: G. K. Hall, 1991).

Ward, Patricia, 'Annie Dillard's Way of Seeing', in *Christianity Today* 22 (1978), 974–75.

Webb, Stephen H., 'Nature's Spendthrift Economy: The Extravagance of God in *Pilgrim at Tinker Creek*', in *Soundings* 77 (1994), 429–51.

Wilde, Dana, 'Annie Dillard's "A Field of Silence": The Contemplative Tradition in the Modern Age', in *Mystics Quarterly* 26:1 (2000), 31–45.

—— 'Mystical Experience in Annie Dillard's "Total Eclipse" and "Lenses"', in *Studies in the Humanities*, 28:1/2 (2001), 48–81.

Wilson, A. N., *Iris Murdoch: As I Knew Her* (London: Hutchinson, 2003).

Woolf, Virginia, *A Room of One's Own* (London: Flamingo, 1994).

Yancy, Philip, 'A Face Aflame', in *Christianity Today* 22 (1978), 960–61.

Index

Religions and Discourse

Edited by James M. M. Francis

Religions and Discourse explores religious language in the major world faiths from various viewpoints, including semiotics, pragmatics and cognitive linguistics, and reflects on how it is situated within wider intellectual and cultural contexts. In particular a key issue is the role of figurative speech. Many fascinating metaphors originate in religion e.g. revelation as a 'garment', apostasy as 'adultery', loving kindness as the 'circumcision of the heart'. Every religion rests its specific orientations upon symbols such as these, to name but a few. The series strives after the interdisciplinary approach that brings together such diverse disciplines as religious studies, theology, sociology, philosophy, linguistics and literature, guided by an international editorial board of scholars representative of the aforementioned disciplines. Though scholarly in its scope, the series also seeks to facilitate discussions pertaining to central religious issues in contemporary contexts. The series will publish monographs and collected essays of a high scholarly standard.

Volume 1   Ralph Bisschops and James Francis (eds):
            Metaphor, Canon and Community. 307 pages. 1999.
            ISBN 3-906762-40-8 / US-ISBN 0-8204-4234-8

Volume 2   Lieven Boeve and Kurt Feyaerts (eds):
            Metaphor and God Talk. 291 pages. 1999.
            ISBN 3-906762-51-3 / US-ISBN 0-8204-4235-6

Volume 3   Jean-Pierre van Noppen: *Transforming Words.*
            248 pages. 1999. ISBN 3-906762-52-1 / US-ISBN 0-8204-4236-4

Volume 4   Robert Innes: *Discourses of the Self.*
            236 pages. 1999. ISBN 3-906762-53-X / US-ISBN 0-8204-4237-2

Volume 5   Noel Heather: *Religious Language and Critical Discourse Analysis.*
            319 pages. 2000. ISBN 3-906762-54-8 / US-ISBN 0-8204-4238-0